Rounding of Income Data

T0317011

SCHRIFTEN ZUR EMPIRISCHEN WIRTSCHAFTSFORSCHUNG

Herausgegeben von Peter M. Schulze

Band 9

PETER LANG

Frankfurt am Main · Berlin · Bern · Bruxelles · New York · Oxford · Wien

Jens Ulrich Hanisch

Rounding
of Income Data

An Empirical Analysis of the Quality
of Income Data with Respect to Rounded Values
and Income Brackets with Data
from the European Community Household Panel

PETER LANG

Europäischer Verlag der Wissenschaften

Bibliographic Information published by die Deutsche Nationalbibliothek
Die Deutsche Nationalbibliothek lists this publication in the
Deutsche Nationalbibliografie; detailed bibliographic data is
available in the internet at <http://www.d-nb.de>.

Zugl.: Frankfurt (Main), Univ., Diss., 2006

D 30
ISSN 1437-0697
ISBN 3-631-55687-X
US-ISBN 0-8204-8721-X

© Peter Lang GmbH
Europäischer Verlag der Wissenschaften
Frankfurt am Main 2007
All rights reserved.

Printed in Germany 1 2 3 4 5   7

www.peterlang.de

Preface

This doctoral thesis is a result of my work as a participant of the EU project "Change from Input Harmonisation to Ex-post Harmonisation in National Samples of the European Community Household Panel" (CHINTEX). This work was financed by the European Community under Contract IST-1999-11101.

The data were kindly provided by Statistics Finland (Tilastokeskus), the Deutsches Statistisches Bundesamt, the Statistical Offices of Luxembourg, the University of Essex and the DIW Berlin. I especially want to thank Susanna Sandström, Marjo Pyy-Martikainen and Johanna Sisto of Statistics Finland for producing the special Finnish ECHP data base with matched data from registers and interviews.

I am indebted to a number of people for their help and support during the project, especially Professor Leif Nordberg (Abo Akademi, Finland), Markus Jäntti (Åbo Akademi, Finland) and Professor Risto Lehtonen (University of Jyväskylä) for their comments and excellent cooperation and a very nice time in Finland. I want to thank the participants of the CHINTEX conferences, the Basel Workshop of Item Non-Response and Robert Mason for helpful comments. Also, four anonymous reviews and Professor Regina T. Riphahn's comments have been useful.

My gratitude goes to my supervisor Professor Dr. Ulrich Rendtel. Without his initiative this work would not have been started. And I want to thank the other members of the board of examiners, Professor Dr. Uwe Hassler, Professor Dr. Hans-G. Bartels and Professor Dr.

Bertram Schefold. Also, I want to thank my former colleagues at the Institute of Statistics and Mathematics, in particular Dr. Thomas Neukirch, PD Dr. Andreas Behr, PD Dr. Egon Bellgardt and Ivo Marek but also many others for fruitful discussions and criticism.

Last not least, I am very grateful to my significant other, Dr. Silvia Schiemann, for her patience and kind encouragement.

Contents

List of Figures

List of Tables

Notation

symbol	domain	label
$\mathbb{N}$		the set of natural numbers
$\mathbb{Z}$		the set of integers
$\mathbb{R}$		the set of real numbers
$\mathbb{X}$		the target population of x values
N	$\mathbb{N}$	sample size or number of observations
i	$\mathbb{Z}$	number of individual
j	$\mathbb{Z}$	(used for different purposes)
$b, b(y)$	$\mathbb{N}^n$	number of significant digits (of y-value)
X	$\mathbb{R}^n$	random vector or skalar of income variable x
w	$\mathbb{R}^n$	vector or value of design weights
x	$\mathbb{R}^n$	accurate vector or skalar of income variable x
Y	$\mathbb{Z}^n$	random vector or skalar of income variable x
$Y(X)$		the set of possible rounded observations given X
$X(Y)$		the set of possible accurate observations given Y
y	$\mathbb{Z}^n$	observed vector or skalar of income variable x
z	$\mathbb{R}^n$	observed vector or skalar of non-income variable z
A	$\{0,1\}^n$	binary logical condition
ϵ		error term
ϵ_r		rounding error
$\bar{x}$		empirical mean value of x
μ		theoretical mean
s_x		empirical standard deviation of x
σ		theoretical standard deviation
x_{min}		minimum value of x
x_{max}		maximum value of x
x_p		percentile p of x
Q1		first quartile (of x), identically to $x_{.25}$
Q2		second quartile (of x), median, identically to $x_{.5}$
Q3		third quartile (of x), identically to $x_{.75}$

Abbreviations

adj.	adjusted
AIC	Akaike's Information Criterion
approx.	approximately, approximated
BHPS	British Household Panel Survey
DEM	Deutsche Mark
CAPI	computer aided personal interview
cf.	[from latin] compare
CHINTEX	Change from Input Harmonisation to Ex-post Harmonisation
CIRCA	Communication and Information Resource Centre Administrator
coeff.	coefficient
cum. prc.	cumulative percent
DEM	Deutsche Mark (national currency in Germany prior to EUR)
dev.	deviance
d.f.	degrees of freedom
ecdf	empirical cumulative distribution function
ECHP	European Community Household Panel
e.g.	[from latin "exempla gratia"] for example
err.	error
EUR	Euro
EU-SILC	European Survey on Income and Living Conditions
FIN	Finland, Finnish
FIM	Finmark (national currency in Finland prior to Euro)
GER	German, Germany
GSOEP	German Socio-Economic Panel
i.e.	[from latin "id est"] that is
i.i.d.	independent identically distributed
KDE	kernel density estimation (or estimator)
ln	logarithm
LUF	Luxembourgian Francs (national currency prior to EUR)
LUX	Luxembourg
MAD	Mean Absolute Deviation
OLS	Ordinary Least Squares

p.a.	per annum
p.m.	per month
PDB	Production Data Base
prc.	percent
PSELL	Panel socio-économique / Liewen zu Lëutzebuerg
sig.	significance, significant
SOEP	Socio-Economic Panel
std.	standard
UDB	User Data Base
Var	Variance

CHAPTER1

Rounded Values

1.1 Introduction

Response behavior and questionnaire design are cornerstones for a survey. Income values sampled from an empirical income distribution are often assumed to be continuous or at least of interval-scale. Survey participants are expected to edit accurate values in response to income questions, but in fact they often provide more or less imprecise values: Most observations are rounded or in the form of income brackets. Information from rounded values and income brackets is of inferior quality compared to precise data.

The quality of income data is a fundamental issue for every European social survey, e.g., the European Community Household Panel (ECHP) and its follow-up project, the European Community Statistics of Income and Living Conditions (EU-SILC). Aspects of quality and lack of quality will be shown in Chapter Two.

Some results of this thesis are specific for these surveys but some can be generalized for others. For example, the rounding effects on distributions are more general, while the trend of using such response types during panel participation (panel effect) is more survey-specific. See Chapter Two for a detailed discussion of the effects of rounding, and Chapter 6 for an analysis of the relation between various factors and rounding.

Collecting data by interviewing is not an easy task. The sample person must be motivated to respond and needs to have sufficient skills and enough time to answer the long list of questions he or she is asked in the interview successfully. Questions regarding income are especially difficult because many different figures have to be produced from memory and edited in the format required in the questionnaire. This could motivate for people to edit rounded values, because it is faster and requires less knowledge.

Not much empirical research specifically on rounding of income data has been done. One reason for this lack of publication could be, that rounding is usually discussed as either a more technical problem in computation, or as a phenomenon in psychology. Perhaps a more important reason is, that rounding and bracket usage cause only minor problems compared to non-response: At least, some information is gathered, thus inaccurate data are better than none. And from a technical point of view, rounded values can be used just like continuous values. Another reason could be a lack of available data to compare rounded with non-rounded data. However, a very special situation involving the European Community Data Base for Finland (see Section 3.1.3 for details) opens up the chance to analyse rounding in more detail than usually possible.

Information about the incomes of individuals and household are required for a number of purposes. Official and government statistics need data from a majority of the citizens for taxation and social transfers. These data are collected regularly and put into administrative registers. Research institutes need data for economic and socio-economic research, for policy recommendations, for inter-temporal and international comparisons. Because non-government organizations usually do not have access to administrative records and official statistics, they often have to collect the data through surveys. But even official agencies need survey data, for example, when the desired information cannot be obtained from register sources. A major project of this kind was the European Community Household Panel (ECHP), which sampled about 60000 households from over a dozen countries of the European Community. It followed a panel design, which has the advantage to deliver data about household dynamics and individual change. The amount and quality of data collected by different instruments such as administrative records, surveys, panel surveys can be very different. In income statistics the main concern arises from discrepancies found in comparison of register and survey data. In the European Community, some countries already use register data for important economic statistics and research, while others use survey data. These data will be compared in the EU. If discrepancies between the values for the same individuals occur within a country, i.e., the value from registers and from the survey interview would be very different, then it would be the question whether it was possible to compare the two different samples at all, or if the data would not be sufficiently harmonized to allow comparisons on substantial level.

Some suggestions and methods on how to work with inaccurate data will be discussed and briefly reviewed in Section 2.3. The frequency and impact of rounding and usage of income brackets on income data has been researched only sparsely.

The main purpose of this thesis is to show how statistics are affected. We study the quality of data in the ECHP, look for factors which have an impact on accuracy of data, and suggest how to improve data quality in future surveys.

1.2 The CHINTEX project

This thesis paper is the result of my participation in the research project CHINTEX (an acronym for "Change from Input Harmonisation to Ex-post Harmonisation").

The project was carried out in co-operation of an international consortium of research institutes and national statistical institutes in a collaborate attempt to analyze the attained level of comparability and harmonization in the European Community Household Panel: The DIW in Berlin (German Institute for Economic Research), the Federal Statistical Office Germany (Statistische Bundesamt) in Wiesbaden, Johann Wolfgang Goethe Universität (Institut für Statistik und Mathematik) in Frankfurt – Germany, the University of Essex (Institute for Social and Economic Research), CEPS/INSTEAD in Differdange – Luxembourg, Statistics Finland (Tilastokeskus) in Helsinki – Finland, and Åbo Akademi University in Turku – Finland.

Many people involved in the project have generated reports and publications based on their work in the project, covering various topics within the framework of the CHINTEX project. Because it was agreed to split work among project partners, topics like *item non-response* and *attrition* are only briefly discussed in this thesis. Please refer to the following CHINTEX papers on these topics (list not necessarily complete):

- Unit non-response, attrition and attrition bias: Neukirch (2002), Behr et al. (2003b), Sisto (2003), Behr et al. (2003a), Basic (2003), Marek (2002) and Pyy-Martikainen and Rendtel (2003).

- Measurement error, comparison of interview and register data, respectively: Nordberg et al. (2001), Hovi et al. (2001), Jäntti (2004).

• Calibration and weighting to reduce attrition and non-response errors: Neukirch (2003), Harms (2003b), Harms (2003a).

• More information about the project and publications is available at the project internet website: http://www.destatis.de/chintex/.

The Chintex project is now finished and a publication with results from the teams is available: Statistisches Bundesamt (2004).

1.3 Hypotheses

For the aims of this thesis, it is necessary to formulate hypotheses on rounding, discuss¡ them and analyze the available data with respect the hypotheses. A number of different methods will be applied, but the focus is on producing answers or at least additional empirical evidence regarding the hypotheses.

The first hypothesis is, that rounding has relevant effects on statistics like the distribution of values and statistical aggregates and commonly used statistics like income mobility and poverty measures. Here some simulation and experiments shall give answers.

If rounding has some effects on univariate statistics, it is the question whether rounding is either random or can be related to covariates that are helpful in predicting rounding behavior. Therefore some explicit covariates are analyzed. Regarding household panel surveys, these covariates can come from the following groups:

• Interview-related factors: We expect that the *mode of interview* is important, because personal interviews are different from proxy interviews, and face-to-face interviews are different from phone interviews. Interviewees are probably less reluctant to disclose income figures in a face-to-face interview, and proxies often have to make a rough guess. *The respondent-interviewer relationship* and the change of interviewers is a known factor in explaining non-response (Rendtel, 1995), but it is less likely that it has an influence on response rounding. The *question design* is important, of course, but experimental methods might be necessary to understand the effect of question design. *Time of year* could be important because of taxation reasons. Many persons have to fill in their tax declaration, and this often happens in the first quarter of the year. For this it is necessary to go through a lot of income-related values, and it is possible that persons better remember these figures shortly after having filled out their tax forms.

• Panel-related factors: *Panel conditioning* is a well-known factor for change of response behavior, but in two different directions. After the first wave, interviewees know the questions and could prepare notes and documents ahead for the next interview. This phenomenon has been reported by interviewers. And, the novelty of being interviewed becomes routine and their response behavior – especially with respect to non-response, but also to rounding – might be different than at the beginning of the panel. These factors are believed to improve reporting, but another factor might deteriorate the quality of responses: People get bored when being asked the same questions over and over and become less diligent reporters.

One additional question is, whether cooperation can be related to other covariates or not. And, assuming that respondents are learning from the interview process, it is of interest, whether the response type was stable or how it changed in following waves.

• Income-related factors: It is very likely that persons remember only the first few digits of a number. Thus, values are probably reported with a relative precision, or, in other words, with a certain number of *significant digits*. In addition, more complicated or just obscure income components are perhaps reported with lower precision than very important ones like gross earning from main job.

There are other factors known to have an impact on (item and unit) response probability. E.g., the age and gender of the head of household, the household composition (and changes thereof), the number of interviews, head of household is a participant since first wave, change of marital status (separation of a couple), unemployment or expected job loss, occupational status, income and income types, reluctancy to report household income and assets, and migration background (East-West or immigrant). The number of factors seems large, and the relevance, significance and direction of effects varies. We have to restrict our analyses to some selected few factors.

1.4 Approach

In Chapter Two we propose a working definition of "rounding". A review of the literature dealing with the topic of rounding and use of income brackets gives an overview of what has been researched in this area. The focus of this thesis is not to provide the "final statistical model" for rounded and interval data. Depending on the assumed nature of the rounding process, one or the other method seems to be better suited. This thesis gives an impression where rounding error has an impact, how rounding can be described and provides empirical results on characteristics that correlate with rounding behavior.

In the second part of the chapter we assess the effect of rounding on income-related distributions. This is done with some simulations and real data examples. We analyze cross-sectional data (one period, multiple persons) and a mobility measure (change across two periods, multiple persons).

The third chapter starts with a description of the panel data used. Then descriptive statistics with the frequency of three response types for household income follow: Responses as exact values, as rounded values, and as income brackets. We offer an approach to rounding as a sequential process and compare results from four panel surveys.

The use of income brackets as response to the question on household income is the main topic of Chapter Four. Our interest is the frequency of bracket usage and the distribution of income values within bracket boundaries. We compare empirical results from two national samples of the European Community Household Panel (ECHP), the Luxembourgian and the German sub-samples of the ECHP and compare the results from the German ECHP with results from a similar German panel survey, the German Socio-Economic Panel (SOEP). Finally, an improvement for the design of bracket boundaries is sketched.

Comparing data from different origins is the topic of the Fifth Chapter. The motivation for this comparison is the idea that register data are reported accurately and not rounded. Therefore register data can be informative for departures from the true values because of rounding. We compare individual income data from registers and from a survey. This is done for data for one period, and for a mobility measure based on two different periods.

In Chapter Six, probit and logit models for rounding behavior are proposed and estimated. We are investigating various coefficients and find several factors which correlate with rounding behavior, especially gender, job, interview type and the behavior in previous waves.

Finally, we give a comprehensive overview of the results and draw the main conclusions. Some additional figures and information can be found in the Appendix.

CHAPTER 2

The Effect of Rounding on Distributional Figures

While measurement errors are wide-spread in interview-based survey samples (see Biemer et al., 1991), the effect of rounding is a peculiar aspect of the quality of data. In this chapter it is demonstrated that using rounded observations instead of accurate values potentially causes non-ignorable measurement error for inference, in particular in the quantiles of a distribution and on measures of change.

In the first sections, a framework definition for quality of data and accuracy of data in general is given, and a short review of literature dealing with rounding. For the purposes of this work, a definition of rounding is given in the following section. In the final two sections, the impact of rounding on various coefficients and on poverty measures like headcount ratio and the TIP curve is demonstrated.

2.1 The quality of income data

People use the word "quality" for a variety of reasons in science, business and in daily life. Even the meaning of "quality of income data" is rather diverse, and it is not a well-defined concept. It has been pointed out that the term "quality" has been overused and questioned because of the lack of a common definition (Brackstone, 1999).

We will show which aspects are contained in data quality, and later we will give general recommendations to improve data quality in surveys.

2.1.1 A framework for data quality

To discuss aspects of data quality, it can be structured into seven dimensions, e.g., according to Eurostat (2003, Nomenclature on Research in Statistics):

- *relevance* of the concepts and data to particular purposes
- *accuracy* of estimates
- *timeliness*, i.e. the timelag between the data release and the data collection reference period
- *accessibility* to and clarity of the available information
- *comparability* of the information between countries and time
- *coherence* between different sets of concepts and statistics
- *completeness* of the data in specific statistical exercises

The data quality management at Statistics Canada uses a very similar structure. According to them, "quality of data" is defined as a "fitness to use" with six dimensions (Statistics Canada, 2003): *Relevance, Accuracy, Timeliness, Accessibility, Interpretability* and *Coherence*. Therefore, we assume that these dimensions cover the aspects of data quality.

The dimensions are ordered according to their importance. This is important, because the dimensions are not independent of each other. It is possible that conflicts occur in practice, especially, when only a limited amount of time and money was made available for the whole data generation process. Often, trade-offs are necessary. Higher accuracy usually requires more time for preparation and processing, thus data production requires more time which could reduce the timeliness. Generating highly relevant data is more important than offering widely accessible data, which is in conflict in countries where data privacy is an issue. These problems have been and still are being discussed in the statistical community (Holt and Jones, 1998).

Rounding concerns several of these dimensions. In particular, we discuss the effects on the accuracy and comparability of data. Accuracy can be defined, e.g., according to Brackstone (1999, p.5):

> "The accuracy of statistical information is the degree to which the information correctly describes the phenomena it was designed to measure. It is usually characterized in terms of error

in statistical estimates and is traditionally decomposed into bias (systematic error) and variance (random error) components. It may also be described in terms of the major sources of error that potentially cause inaccuracy (e.g., coverage, sampling, non-response, response)."

According to this definition, accuracy is the degree to which a concept is measured correctly using a statistical instrument. Therefore, rounding and the use of income brackets are clearly aspects of accuracy, though they are not the most important factors. Sampling, of course, is one of the very roots of statistical investigation and has the most important impact on accuracy. Much methodological development has been done, because statisticians wanted to know how accurate certain sampling schemes and designs are and how to make best use of the resources at the disposal – especially with respect to time and money (Neyman, 1934).

A statistical instrument may be the vector of observations or a parameter describing the distribution of values or an aggregate like a population total. Some errors may be small on individual level, but sum up to considerable errors in the estimation of population totals. Others could be relatively huge on individual level, but cancel out when aggregated. For agencies who provide panel data, both views can be important – depending on whether it is their duty to provide accurate data at the so-called micro-level with small units, e.g., for individual households, or at the macro-level of large units or the total population. It is not certain how rounding relates to this. It is possible that rounded values and income brackets are quite inaccurate on the micro-level, but this does not necessarily mean that this causes errors on macro-level.

In the remaining parts of this Chapter we will show examples where rounding has an impact, and where not.

2.1.2 Improving the accuracy of data

Whenever people produce official statistics, all parameters which might have an effect on accuracy and other aspects of quality have to be taken into consideration. With respect to accuracy, Brackstone (1999) suggests eight primary aspects of design which require attention. We quote and give some comments:

"1. Explicit consideration of overall trade-offs between accuracy, cost, timeliness and respondent burden during the design stage. The extent and sophistication of these considerations will depend on the size of the program, and the scope for options in light of the program parameters. But evidence that proper consideration was given to these trade-offs should be visible.

2. Explicit consideration of alternative sources of data, including the availability of existing data or administrative records, to minimize new data collection. This issue focuses on the minimization of respondent burden and the avoidance of unnecessary collection."

Sampling data through personal interviews is possibly not the only survey instrument available. For example, secondary sources for income data might be employer records and tax records. Due to privacy reasons, such data are rarely available for processing in a survey. The Finnish sub-sample of the ECHP is one of the rare occasions where such data has been used to assess the accuracy of interview data. Another option is to use auxiliary information for quality control. The G-SOEP already uses some auxiliary data (e.g., regional population totals from other sources) for weighting purposes. Another option is to collect information from other representative surveys for the same population.

"3. Adequate justification for each question asked, and appropriate pre-testing of questions and questionnaires, while also assuring that the set of questions asked is sufficient to achieve the descriptive and analytical aims of the survey.

4. Assessment of the coverage of the target population by the proposed survey frames.

5. Within overall trade-offs, proper consideration of sampling and estimation options and their impact on accuracy, timeliness, cost, response burden and comparisons of data over time.

6. Adequate measures in place for encouraging response, following up non-response, and dealing with missing data."

Regarding points 3 and 6 and income data, some income types might be less known or more sensitive than others. The respondent's cooperativeness is possibly influenced by very sensitive questions during the interview process. A carefully designed set of questions increases the overall response rate and might improve the accuracy of data. For example, many incomes can be measured in different ways. The *employee wage* can be asked for as total "gross" or "net" value. Depending on the national framework and personal circumstances, some individuals know one of the two types of income, some know the other. Instead of asking for just one type, it is common to ask for both. Knowing one type is helpful when the other one has to be imputed, and if respondents tell both values, additional consistency checks can be done.

Concerning question design about gross or net income, asking for one figure is the most simple solution. However, there is a high risk involved that the respondent does not answer the question correctly, because it is too difficult, or he does not answer it at all, therefore providing no information. A more sophisticated option is to split the income value into components which are asked for separately and put together during data processing. This is the usual procedure for household income in the ECHP. Missing information on individual income components can be imputed separately and the overall amount of information is greater. The drawback is a high interview burden due to income questions.

If only one value is asked for, and the respondent does not answer the initial question, then it is possible to use one or more follow-up questions. One possibility for personal wage and earnings is to ask for gross and net income. Another option is to ask for the annual total when the monthly average is not known. These are options used in the ECHP questionnaire. Another option is to offer various pre-defined ranges, and ask the respondent to choose one of the ranges in which the true value perhaps is. While all these options perhaps reduce complete item non-response and therefore increase the accuracy of data, they also increase the tedium during interview. The trade-off between accuracy and respondent burden has to be considered (see point 1.). Also, it is reasonable that additional questions could cause new errors.

"7. Proper consideration of the need for quality assurance processes for all stages of collection and processing.

8. Appropriate internal and external consistency checking of data with corresponding correction or adjustment strategies."

An international survey like the ECHP is often a multi-stage, multi-center study. Many different organizations and persons are involved: National institutes, private institutes which are specialized on official statistics, full-time and part-time employees, scientists and others.[1]

It was one of the main issues of the CHINTEX project to examine the quality of data in the ECHP, and to assess whether the approaches to produce harmonized data have been successful. Indicators for data quality (and especially lack of quality) and methods to improve the quality of data after the sampling steps are investigated. Rounding is a simple yet influential factor for the accuracy of data. Describing the amount of rounding in data could be an additional tool to compare and evaluate the quality of data.

2.2 Response type as a result of the interview process

An interview is a multi-stage process. Based on options generated through the interview design and decisions made by the respondent during the interview, a variety of different types of response is possible. In this section, we briefly discuss the interview process as far as it is of concern for this thesis.

The ECHP interview process

Figure 2.1 gives a simplified overview of the ECHP interview process with respect to the question on normal wage and earnings.

First, a contact with the household has to be established and interviews with the head of household and all household members have to be arranged. Each household member has the choice to refuse being interviewed – which would result in *unit non-response*, the lowest type of response with respect to accuracy. When an individual refuses to participate in all future waves, too, he is called an *attriter*.

During a successful interview, a respondent is asked if he receives specific income components, for example, if he is working in paid employment. If the answer is no, the information has been gained that the person does not receive an income from the specific source. If the answer is yes, the person is asked to tell the income value.

In the following part of the section are excerpts from the blueprint ECHP personal interview, questions on gross wage and earning (Eurostat, 1999b, p. 58-60).

---

[1] In Section 3.1.2, the ECHP will be described in more detail.

Figure 2.1: Interview Process and Responses

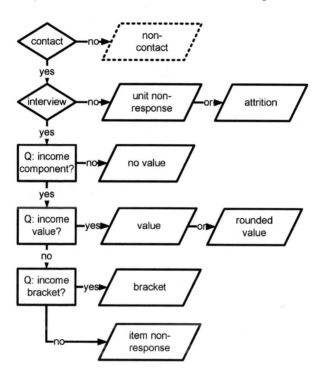

"Q130: We would like to ask you about any changes of your activity that may have occurred during 1995. Here are the categories to describe your main activity status.

Main activity: job or business	Code
Paid employment, whether full-time or part-time	01
Paid apprenticeship or training under special schemes related to employment	02
Self-employment (with or without employees)	03
Unpaid work in family enterprise	04"

[...]

If codes 01, 02 or 03 from above list were valid for the whole year of 1995 or at least some of the months, the interviewer went into details:

"Q132: Now we would like to ask about your income in 1995.

Can we begin with any income you have had as an employee, including both casual or temporary work and any regular work. Did you at any time in 1995 receive a wage, salary or other form of pay for work as an employee or an apprentice?"

The question could be answered by yes, no, or no answer. If this questions was not answered with "no", then the interviewer asked the respondent to provide the specific level of income:

"Q133: During 1995, what were your normal earning *per month* worked?

You are requested to give the gross amount, that is the amount before tax and contributions to social insurance are deducted, and the net amount, that is the take-home pay.

Gross amount per month in NC: (1 - 99999990) or missing
Net amount per month in NC   (1 - 99999990) or missing"

In this question, the type of income which is asked for was described in detail. But the respondent was not told to provide the answer with a certain level of precision. The respondent was free to answer with any accurate or rounded value.[2]

If the individual did not give a value, then in the German ECHP interview he (or she) was asked to chose one from a list of pre-defined income brackets. Asking this follow-up question was a standard procedure for household income interviews, but not for personal gross wage and earnings. This was a deviation from the ECHP blueprint questionnaire.

In case the individual had not answered with a valid gross or net income per month, he was asked to give an estimate for the annual total (gross or

---

[2] Outside the ECHP, studies have analyzed the overall level of accuracy gained by certain question designs. In particular, new or alternative techniques show promising results in experimental studies, like the use of *implicit brackets* (Moore and Loomis, 2001).

net). A brief empirical analysis of the response types can be found in the Appendix, Section A.2.2.

After these income questions, the interview continued to ask for how many month this income was received, whether there were extra payments, how much, and so on. Therefore, the blueprint questionnaire explicitly or implicitly offered many different valid response possibilities:

- non-contact
- unit non-response
- not eligible / no value
- value / rounded value (net or gross, monthly or annual)
- income brackets
- item non-response

It is notable that the achieved level of information gained is not totally concordant with the interview burden: If the respondent shows full cooperation, then all follow-up questions were skipped, especially questions on net values and income brackets. Full cooperation is one of the fastest ways to complete the interview.[3]

2.3 Rounding in statistics, a short review

2.3.1 Early literature on the effects of rounding

The effect of rounding and *grouping* of data has been analyzed from the early years of modern statistics on, because of a simple reason: Data were often aggregated, tabulated and thereby rounded or grouped before being processed further. Often, statisticians received only pre-aggregated and tabulated data with finite precision and had to work with the reduced amount of information therein. In addition, it was a matter of efficiency to work with aggregated parameters instead with raw data.

Sheppard (1898) wrote an article on the effect of grouping on the moments of a normal distribution. He stated that the effect on the mean was negligible under most circumstances, while the variance estimation was biased by a factor $1/12w^2$ proportional to the squared rounding interval w. Hence, he recommended what is now known as *Sheppard's Correction*, a heuristic

---

[3] More discussion on the relation between cooperation and response types can be found in Section 6.1.4.

to calculate an unbiased estimator of the variance in the presence of rounding error. This is especially useful in regression analysis. If a variable is measured with error and used as an explanatory variable, then the slope coefficients – when estimated with the ordinary least squares method – underestimates the true slope (Fuller, 1987, Section 1.1). This is called "attenuation bias".

Tricker (1984) analyzed the effect of rounding on other distributions than the normal distribution,[4] and concluded that the bias is not only dependent on the measurement error introduced by rounding, but also on the exact position of the (accurate) mean within the *rounding lattice*[5], and especially the type of distribution. Rounding has a much higher impact on the moments of skewed distributions than on symmetrical ones. For symmetrical distributions, the first moment is rather unaffected and only the second and higher moments are influenced by rounding. But in other cases, for example log-normal, gamma, exponential and other skewed distributions, rounding has a distinctive impact.

2.3.2 Literature on the reasons and types of rounding

An early paper on rounding due to measurement scale was written by G.U. Yule, who analyzed scales like body height, thermometer readings and weightings (Yule, 1927). People reading from scales with finite precision tend to prefer certain digits, which in turn has an impact on the distribution of final digits. If data is not sampled by scientists and field-work personal, but by students or untrained staff, then the data is often of low quality in many respects. Not only rounding, odd distributions of final digits, but also a high number of identical observations cause problems. For example, date or birth in some regions does not follow more or less the uniform distribution, but instead lots of values are heaped on a small number of days. This *heaping* is caused by the fact that in some states (like some regions in Turkey) parents do not give the exact date of birth for young

---

[4] Early authors, for example Eisenhart (1947), treated rounding and its effects with respect to the normal distribution only.

[5] The rounding lattice is the usually even-spaced subset of rounded values. For example, Tricker states that the bias for symmetrical distributions – like normal and Laplace – is zero when the accurate mean coincides with either the center or the border of the rounding intervals (Tricker, 1984, p. 384).

children. Instead the date of registration or some other fixed day is used by the authorities for all children whose birth is being registered upon an other fixed day.

Scale measurements are not necessarily rounded to multiples of five or ten. In some cases, values are multiples of other measurement units. For example, if body height is measured in inches and then edited in centimeters, the distribution of observed values will not look rounded on first view – but the problem is only hidden and not solved yet. The same effect happens when values are transformed into other units. A very important example is the transformation of many European Currencies into the Euro: If historic data involving monetary amounts (in national currencies) has been transformed into Euro data, then it is difficult or impossible to determine whether the data was originally rounded or not.

2.3.3 Benford's Law and rounding

Someone could argue that a round value is not necessarily the result of human rounding, but is naturally round. In fact, if we would draw uniformly distributed random integer numbers from a certain span of values, say, 1 to 999, then 99 of them would be multiples of 10, and 9 values would even be multiples of 100: The numbers 100, 200, 300,... 900. It is the question what natural amount of rounded data we would expect in a random sample of values.

This question is related to another topic: The distribution of first digits in *natural numbers* and *Benford's Law of Anomalous Numbers*.[6]

In 1938, Benford noticed that pages of logarithms corresponding to numbers starting with 1 were more worn out than other pages. He then analyzed data from very different sources such as the length of rivers, baseball statistics, numbers in magazine articles and the street addresses of the first 342 people listed in the book *American Men of Science*. Across all these sets of "natural numbers", the number 1 turned up as the first digit about 30% of the time, and the other digits were less frequent. He found a similar pattern for the second digit distribution.

---

[6] This so-called law was named in honor of Benford (1938), though in fact the main content of his article was based on the even older "Note on the Frequency of Use of the Different Digits in Natural Numbers" by Newcomb (1889).

Benford found out that the distribution of first digits in real samples usually does not follow an uniform distribution. In most cases, the first digits 1, 2, 3 are encountered more often than the digits 7, 8, or 9. The idea of Benford's Law is, that each digit is usually encountered more often than the next one. An intuitive explanation for this is the cards in the hat example, which is explained in the Appendix, Section A.4.1.

More than a century after Newcomb's article, Carslaw (1988) applied Benford's Law to accounting data. With some math, the general formula for the probability of the nth digit being equal to j can be calculated (Nigrini and Metternaier, 1997). Since then, it has become a tool among auditors to detect accountancy fraud and irregular patterns in financial data and many references on Benford's law and its application have appeared.

However, Benford's law in its original form assumes that the values are fairly evenly distributed on a linear or logarithmic scale. Income, however, does not follow that distribution.

But when people round data, they change the natural distribution of digits. The second (and the following) digits are more often equal to zero than expected for continuous values (such as values sampled from a theoretical distribution). Therefore, the frequency of other digits has to be lower than expected.

By comparing the distribution of certain digits such as the second digit or the final digit(s), oddities and deviations from natural (accurate) numbers can be detected.

2.3.4 A psychological model for rounding

Respondent knowledge is rarely a yes/no issue. A respondent often has a more or less accurate idea of things that matter to him, like wage and earnings. Therefore, respondent knowledge is often a matter of accuracy. The reason why humans tend to round values and remember only a few digits might be explained by the psychological theory of *cognitive reference points* by Rosch (1975). Regarding amounts of money, people tend to remember the magnitude of a value (usually, as a magnitude of 10) and the first digit(s) and forget the rest. If they have to respond the amount from memory, then they edit zeros for digits they do not remember and therefore produce a rounded value. If they do not know the value at all and take a guess, then they produce a random number which, according to results from experimental psychology, is often highly rounded; cf. Brugger (1997). As a side note, rounding is not necessarily the cause for errors in data – sometimes it is a side-effect. To edit a value, the reporter is not only required to have sufficient knowledge, he needs to be motivated to cooperate, too. At least three reasons are possible why an interviewee reports a rounded value:

- The accurate value is a round value.

- The accurate value is not round, but the respondent does not know it exactly and reports a rounded value or guesses the value.

- The respondent does not know the accurate value at all or does not understand the question and makes up a value as a guess to hide his ignorance.

Some researchers come to interesting results, which are also helpful in the analysis of rounded responses. For example, Schräpler (2004) has written an article about the motives for item non-response in income questions, and introduces an approach to separate "don't know" from "refuse to answer" in the BHPS (British Household Panel Study) and the GSOEP. This bears some similarities to the difference between precise and rounded answers. Schräpler found evidence for the assumptions that interviewee cooperation is a continuum between no cooperation and full cooperation. The two frameworks he deployed to explain respondent behavior are rational choice theory (Esser, 1993) and cognitive theory (Tourangeau et al., 2000; Tourangeau, 1984). In rational choice theory, it is assumed that respondents choose their response type, and their decision is based on the information they currently have about the interview and the survey and what consequences they expect for the different types of response. With reference to rounding, it is an open question whether (the degree of) rounding is an indicator for cooperativeness, too.

Cognitive theory assumes that the interview is a multi-stage process, from interpreting and understanding the question, retrieving the knowledge necessary to answer the question, to editing the question into the final format, thereby producing an answer.

Rounding is an aspect of knowing the data and editing the answer, so it touches both rational choice theory and cognitive theory, and the aforementioned theory of cognitive reference points.

2.3.5 Hypothetical factors with an effect on rounding

The propensity whether a value is rounded or not may be affected by a number of factors. Some are listed below but specific factors will be discussed in later chapters.

- Measurement instrument.
- Each question has a smallest unit of precision and a maximum number of digits for recordings, this limits the accuracy.
- The measuring unit is of importance. If respondents have to use unfamiliar or new measurement units, e.g., meters instead of imperial feet, then the rounding behavior could be different.
- Interview technique.
- A stimulus like "please estimate" in the question could encourage respondents to respond with a rounded value.
- The question context plays a role, for example, previous questions could have an impact by focussing the respondents attention on a certain part of his memories or increase his willingness to disclose income details.
- Panel conditioning.
- As people get acquainted to a specific survey or interviewer, they might have more trust and give more accurate answers.
- Previous knowledge of questions could cause that respondents become more sensitive to specific income values.
- People become bored during the interview and do not want to answer the same questions again every time. They try to rush through the interview and thereby do not answer questions carefully.
- Level of difficulty.
- The chance that the respondent can provide a specific information requires that the person is familiar with it. It does play a role whether he needs this information frequently, or if he has used it only recently.
- The more digits, the more difficult to remember. Usually, longer values are reported with lower absolute accuracy.

- Data processing.

- If a value is the sum of values of which some are rounded and some are not, the result does often not seem to be rounded although it contains an error component due to rounding. Adjustments, sums and imputation can have a masking effect.

This is not an exclusive list, and some or all of these factors can possibly play a role. In addition to these general factors, individual factors are probably important. Some persons have a good memory for figures, others can only remember the overall magnitude of a value but not the single digits.

Taking these things together, we assume that rounding cannot be contributed to a single factor. Possibly, a combination of several factors can be useful to predict rounding behavior. An immediate consequence is, that the probability to provide a rounded value is not homogeneous for all persons in a sample.

2.3.6 Literature on methods to use rounded data

Rounding is not only a psychological phenomenon: Processing of data often requires rounding on a technical level, it is simply necessary to squeeze continuous variables with an arbitrary or even infinite number of digits into a value with finite precision. This is a topic in computer programming and numerical algorithms. Calculations involving rounding can be technically computed using standards like IEEE Task P754 (1985) which guarantee consistent rounding across algorithms and processing units and a minimum rounding error. The maximum amount of rounding error in computational problems is often less than the value of the last digit.[7] These rather technical aspects are not discussed in this paper.

Rounded data cause two problems: 1. Rounded data implies that a part of the information is missing. 2. Respondents who like to edit rounded values are probably different from others. Statisticians often ignore this issue of data quality, though it can lead to biased estimates and inappropriate interpretations of results.

These two points are not surprising for persons who are acquainted with missing data problems. In fact, the topic of rounded data has been discussed

---

[7] However, in repeated calculations with rounding steps after each calculation, the total error can grow considerably.

in a somewhat broader context under the keywords of *grouped continuous* or *coarse* data (Heitjan, 1989, p. 164). Heitjan's formal description of the missing data problem of grouped or rounded data is:

> "Suppose that the random variable $\mathbf{x}$ is distributed according to a density f in a sample space χ, which is partitioned into a collection of disjoint measurable sets $\{S_i\}, \chi = \cup S_i$. Suppose that instead of observing $\mathbf{x}$ exactly, one receives the datum $\mathbf{y} = \mathbf{y}(\mathbf{x})$, where $\mathbf{y}(\ )$ is a function that conveys the identity of the subset S_i of χ into which $\mathbf{x}$ has fallen.[...]"

According to this definition, coarse data includes data rounded after only one or a few digits, data measured in brackets, and censored data (e.g., for time intervals). The vector of observed values $\mathbf{y}$ is an incomplete (coarse) information, and $\mathbf{x}$ is the complete information. This way, rounded data, missing data and brackets are all more or less incomplete – and can possibly be treated within the same theoretical framework. The question is how to make use of the observed information, for example, "to draw inference from y to an unknown parameter $\theta \in \Theta$" of the distribution $f(x)$. Missing and incomplete data problems are important areas in the field of applied statistics, though they rarely deal specifically with rounded data.

Dempster and Rubin discussed "the Appropriateness of Sheppard's Correction" in least squares regression and compared it to the naive approach – treating the data as if they were not rounded. They concluded that Sheppard's Correction improved the estimation, but suggested using a full specification of the distribution of all variables – including the rounding procedure – and solving with the EM algorithm[8] Rubin has used so well in missing data situations (Dempster and Rubin, 1983). However, they warn that "*Probability models for rounding errors must be interpreted with great care if they are to lead to sound adjustments for rounding error.*", and this statement is surely true for recent methods, too.

Several statisticians have offered methods to work with rounded data. But the methods are based on assumptions which often do not hold. For example, Manski and Tamer (2002) have published an article sketching a

---

[8] EM stands for Expectation-Maximization, the algorithm is detailed in Dempster and Rubin (1977).

framework for regression with interval data. Their framework requires an assumption of mean independence: The expected value of the complete information is independent of the fact whether the observed value is complete or incomplete, thus $E(y|x_{\text{complete}}) = E(y|x_{\text{incomplete}})$. If the completeness of information is dependent on other observed or unobserved information, the model would not generate unbiased estimates.[9]

Recently, the topic has received new impetus. Lee and Vardeman (2001) have written articles on how to use *quantized* data – e.g., values known with finite precision – in likelihood estimation. And Winter (2002) has investigated the biases when using brackets and suggests methods to analyze "biased interval data", e.g., by extending Manski and Tamer's model.

2.3.7 Applied methods for incomplete data

When working with partially missing or mixed data (e.g. some values are continuous, grouped continuous like rounded values, and interval like income brackets), many standard software packages do not support the researcher with build-in routines for heterogeneity and additional variation due to lack of precision.

Sometimes, methods which deal with missing data can be used for mixed data, too. There are many approaches: delete cases, impute values, estimate separate models, model the mixture, and ignore the problem. In the following section, we briefly sketch such methods.

Case Deletion. Simply ignore units with insufficient quality of data. This method is not recommended in general, because one would throw away useful data.

Single Imputation. Treat interval and grouped interval data as partially missing data and fill in the rest to give exact values, e.g. using one of the following methods.

a) Mean imputation. Intervals are replaced by the arithmetic mean of the interval, which implies that rounded values will NOT be changed, and interval data will be replaced by the middle of the interval.

b) Plug-in methods. The mean is estimated using some plug-in estimation for the distribution of values within the interval limits. For example, assumptions about the distribution of the latent value could be used, possibly

---

[9] This is related to R. Moffitt's dichotomy of *missing on observables* and *missing on unobservables*, cf. Fitzgerald et al. (1998).

extended by using the correlation with other characteristics. Plug-in methods generate a distribution of values, and either the mean or a randomly drawn value can be used for the imputation.

Multiple imputation. Single imputation has the drawback that the variance and standard errors of the statistics are not correctly estimated. The standard errors would have to be adjusted to account for the imputation method. The idea of multiple imputation is simple, see e.g., a summary by (Faris et al., 2002, p.186):

> "Multiple imputation methods randomly draw observations from a fitted distribution for the covariates and the outcome variable. For each imputed data set, the missing data are filled in with values drawn randomly [with replacement] from the distribution. Analyses are performed on each data set as though the data had been completely observed. The results of these analyses are then pooled to provide point and variance estimates for the effects of interest."

Of course, multiple imputation cannot always be used with success. A disadvantage is that the choice of the method to create imputed values is important. For example, multiple imputation does not work with mean imputation, because the imputed sets of data would be identical. A simple approach to impute rounded data would be to select a value from the set of possible values. E.g., when the value 600 was provided by the respondent, the imputed values should be from the range 550 to 649.

Often, a parametric approach is chosen, where a predictive distribution of the variables whose values are missing is used. If the values are not missing at random, but correlated with the true missing value, or with the sampling probability (i.e., persons with missing data have a lower sampling probability than persons with complete data), then this predictive posterior distribution must include these mechanisms. Clearly, in complicated data situations with lots of different variables missing and the missing values are not missing at random, finding a suitable joint predictive posterior distribution can be quite hard. In these cases, researchers often use simpler approaches. In the case of the ECHP, the program IVEware was used. Within the CHINTEX project, Spiess and Goebel (2004) discussed and evaluated the performance of this software with respect to imputation. As one conclusion, they found out (and confirmed previous results by other researchers) that it is preferable to use as many information as possible when creating imputed values.

Hot deck imputation is a non-parametric alternative. "The basic idea of the hot deck method is that for subjects whose X is missing, an X is imputed by simply choosing at random from among validation sample members with matching Y and Z." (Reilly, 1993), where Z are covariates like age, gender or job type which are used to stratify the data.

The first drawback of this method is that the number of observations in the group of sample members with matching Y and Z can be quite small when the number of groups is high. The second problem is the assumption that the data is missing at random, i.e., the units with missing data could be a random sub-sample from the study population. However, this assumption is difficult to confirm, given the fact that we do not have data missing, but also that not all information available on the subjects is surveyed, and some hidden effects exist which can cause biases in imputation approaches.[10]

Several multiple imputation methods are described e.g. in Little and Rubin (2002) and Schafer (1997).

Separate Models. In this approach, the data are separated into partitions with identical type of precision (e.g., complete, incomplete). For each partition, an appropriate method indicated is used, and the results are combined.

Latent variable model. Rounded and interval data could be modelled as a latent variable problem. For incomplete data, the true value of X is unknown, but the observed value provides at least a partial information which, for example, can be used in a maximum likelihood model.

Schweitzer and Severance-Lossin (1996) have written a working paper with such an approach. They used a Generalized Methods of Moments to investigate and describe the occurrence of rounding in the Annual Demographics Supplement to the Current Population Survey (CPS) on a range of different statistics.

Another proposal, the **coarsened data model**, was made by Heitjan and Rubin (1991, p. 2247). The coarsened data model assumes an underlying

---

[10] In Chapter 6, we analyse several possible effects with respect to correlation with rounding behavior.

variable X and a parameter vector θ which is required for estimating: $Y \sim f(x|\theta)$. This is a good example for many coarse data situations, e.g. readings from a scale with finite precision or age reported in years.

For a coarsened data likelihood, consider another variable G which holds the information about the coarseness (or precision) by which X is reported. The distribution of G can be modelled using a parameter vector γ and assuming a distribution function $G \sim h(X, \gamma)$. The random variable G determines the mapping of $X \rightarrow Y$. The model is not limited to rounded variable, but could also include other coarse or incomplete data types, too, for example censored data.

In the rounded data situation, G is not directly observed, but can be infered from Y. Y given $(X, G) = (x, g)$ has a conditional distribution which can be used in likelihood analysis. The advantage of this method is that it is compatible to common maximum likelihood approaches, and could therefore be implemented in the statistical software GAUSS, for example. The disadvantage is that it requires assumptions and a model how to infer from Y to X using G.

Ignore the problem. This is by far the most common approach. In some situations, when data are only slightly rounded and the methods are not particularly sensitive to this measurement error, it does not necessarily introduce a great additional error or bias. However, at least a simulation study should be applied to analyze the effect of rounding on the results. If only a few data are rounded and rounding is random, that means not correlated with either the true value of the rounded variable or other variables which are used in the analysis, then the effect of rounding could be negligible. The simulations in Section 2.6 demonstrate some situations when rounding is negligible and when it is not.

Remark: The topics *rounding* and *interval data* are covered in many different areas of literature, and this review could only give an incomplete overview. However, empirical results on the extend of rounding in actual panel surveys are rare, and the amount of rounding in survey data is rarely described at all.

2.4 Types of human rounding in interviews

Rounding can happen in various ways. Almost any value encountered in empirical research has been rounded in one way or the other. Respondent rounding is only one of several origins of rounding.

In interviews (oral or questionnaire-based), rounding is often a phenomenon with a psychological background. Characteristics like time intervals, amounts of money, fractions, and scale measurements are often rounded, for example:

- Time and time intervals are rounded to full weeks, month, or year.

- Amounts of money are rounded to multiples of 1, 10, 100, 1000, etc.

- Fractions (in percent) are rounded to integers, especially multiples of 5 or 10.

- Depending on education and cultural background, people round values to integer multiples of typical measurement units like
  - meter and centimeter or miles, feet and inches
  - Euro, Dollar or other national currency units
  - kilo or pound

- Scale readings have a finite precision (e.g., digital scales).

The difference between mathematical rounding during data processing and "human" rounding during interviews is, that in the first case the level of rounding is usually known and all values are subject to the same type, e.g., rounding to next integer. But in the latter case, the rounding process is not determined and can lead to different results:

- Rounding after decimal point: Most people would round 99.90 to 100, but it could also be truncated to 99.

- Rounding of odd to "next even" number: 2949 could be rounded to 2950, 2900, or 3000.

- Rounding to "next" amount with a fixed number of significant digits. 8514 could be rounded after 1 digit $\rightarrow$ 9000, after 2 digits $\rightarrow$ 8500, or after 3 digits $\rightarrow$ 8510.

- In a very similar way, figures can be rounded to "next" multiple of a fixed rounding unit, e.g., 100. 8514 would be rounded to 8500, 123456 to 123500.

- Rounding does not have to be "mathematical" rounding. Some persons could always round up or down, or round only small amounts (e.g., round 9 and 11 to 10, but do not round 8 or 12).

As a result, data provided by different interviewees are often a mixture of values which are rounded in different ways. These data can not be treated as data rounded by a simple mathematical process.

2.5 The rounding indicator

2.5.1 Definition

Our rounding indicator takes the incidence and the intensity of rounding into account and provides the number of significant integer digits until all following digits are equal to zero (assuming all income values are integers). This indicator is denoted as $b = b(y)$, a function of the income value y provided by the respondents. Examples are: $b(2) = b(300) = b(7000) = 1$ and $b(11) = b(170) = b(6800) = 2$.

To further explain our approach, consider a sequential rounding process: An interviewee who decides to report a value edits the value digit by digit, starting with the highest digit. After each digit, he decides whether he continues editing, or if he rounds the actual digit and fills out "zeroes" for all remaining digits. This way, he produces any combination of non-zero and zero digits.

b is always less or equal to the total number of digits of x. With numerical methods, b can be calculated as follows: If d is the greatest integer value so that $x \bmod 10^d = 0$ where mod is the modulo operator, then d is the number of *final* digits equal to zero. b can be calculated by subtracting d from the value's total number of digits (for simplicity, disregarding digits after decimal point).

For some analyzes, a dichotomous $\{0, 1\}$ indicator for rounding behavior is required. In these cases, a capital B is used followed by a number for the maximum number of leading digits of rounded values.

$$B2(y) = \begin{cases} 1 & \text{if } b(y) \leq 2 \\ 0 & \text{else} \end{cases}$$

An alternative indicator is based on whether values are integer multiples of "even" values like 10 or 50. In this case, the greatest value k_r from the set of *rounding bases* $\{1, 5, 10, 50, 100, ...\}$ is determined, so that $y \bmod k_r = 0$, where mod is the modulo operator. For a dichotomous indicator of rounded and not rounded values, a specific base number is chosen, e.g., 100. Values which are multiples of this base number are called "rounded".

While this is a simple and easily understandable approach, the results are difficult to compare across countries, data with different numeraires and even across different time periods. One reason is the inflation: The value of the rounding bases is different (e.g., with respect to purchasing power). In Luxembourg, for example, rounding by 100 LUF surely has a lower impact on rounding statistics than rounding by 100 DEM in Germany.

In many data situations, both indicators are highly correlated. For Finnish incomes, which are in the range of several thousand to ten thousands Finmark (former national currency in Finland, abbreviated FIM), $b = 1$ corresponds to rounding by 1000 or 10000 FIM.

Sometimes, we refer to round values as *rounding points*, and to the set of possible rounded values as the *rounding lattice*.

2.5.2 An example

Regardless which indicator is used, a major part of income data in interviews is reported with rounded values. In Figures 2.2 and 2.3, the relative frequencies of rounded values in average gross wage and earnings according to either survey or register data of the Finnish sub-sample of the ECHP is compared. Register values are taken as accurate values and are therefore believed to have the advantage of being not subject to rounding or editing errors by respondents. It was a unique chance to use them here for comparison.

As you can see in Figure 2.2, most income values (95%) reported in the survey can be divided by 5, but only about one third of the register data. Further, the number of survey data which can be divided by rounding bases 10, 50 or 100 is well over 90%, but the number of register data which can be divided by these numbers is very small. Almost 50% of survey data are even divisible by 1000 FIM, which is about 160 Euro – hardly an amount of inaccuracy which can be ignored.

Figure 2.3 shows that about for example 90% of the income data in registers have three or more leading digits, while only about 21% of the survey data (average wage and earnings of the Finnish sub-sample of the ECHP) do have 3 or more leading digits. Most survey values have only 1 or two (about 70%) significant digits, while most register values have 4 or 5 significant

Figure 2.2: Frequency of values which are multiples of even numbers k

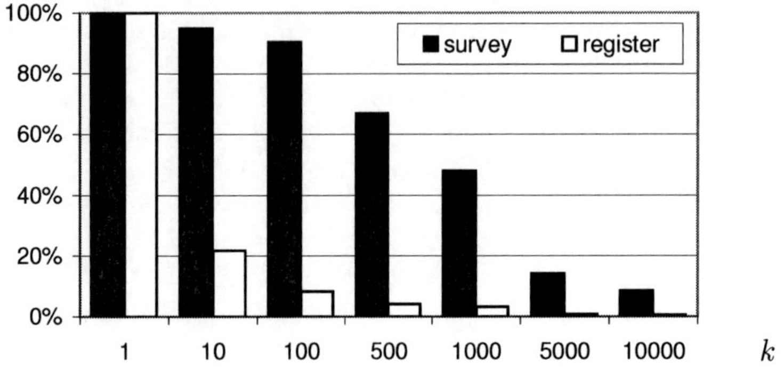

Data: Fin-ECHP, gross wage and earning, wave 3 (1996), N=4437 (survey), N=7747 (register).

digits. Even if one assumes that register data are not "true" data, register data is possibly more accurate than survey interview data. Of course, one potential cause for this difference is the fact that register data are annual totals, while the respondents in the survey interview were asked to provide monthly averages. In Section 5 of this thesis, differences between register and survey data are examined in more detail.

In the European Community Household Panel, rounding of income figures is clearly a common feature, as demonstrated by the previous figures. Also, a look at the distribution of income data would reveal considerable heaping at the rounding points.

Figure 2.4 shows a *kernel density plot* [11] for the net disposable household income data. Figure A.3 in the appendix shows a similar plot for the personal gross wage and earning.

The figure shows the smoothed density of incomes up to 30000 FIM. Ob-

---

[11] Cf. Silverman (1986) or Wand and Jones (1995) for an introduction to kernel density estimation. A brief introduction to kernel densities and a method to take rounding into account is presented in Section 2.6.3 of this thesis.

Figure 2.3: Frequency of values accurate by at least b significant
digits

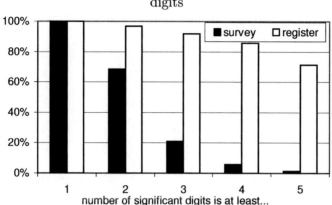

Ordinate: Relative frequency of income data which is a multiple
of k. Data: Fin-ECHP, gross wage and earning, wave 3 (1996),
N=4437 (survey, monthly value), N=7747 (register, annual value).

viously, it is a curve with many local peaks, which always coincide with
multiples of 1000 or 10000 – the global maximum is at 10000. The smooth-
ness of the curve can be modified by changing the bandwidth parameter.
With a greater bandwidth parameter, the presence of rounded value would
eventually be hidden.

Figure 2.5 shows the same data with a different bandwidth. In this figure,
the distinct peaks at 10000 and 15000 are still indicated but the peaks at
each multiple of 1000 are no longer visible.

2.5.3 Denotation of accurate and reported income

The reported income is denoted as y, and the accurate income (usually
unobserved) is denoted as x. Subscripts are used if necessary, for example,
y_i is the reported income for unit i.

The accurate and the observed income can be different because of rounding
and of other reporting errors. As long as we do not take other types of
measurement error into account, x_i is not necessarily the "true" value.

Figure 2.4: Empirical density of household income (1)

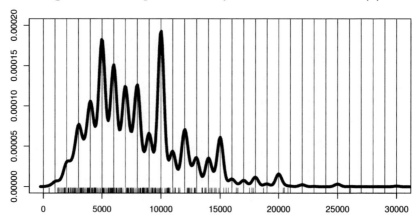

Kernel density estimation (using a gaussian kernel and a bandwidth of 250) of household income (FIM). Data: Fin-ECHP 1996.

Because not all observations y are rounded, we sometimes use y_r for the sub-sample of round observations. It can be argued that it is not possible to know whether a value has been rounded by the respondent, or if it is truly a round value and has been reported exactly, so $y_r = x$. This case is called "employer rounding", while the more typical case $y_r \neq x$ is called "employee rounding". In Germany, due to tariff agreements, which rarely produce rounded values, employer rounding is very rare among non-self-employed persons.[12] In other countries, rounded wages are perhaps more frequent.

2.5.4 The rounding error

Given x and b, both the response y and the absolute rounding error $|x - y|$ are defined. If only y is known, b can be calculated and the precise value x is at least known up to an interval depending on y and b.

---

[12] Source: Personal communications with Stephan Bender, German Institute for Employment Research, IAB.

Figure 2.5: Empirical density of household income (2)

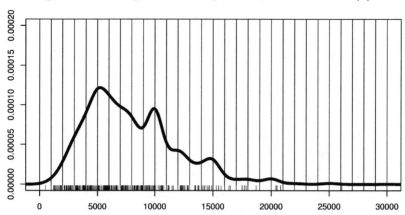

Kernel density estimation (using a gaussian kernel and a bandwidth of 640) of household income (FIM). Data: Fin-ECHP 1996.

When a rounded value y_r is reported, we do not know the accurate value x. But we can assume that x is in an interval $[x_l, x_u] = X(y_r) \subseteq \mathbb{X}$ so that $Y_r(X(y_r)) = y_r$. Here, $Y_r(X)$ is the rounded value (or set of rounded values) Y_r given X, $X(y_r)$ is the set of all possible values of X whose rounded value is equal to y_r, and $\mathbb{X}$ is the set of all possible values of X.

To specify the width of the interval $X(y_r)$, the rounding indicator k_r from Section 2.5.1 can be used.

Assuming mathematical rounding (rounding to nearest value $y_r = i \cdot k_r$, $i \in \mathbb{Z}$), the interval which covers the possible accurate values is $X(y_r) = [y_r - \frac{k_r}{2}, y_r + \frac{k_r}{2}]$.

Example: $y_r = 480 \Rightarrow k_r = 10$ and $x \in [475; 485]$.

Of course, this assumes that the value provided by the respondent is indeed a rounded version of the true value. In the presence of other measurement errors, it is not possible to separate a rounding effect completely from other types of measurement error without making assumptions about the cognitive details of the rounding process. Therefore, some simplifications are necessary.

The *rounding error* $\epsilon_r = y_r - x$ is the difference between an accurate value and the reported value with rounding. Sometimes, we use the absolute rounding error $|\epsilon_r|$. The value of k_r is an upper limit for the absolute rounding error.

Sometimes the *relative rounding error* $(y_r - x)/x$ is a reasonable quantity. Rounding is a special kind of measurement error, but it is not the only measurement error – in fact, rounding error and other measurement errors can hardly be separated properly. Thus, if any person does not know the "true" value x, but only an estimate $x' = x + \epsilon$, and then rounds this value to $y_r = y + \epsilon_r$, then of course $y_r = x + \epsilon + \epsilon_r$ and ϵ_r is possibly dependent on ϵ and x. It would not be possible to separate ϵ from ϵ_r when only y_r has been observed.

2.6 The impact of rounding on an empirical distribution

In this section, we want to demonstrate some immediate effects of rounding on an empirical distribution when a rounded value $y_r = y_r(x)$ is observed for the value of the x-variable.

2.6.1 Immediate consequences

(1) Rounding implies a loss of information about the true values. As an effect, OLS estimators using observed data as substitutes for true (not rounded) values could be biased, even in large samples. Knowledge on this topic is scattered across literature, but some papers are quite comprehensive, e.g., "Effects of Rounding or Grouping Data" (Eisenhart, 1947, Chapter 4) which illustrates (analytically, graphically, and with examples) several statistics of small and large numbers of technically rounded observations from normal populations (e.g., mean, variance, Student's t).

(2) Rounding has immediate effects on the ordering of values. After rounding (or grouping), a continuous variable is only partially ordered. If some people report rounded values and others do not, or if values are reported with different levels of rounding (by 10, by 1000), then it could even happen that $x_i > x_j$, but $y_i \leq y_j$. Strictly speaking, this violates the qualities of an ordinal scale.

(3) Rounding has a major impact on the quantiles y_p of an empirical

distribution, and all statistics based on these, for example the Gini coefficient of inequality. We will illustrate this in a simulation study.

(4) An estimation of the underlying distribution using kernel density estimation has very different results depending on how much the values have been rounded. Depending on the bandwidth used with the kernel method, peaks will show up at several rounding points, and the true peaks are shifted (see Figure 2.6).

As an useful side-effect, kernel density plots with relatively small bandwidth may be used as an explorative method to detect rounding points. For example, Figure 2.6 shows a kernel density plot for simulated data. It can be easily seen that the density plot for rounded data has many evenly spaced local peaks. This is an indicator for rounding in data.

Figure 2.6: Density of rounded and true values (simulation)

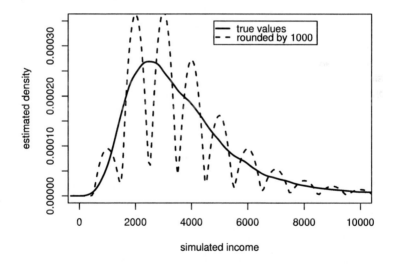

Kernel density estimation (with Epanechnikov kernel, bandwidth of 1000). Data: Simulated log-normal distribution, $\ln(X) \sim \mathcal{N}(\mu = 8.0863, \sigma = 0.5268)$.

Also, automatic bandwidth selection, a technique which is commonly used for kernel density estimates, is affected negatively by rounding: Rounding points become modes for automatic bandwidth selection (Schweitzer and Severance-Lossin, 1996, Section 5.3).

(5) The measurement of change of a variable is of major interest in longitudinal studies. An individual additive measurement error ϵ_i would cancel out when serially correlated, but rounding error does not:

$$
\begin{aligned}
Y_{i,t} &= x_{i,t} + \epsilon_i + \epsilon_{r,t} \Rightarrow \\
Y_{i,t+1} - Y_{i,t} &= (x_{i,t+1} + \epsilon_i + \epsilon_{r,t+1}) - (x_{i,t} + \epsilon_i + \epsilon_{r,t}) \Leftrightarrow \\
Y_{i,t+1} - Y_{i,t} &= (x_{i,t+1} - x_{i,t}) + (\epsilon_{r,t+1} - \epsilon_{r,t})
\end{aligned}
$$

i indicates the individual unit, ϵ_r is the rounding error, and ϵ_i is the individual measurement error.

If $\epsilon_{r,\tau} = \epsilon_r$, then the rounding error would disappear. However, the rounding error $\epsilon_r(x)$ is dependent on the position of value of x on the rounding lattice. And if an interviewee does not know the accurate value $x_{i,t}$, but only the accurate value plus an individual error ϵ_i, then the rounding error ϵ_r is created by mapping $(x_{i,t} + \epsilon_i)$ on the rounding lattice.

Therefore, rounding error does not vanish, it is not even additive, and it does not fit into typical measurement error models, e.g. Fuller (1987).

2.6.2 Impact on cross-sectional income distribution

We want to show the impact of rounding on distributional parameters. First, simulated rounding is applied to simulated data. In these simulations, other types of measurement error (e.g., misreporting and heaping effects other than rounding) are not taken into account. Later simulations use more empirical information, and finally, empirical data is analyzed.

Simulation 1: German household income

The net disposable cash income (in DEM) per household in the G-ECHP data set 1994 (disregarding weights) is approximated with a log-normal distribution $\ln(X) \sim N(\mu = 8.0863, \sigma = 0.5268)$, thus $E(X) = 3733.34$

$Var(X) = 2111.40^2$. Then 10000 random values X_i are drawn independent and identically distributed (i.i.d.). Descriptive statistics are calculated at different levels of rounding (Table 2.1).

Table 2.1: Simulation 1: Simulated G-ECHP household income

rounded	x_{min}	$x_{0.25}$	$x_{0.5}$	$\overline{x}$	$x_{0.75}$	x_{max}	s_x	MAD
by 1	268	2275	3246	3729.3	4630	39745	2113.1	1651.6
by 100	300	2300	3200	3729.3	4600	39700	2113.4	1630.9
by 1000	0	2000	3000	3728.8	5000	40000	2133.6	1482.6

Rounded: Values were rounded to nearest multiple of this rounding base. $x_{\min}$: Observed minimum of rounded values. $x_{0.25}$: First quartile of rounded values. $x_{0.5}$: Second quartile or median of rounded values. $\hat{x}$: Mean value of rounded values. $x_{0.75}$: Third quartile of rounded values. $x_{\max}$: Maximum of rounded values. s_x: Standard deviation of rounded values. MAD: Mean absolute deviation of rounded values. Data: Simulation.

In this simulation, rounding to the nearest 1000 affects many statistics: the minimum, maximum, upper and lower quartiles are shifted by up to -275 and $+370$, and the median by -246. The standard deviation and the mean value are barely changed at rounding by 100, but at the highest rounding level, by 1000, the standard deviation changes by $+20.5$. The median absolute deviation (MAD), used as a "robust" measure for deviation, is 1482.6 instead of 1651.6.

Of course, these results are more or less random because the variance between individual simulations is rather high, even given the sample size of $n = 10000$ random values in the simulation. In a different simulation run, they would be different. Therefore, we want to demonstrate the effect of rounding on the quartiles $x_{0.25}$, $x_{0.5}$ and $x_{0.75}$ in repeated simulations with independent (pseudo-)random samples.

Simulation 1a: German household data, repeated runs

Figure 2.7 shows three times three scatter plots, one for the 25% quartile, one for the median, and one for the 75% quartiles. In each of the one hundred simulation runs, we compare the quartiles computed for accurate and data rounded (mathematically) after one (two or three) significant digits. Because each run uses a different random sample from the distribution, the accurate quartiles are slightly different.

Each comparison is represented by one circle in the respective scatter plot. For easier comparison, the equivalence line is added to each plot. If rounded and non-rounded data would generate the same results, each circle would be exactly on this line.

For data rounded after three digits (upper three scatter plots), the quartiles for rounded and non-rounded data are close to each other, although a slight step function is visible. When rounding after two digits, the step size is large ($100/2200 \approx 4.5\%$) and introduces a lot of variation between the true quartile and the observed quartile. In fact, the variance caused by rounding seems to be bigger than the variance between simulations caused by random sampling. The observed variance, however, is very small. Most values fall into a small number of categories, and the span of the observed (rounded) quartiles is sometimes even greater than the range of the accurate quartiles.

In the lower row, results for rounding after one digit are shown. Here, the quartiles for rounded data are degenerated to a point distribution which is, depending on the position of the accurate quartile relative to the rounding point, severely biased.

Simulation 1b: German household data, random rounding

Someone could argue that Simulation 1 (and 1b) is making too strict assumptions. In reality, instead of N values all being rounded by the same amount, a mixture of different types of rounding is observed.

The result of a bootstrap-type simulation shows the estimated distribution of the five quantiles (minimum, first quartile, median, third quartile, and maximum) and the mean when each value has been subject to a random type of rounding. Each value is individually and independent from the others rounded after 1, 2, 3 or 4 digits. A pseudo-random function rounded a value after 1 digit with 25% probability, after 2 digits with 60%, with 10% probability after 3 digits, and all other values, about 5%, are rounded after 4 digits. These probabilities are similar to the empirical rounding probabilities in the German ECHP data (source: own calculations). We use one set of simulated values from Simulation 1 and calculate the statistics 500 times, each time with different (randomly determined) mixture of rounding types.

Figure 2.7: Scatter plot of rounded vs. non-rounded values in Simulation 1a

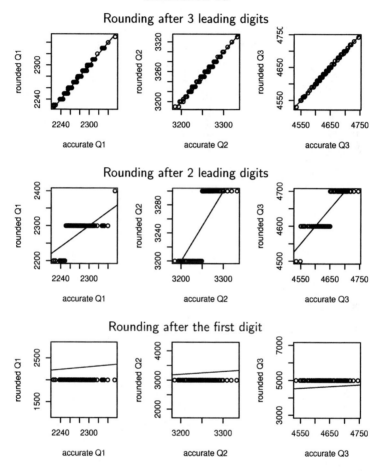

The circles indicate results of individual simulations, the solid line marks the line of equivalence between values based on rounded or accurate values. Note: The limits for the ordinates are not identical in wave 1, 2 and 3. Data: Simulation with n=100 runs with 5000 values each.

The only difference in these simulation runs is which values are rounded by what degree. The results are shown in histograms in Figure 2.8.

Figure 2.8: Results of Simulation 1b

Histograms for statistics in each simulation run

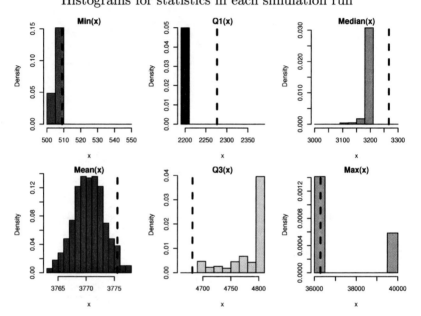

The histogram shows the frequency distribution of the empirical statistics for minimum, maximum, quartiles and mean in Simulation 1b. The intersected line indicates the location of the statistic for accurate values.

The quartiles are frequently located on the lattice of rounded values. The second quartile is always 2200, the histogram degenerates to a single bar. The other statistics are distributed over some range. Except for the mean, no statistic looks like a normal (Φ) distribution, and do not even seem to be symmetrical around the true value.

Thus, rounding causes a non-normally distributed error term and bias (caused by a shift towards nearby rounding points) in the estimation of quartiles. This is demonstrated in Figure 2.9. It shows the distribution of the estimated quantiles based on the $n = 100$ simulations runs from Simulation 1a. The plot is constructed by sorting the quartiles x_{jq} calculated in the simulation, with $j = 1\ldots 100$ and $q \in \{0.25, 0.5, 0.75\}$, in ascending order for each quartile, and then plotting the 100 resulting values $x_{q,(j)}$ against the theoretical values $F^{-1}\frac{1}{n}, F^{-1}\frac{2}{n}\ldots F^{-1}\frac{n}{n}$ of the standard normal distribution. If the values follow a normal distribution, then the resulting scatter plot should follow a diagonal line.

For 3 digits, the simulated distribution is close to a normal distribution and according to a Kolmogorov-Smirnov Test we do not reject the hypothesis that the 100 values are sampled from a normal distribution. For more rounded values (less digits), the distribution is more degenerate and does no longer look normal distributed. Given the result of the Kolmogorov-Smirnov test, we reject the hypothesis that the statistics for values rounded after 1 or 2 digits could be sampled from a normal distribution.

This result implies that not only the rounding error for individual values does not conform to typical measurement error models like Fuller (1987), but also certain statistics based on rounded errors are unusual (not following a normal or a related distribution).

Simulation 2: German personal income

The German personal gross wage and earning in the G-ECHP data 1994 (disregarding weights) can be approximated with a log-normal distribution with parameters $\ln(X) \sim N(\mu = 8.1700, \sigma = 0.4865)$. From this distribution, 10000 random values are drawn. The resulting simulated incomes are rounded by 1 (not rounded at all), 100, and 1000.

Table 2.2: Simulation 2: Simulated G-ECHP data, personal income

rounded	x_{min}	$x_{0.25}$	$x_{0.5}$	$\overline{x}$	$x_{0.75}$	x_{max}	s_x	MAD
by 1	686	2541	3533	3980	4904	24580	2056.42	1674
by 100	700	2500	3500	3980	4900	24600	2056.68	1631
by 1000	1000	3000	4000	3981	5000	25000	2077.80	1483

Figure 2.9: Results of Simulation 1a: Q-Q Plots

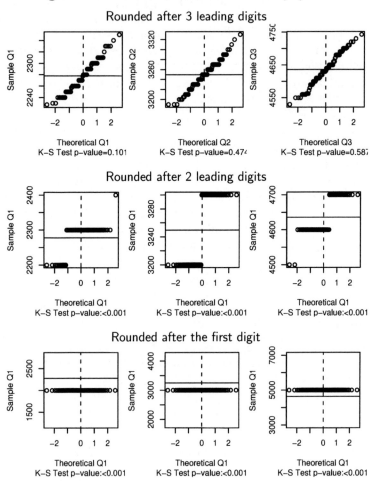

The plots show individual Q-Q plots for the simulated distribution of the 1st, 2nd (median) and 3rd quartile against the normal distribution. The solid line indicates the theoretical quartile and the intersected line shows the median for the estimated quartile across the simulations. Data: Simulation with n=100 runs with 5000 values each.

The results (Table 2.2) are very similar to simulation 1: Percentiles are heavily affected, mean and standard deviation are almost unaffected, the mean absolute deviation (MAD) drops. This is not surprising because the distribution of the random variables is very similar.

Simulation 3: Finnish household income

In this simulation, the household net disposable income in the Fin-ECHP data 1994 is approximated with a log-normal distribution. This distribution has the parameters $\ln(X) \sim N(\mu = 9.0843, \sigma = 0.5788)$. 10000 random values are drawn from this distribution. The resulting simulated incomes are rounded by 1 (not rounded), 100, and 1000.

Table 2.3: Simulation 3: Simulated Fin-ECHP data, household income

rounded	x_{min}	$x_{0.25}$	$x_{0.5}$	$\overline{x}$	$x_{0.75}$	x_{max}	s_x	MAD
by 1	826	5938	8832	10530	13130	111200	6867.3	4980
by 100	800	5900	8800	10530	13100	111200	6867.1	4893
by 1000	1000	6000	9000	10530	13000	111000	6873.3	4448

In this simulation, the minimum, 3rd quartile and standard deviation are only slightly affected (Table 2.3). As in the previous simulations, the MAD decreases. Rounding to multiples of 100 and 1000 does not seem to affect these distribution statistics as much as the German data in the previous simulations.

An explanation for this is that Finnish incomes are nominally higher than in Germany, partially because the former national currency in Finland, the Finmark (FIM), was about 3.04 DEM (the fixed exchange rate at the time when the national currencies converged into the Euro). We cannot compare rounding of German and Finnish data on the same real rounding level, because in Germany no one would round to the nearest multiple of 3040 FIM.

Simulation 4: Rounding of register income (household)

Instead of creating random variables, in this simulation register-based values are used and rounded artificially. The data is from the Fin-ECHP 1996 household dataset, the income variable is *annual* household net disposable income (in national currency). These are empirical data, only the rounding process has been simulated. Values of 450000 FIM and above or 0 FIM and below have been excluded from this simulation. The incomes are rounded by 1 (no rounding), 100, 1000 and 10000.

Table 2.4: Simulation 4: Rounding Fin-ECHP household register data

rounded	x_{min}	$x_{0.25}$	$x_{0.5}$	$\overline{x}$	$x_{0.75}$	x_{max}	s_x	MAD
by 1	170	90150	140200	150400	195700	449100	79774.3	77680
by 100	200	90130	140200	150400	195700	449100	79774.2	77688
by 1000	0	90000	140000	150400	196000	449000	79776.2	77095
by 10000	0	90000	140000	150500	200000	450000	79790.2	74130

In this example, rounding has only minor effect on the descriptive statistics. Percentiles, mean and standard deviation undergo small relative changes. Only rounding to the nearest multiple of 10000 notably changes the MAD and the third quartile.

An explanation why the effect of rounding here is much smaller than in previous simulations is the fact, that the quartiles of the original distribution already are close to multiples of 10000 (1st quartile, median, maximum). Thus, the shift from accurate to rounded values is relatively small.

The effect of rounding on the percentiles and statistics based on percentiles is obviously dependent on the distance of the percentiles to the nearest rounding points. The closer the percentiles are to these rounding points, the smaller is the effect of rounding on the percentiles.

Simulation 5: Rounding of register income (personal)

This experiment is similar to simulation 4, but with annual gross wage and earning from the Fin-ECHP. Values 300000 FIM and above or 0 FIM have been excluded.

As in simulation 4, the effect of rounding is very small. Note that in this simulation experiment the MAD increases, if values are rounded to nearest 1000 or more.

Table 2.5: Simulation 5: Rounding Fin-ECHP personal register data

rounded	x_{min}	$x_{0.25}$	$x_{0.5}$	$\bar{x}$	$x_{0.75}$	x_{max}	s_x	MAD
by 1	2	41210	68660	77940	98540	2997000	77062.5	42141
by 100	0	41200	68700	77940	98500	2997000	77062.5	42106
by 1000	0	41000	69000	77940	99000	2997000	77063.4	42995
by 10000	0	40000	70000	77970	100000	3000000	77223.9	44478

Result for Simulations 1-5

In a series of simulations, we first fitted the survey incomes to a log-normal distribution. From this log-normal distribution we took $N = 10000$ random numbers which were then rounded according to an artificial rounding scheme.

It turned out that the means and variances are almost stable under this procedure. Quantiles which are far away from rounding points may be badly estimated, while quantiles closer to rounding points are not affected that much. The maximum rounding error is determined by the degree of rounding. This result is in accordance with literature, see, e.g. Eisenhart (1947). Eisenhart analyzed the effect of rounding after a fixed number of digits or decimal point on the normal distribution.

Information about the amount of rounding in empirical data is helpful to assess the precision of quantile estimates. When data contains a high amount of highly rounded data, the empirical quantiles are less precise. Rounding must be considered when comparing two samples.

To describe the parameters of an empirical distribution, the mean value or a robustified mean (e.g., without the highest and lowest 5% values) could be more robust than quantile-based statistics with respect to the measurement error due to rounding. The latter are perhaps robust against extreme values and certain measurement errors, but surely not robust against rounding error.[13]

---

[13] In fact, quantiles are not the only robust type of statistic which is vulnerable to rounding. Robust tests like Wilcoxon rank sum tests are affected by rounding, e.g. because ties tend to occur more often.

2.6.3 Excursion: From histograms to kernel density estimation

Often, an empirical distribution $h(y)$ is thought to be a realization of an unknown theoretical distribution. To describe the theoretical distribution, it is a common approach to chose a distribution function $f(Y|\Theta)$ and specify or estimate parameters Θ based on the observed distribution function $h(y)$.

For empirical data, it can be difficult to choose the right distribution family, and a misspecified f leads to bad results. As an alternative, nonparametric approaches can be used. The simplest nonparametric estimator for the density is a histogram. A comprehensive introduction to nonparametric density estimation can be found in Silverman (1986).

Figure 2.10: Example: Two Histograms for the same values

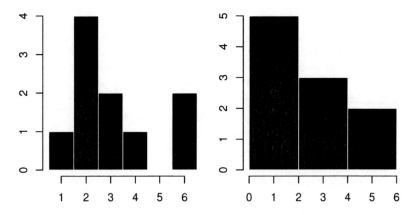

Left: Histogram with even breaks at $1.5, 2.5, ..., 7.5$ and bin width 1. Right: Histogram with even breaks at $1, 3, 5, 7$ and bin width 2.

It is important to chose the bin width and bin breaks wisely. Greater bin width means more points are put into the same bin. Shifting the grid a little bit may result in very different figures. The results are obvious: The two histograms in Figure 2.10 differ with respect to the number and location of modes.

While being attractive because of simplicity in construction and interpretation, a histogram has at least three major restrictions: (1.) it depends on the width and break points of the bins, (2.) it is not smooth but is quite edgy and (3.) the bins are equal to the brackets. In fact, histograms are like rounded data. When the bin widths are chosen carefully, then a histogram might be a very good choice.

The first two problems can be alleviated by using *kernel density estimators* (KDE). A very simple kernel density estimator $\hat{f}_H(x)$ can be constructed by centering bins at each point of a grid or each data point instead of using fixed bins. For each point x_i, the number of observations y_i up to a certain distance h are counted and normalized:

$$\hat{f}_H(x) = \frac{1}{nh} \sum_{i=1}^{n} \frac{\mathbf{I}(|x_i - x| < h)}{2}$$

This is also called a kernel density estimator with rectangular kernel, or a box kernel density plot. It is more flexible than a histogram, but the resulting estimate is not smooth. It is likely that the resulting plot has a step-wise shape and many lokal peaks (see Figure 2.11 with the same data used in Figure 2.10). An improvement is the use of smooth kernels: Values which are farther away from the data point are used with lesser weight than values which are closer:

$$\hat{f}_H(x) = \frac{1}{nh} \sum_{i=1}^{n} K\left(\frac{x_i - x}{h}\right)$$

$K(\cdot)$ is the so-called kernel function. A large number of kernel functions exist. A good introduction to kernel density estimation, the various kernels and methods and the choice of optimal bandwidth is "Density Estimation for Statistics and Data Analysis" by Silverman (1986), but the honor of inventing kernel density estimation was earned by Rosenblatt (1956) and Parzen (1962).

Figure 2.11: Example: Two kernel density plots for the same values

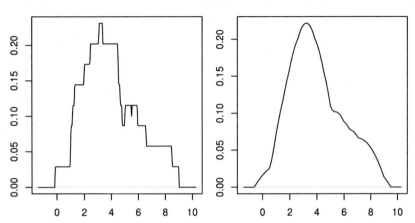

Kernel density estimator of values x, bandwidth 1. For the left plot, a rectangular kernel was used, and an Epanechnikov kernel for the right.

Suggested extension of kernel density estimation for rounded values

The drawback of ordinary kernel density estimation is the fixed choice of bandwidth and kernel. But for rounded data, we would like to use greater bandwidth for highly rounded values, and smaller bandwidth for accurate values.

Kernel density estimation is additive: Given the same kernel function and bandwidth parameter, the KDE $m(x)$ for a set of values $\mathbf{x} = (x_1, \ldots, x_{n-1})$ is equal to $\frac{n-1}{n}m(x|\mathbf{x}') + \frac{1}{n}m(x|x_n)$ (the kernel density estimator is the sum of kernel densities of individual sample values).

This could be used for an customer-designed approach to smooth data rounded by different degree, such as income data. We sketch a simple algorithm below.

The set of values is split into three (or more) different sub-sets $\mathbf{y}_a$. The first set y_1 is the set of values rounded by very high amounts, e.g. rounded to multiples of 1000. The second set contains values rounded by a considerable amount, e.g. values rounded to nearest multiple of 100. The last set is the set of values which seem to be accurate, or rounded by negligible amount. For Euro, income values rounded by 10 or less are in this sub-set.[14]

For each set, a kernel density estimate $m_a(x)$ with a bandwidth according to the level of rounding is used. The set of "accurate" values is smoothed very little, while a greater bandwidth is used for the set of heavily rounded values.

In the last step, the three kernel density estimates are put together by calculating a weighted sum of the three kernel density estimators.

$$(2.1) \qquad \hat{m}(x) = \sum_a w_a m_a(\mathbf{x}_a)$$

The weights w_a have to be determined. The simplest (but not the optimal) solution is to use weights proportional to the number of sample values in each set $\mathbf{y}_a$.

We demonstrate an example using Lux-ECHP personal gross wage and earnings data from 1996 (national currency LUF). We divided the data into separate sets:

i) Values which were multiples of 10000, ii) values which were multiples of 1000 (but not 10000), and iii) all other values. Using the binned KDE (the bkde function) algorithm in the statistical software R,[15] an KDE for each set was calculated, using a bandwidth of 50000 for the first set, a bandwidth of 20000 for the second, and 10000 for the third set.[16] The three densities are shown in Figure 2.12 below. It is easy to see that the three densities are different. One reason is that the frequency of rounded values

---

[14] These sets are not necessarily disjunct: For some values, it is not clear whether they are rounded by 100 or 1000. The set of such values could be shared among both sets.

[15] R is a language and environment for statistical computing and graphics, see R Development Core Team (2004).

[16] The bandwidths chosen are a compromise to smooth the gaps between rounding points on one hand and smooth sparse areas on the other. Therefore, it was not advisable to use bandwidths based on rounding level multiplied by a fixed factor.

is higher for high incomes, but another reason is the different bandwidth selection used for the kernel density function.

Figure 2.12: Kernel density plots for three sets of values

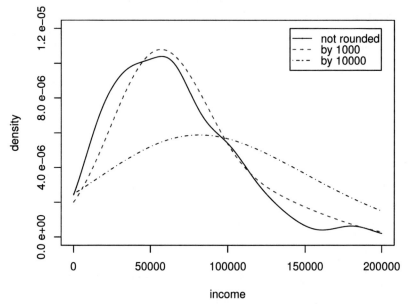

income

Kernel density estimator of incomes (gross wage and earnings) in Lux-ECHP 1996. Separate KDE were calculated for values which were accurate or rounded by less than 100, multiples of 1000, or multiples of 10000 (LUF).

If the three KDEs are put together (e.g. by adding them weighted by the fraction of values in each set), we get a new KDE we will call joint KDE. It is not only different from the KDE for each single set, but also from any KDE calculated for the set of all values, as demonstrated in Figure 2.13 below. The thick solid line shows the joint KDE, while the fine intersected lines show different results if KDEs for the same (single) set of data are calculated with different bandwidths between 5000 and 50000. It is easy to see that none of the resulting KDEs is equal to the joint KDE. While some of the different KDEs are close to the joint KDE in the lower two thirds of the income range, all of these KDEs have higher densities in the upper income ranges when compared to the joint KDE.

Figure 2.13: Comparison of different KDE for the same data

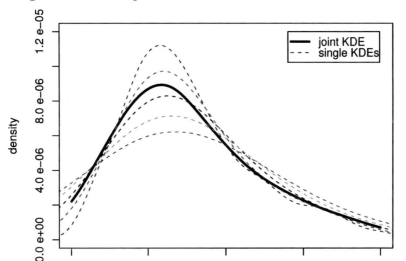

Kernel density estimator of incomes (gross wage and earnings) in Lux-ECHP 1996. The solid line shows the joint KDE based on i)-iii). The dotted lines show KDE for the single data set using bandwidth of 10000, 20000,... 50000.

This example demonstrates that rounding does not only have an impact on KDE estimates, but also that it is possible to take rounding into account by modifying existing algorithms.

The algorithm can be further refined. Usually, some a priori knowledge on the shape of the distribution is known. For example, the distribution of accurate values can be assumed to be roughly log-normal shaped, or symmetrical, or whatever. In this case, the kernel function used for individual bins does not have to be symmetrical. Instead, for example a normalized segment of the theoretical distribution of values between the lower and upper limit of the bin could be used.

2.6.4 Impact of rounding on measures of change

In longitudinal studies, the measurement of change of a variable is important. The effect of rounding has a big impact on the measurement of change, as will be demonstrated in this sub-section.

In the previous simulations, data was rounded by fixed amounts. While this is a straightforward approach, it fails when the range of values is very wide, and some values have only a few digits and others have more. It is not reasonable that a millionaire would round his income by the same fixed amount as a beggar.

Simulation 6: Effect on measures of change

In a new experiment, all random draws from a log-normal distribution are assumed to increase by 16 percent.[17] Then each income figure is rounded separately for the corresponding year, and the relative increase is calculated with respect to the rounded values. Here we use a different rounding strategy that serves as a model for the respondent behavior: The respondents are assumed to remember only a certain number of leading digits and forget about the rest which is rounded to zero. Thus we obtain y^*_{1995} and y^*_{1999}, the rounded incomes for the respective years. Finally we calculated the individual mobility of incomes for every person:

$$m = \ln(y^*_{1999}) - \ln(y^*_{1995})$$

As a reference, the expected mean mobility for a fixed increase rate observed without rounding is $(\ln 1.16) = 0.1484$.

The result is shown in Table 2.6. Rounding after 3 or more leading digits leads to rather small errors, most values are close to the expected value $m = 0.1484$. Thus, slightly rounded values still show the true changes.

---

[17] The parameters were chosen to fit well to Finnish monthly household net disposable cash income and the national nominal increases of incomes.

Table 2.6: Simulation 6: Mobility of wage and earning

	m_{min}	$m_{0.25}$	$m_{0.5}$	$\overline{m}$	$m_{0.75}$	m_{max}	s_m
B=4	0.1475	0.1483	0.1484	0.1484	0.1485	0.1493	0.0002
B=3	0.1406	0.1477	0.1484	0.1484	0.1491	0.1570	0.0018
B=2	0.0800	0.1431	0.1490	0.1489	0.1542	0.2076	0.0174
B=1	0.0000	0.0000	0.1335	0.1533	0.2231	0.6931	0.1806

With increasing levels of rounding, the mean mobility is the same, but the quartiles and extremes move away from the true value. When extreme rounding occurs, e.g., $B = 1$, then a lot of zero changes are observed, which means rounding "hides" the income change. Only when the (cumulated) income change is great enough that the next rounding point is reached, a real income change would be observed. However, this change could possibly exceed the real change within the previous period by far. In the above simulation this is expressed by the fact that the third percentile is 0.2076, much greater than the actual change, and the maximum value is a staggering 0.6931.

Rounding to 2 significant digits causes an error which could be described as tolerable, see Table 2.6.

The observed standard deviation of the income changes rises by a factor 10 when the level of rounding is increased by one digit. This is related to Sheppard's result, that the observed variance of a distribution is biased by a factor proportional to the squared rounding interval.

In a real-data situation, we do not observe a single rate of change, but instead a mixture of different changes. It is not clear whether the effect of rounding would be the same. The marginal distribution of rounded an accurate changes could be less different from each other because negative and positive errors due to rounding would partially cancel out each other.

Simulation 7: Mobility of rounded income (personal)

Finally, we take the original income data for years 1995 (already used in Table 2.5) and 1999 from the Finnish register data. We subject the values to artificial rounding and calculate the income mobility $m = \log(x_{1999}) - \log(x_{1995})$ for original values and for values rounded by different methods.

In Table 2.7, the values were rounded to fixed rounding bases. Rounding by 1 in the first row equals no rounding, while rounding by 50,000 (FIM) means severe rounding of values with a medium value around 100,000 FIM. At rounding up to 1000 FIM, the quartiles, mean and standard deviation for mobility are almost identical. For rounding by 10000 FIM, the values are somewhat different at the third or digit after decimal point. Only for the highest amount of rounding in the table, rounding by 50,000 FIM, the values are considerably different from the accurate values.

A comparison with the results from the previous simulation shows, that the situation is different. Here we used empirical values with individual growth rates ranging from very low to very high changes (though on the average not much different from $\ln 0.14 \approx 16\%$).

Table 2.7: Simulation 7a: Mobility of wage and earning (register data)

rounded	m_{min}	$m_{0.25}$	$m_{0.5}$	$m_{0.75}$	m_{max}	$\overline{m}$	s_m
by 1	-0.6319	0.0300	0.0620	0.1047	0.9273	0.0696	0.1287
by 10	-0.6318	0.0300	0.0620	0.1047	0.9272	0.0696	0.1287
by 100	-0.6321	0.0302	0.0620	0.1047	0.9274	0.0696	0.1287
by 1000	-0.6292	0.0306	0.0619	0.1051	0.9243	0.0697	0.1287
by 10000	-0.6368	0.0300	0.0645	0.1091	0.9208	0.0697	0.1296
by 50000	-0.6990	0.0000	0.0000	0.1761	1.0000	0.0697	0.1509

m_{min} to m_{max} are quartiles and s_m is the empirical standard deviation of m. The mean is written in column titled $\overline{m}$. The first column indicates the level of rounding, specifically the rounding base by which the income values were rounded.

In the second table (Table 2.8), the values were rounded after a certain number of significant digits. Rounding after four digits is the least rounding in the table, and rounding after 1 digit is the most rounding. The values in the rows for rounding after three and four digits are almost identical, and also very similar to the values in the first rows of the previous table. This means that rounding after three and four digits is negligible, as is rounding by 1000 FIM or less. Rounding after two digits, however, seems to have an effect on the figures, almost similar to rounding by 10000 FIM. And rounding after the first digit considerably alters the values. It is quite interesting that many observed values are now equal to zero (e.g., both the median and the 25% quartile are equal to zero). This means that a high level of rounding hides a low income mobility, and instead of small mobility values zero change would be observed.

Table 2.8: Simulation 7b: Mobility of wage and earnings (registers)

rounded	m_{min}	$m_{0.25}$	$m_{0.5}$	$m_{0.75}$	m_{max}	$\overline{m}$	s_m
4 digits	-0.6319	0.0300	0.0620	0.1047	0.9272	0.0696	0.1287
3 digits	-0.6313	0.0306	0.0619	0.1047	0.9272	0.0697	0.1287
2 digits	-0.6226	0.0300	0.0637	0.1068	0.9208	0.0699	0.1291
1 digit	-0.6990	0.0000	0.0000	0.1761	0.9208	0.0698	0.1630

m_{min} to m_{max} are quartiles and s_m is the empirical standard deviation of m. The mean is written in column titled $\bar{m}$. The first column indicates the level of rounding, specifically the number of significant digits after which values were rounded.

This means that we cannot know for sure that a person had no income change between two periods when zero change is observed and both reported income values are rounded. In this situation, inaccurate data are close to missing data.

In a survey situation, the data reported by interviewees are not all rounded by the same degree. More often, some values are rounded after one digit, others after two or more, and some values are not rounded at all. In the Finnish ECHP household data, personal gross wage and earnings (here: using values over 1000 FIM only) were returned with one or more significant digits. The empirical frequency for the sample data used in this section is given in Table 2.9.

The third table (Table 2.11) shows a result when random rounding is applied. This random rounding simulates the empirical fact that the values were rounded differently and the observed data are a mixture of values rounded to different degree.

In our simulation, each register value $x_{i,t}$ was rounded after one or more

Table 2.9: Frequency of rounding after certain number of digits

no. of digits	1	2	3	4	5
frequency (%)	0.315	0.475	0.152	0.044	0.014

Data: Fin-ECHP 1996, personal gross wages and earnings over 1000 FIM.

significant digits. The number of digits after which the income was rounded was determined by a random variable $B_{i,t}$ which simulates the frequency of rounding in the Fin-ECHP personal interview. Because some register data are already round and simulated rounding sometimes creates a value with less significant digits than intended (e.g., rounding 101 after two digits results in 100, which has only one digit), we have to use slightly different probabilities as shown in Table 2.10.

Table 2.10: Probability of rounding for Simulation 7c

B	1	2	3	4	5
$f(B_{i,t})$	0.29	0.47	0.17	0.05	0.02

When applied to the given register data, these probabilities result in data with an empirical frequency of rounding similar to the survey data. As in Simulations 7a and 7b, we calculate the resulting income mobilities with rounded data and give statistics for the empirical distribution of these mobilities in Table 2.11. Because simulated rounding is random for each observation, we repeated this process five times for all observations and calculated the median for the results.

When comparing the individual and median figures for the five sets with results in Tables 2.7 and 2.8, we find that one statistic was outside the range of results found in the two simulations with fixed rounding: The mean value ($\bar{m}$) was between 0.702 and 0.729, thereby outside the range of results in the previous tables (0.0696 to 0.0698). Random rounding seems to introduce a little bit more variance into the calculation of the mean value.

The other figures, especially the quartiles, were equal to or close to values found when applying fixed rounding by 10000 and 50000 FIM, or rounding

Table 2.11: Simulation 7c: Mobility of wage and earning (register data)

run	m_{min}	$m_{0.25}$	$m_{0.5}$	$m_{0.75}$	m_{max}	$\overline{m}$	s_m
set 1	-0.6368	0	0.0637	0.1249	0.9208	0.0702	0.1391
set 2	-0.6368	0	0.0635	0.1249	0.9208	0.0704	0.1391
set 3	-0.6990	0	0.0621	0.1249	0.9208	0.0704	0.1428
set 4	-0.6292	0	0.0621	0.1249	0.9237	0.0713	0.1407
set 5	-0.6368	-0.0002	0.0658	0.1328	0.9208	0.0729	0.1439
median	-0.6368	0	0.0635	0.1249	0.9208	0.0704	0.1407

m_{min} to m_{max} are quartiles and s_m is the empirical standard deviation of m. The mean is written in column titled $\overline{m}$. Each set is an independent simulation run with the same register values but different simulated rounding.

after one or two digits to the data.

This was expectable with the rounding probabilities used in this simulation, because most values were rounded after one or two digits, and only a small part of the data were rounded after three or more digits.

Result

The effects of rounding on the observed distribution of changes may be serious, as shown by the simulations above. Rounding may shift percentiles up or down. Percentiles including the median and median deviation, so-called robust measures, change more than the mean and the standard deviation. In simulations, the error is directly related to the level of rounding and to the distance of accurate values to rounding points.

However, these simulations are not realistic under three aspects: Some experiments assumed a constant increase factor for each person, other experiments assumed that persons round in the same way mathematically[18], and all assume that rounding is the only measurement error involved. These assumptions are not guaranteed to hold empirically. There is a considerable

---

[18] It is possible that some persons always round up, and others always round down.

variation in the increase of wages and salaries based on register or survey interview data, as will be shown in later sections. Also the rounding behavior depends on the level of income and on individual factors. Therefore, rounding effects in empirical situations could be smaller (or even greater) than in simulations.

2.7 Impact of rounding on poverty measures

Poverty measures are an important tool to compare income distributions between two different countries or periods. The literature offers many different poverty measures, e.g., axiomatic measures proposed by Sen (1976), Shorrocks (1995), and inequality measures of which a variety is described in detail in Cowell (1995).

In this paper, we simulate the effect of rounding on the headcount ratio, the Gini index and the TIP curve (Jenkins and Lambert, 1997). The headcount ratio is a common and simple poverty measure, the Gini index is well known as a measure for inequality, and the TIP-Curve is a combined measure for the "Three i's of poverty": Inequality, intensity and incidence.

2.7.1 Gini coefficient

The Gini coefficient is a well-known measure for inequality, based on the Lorenz curve.[19] It may be calculated as:

$$(2.2) \qquad G = \frac{2 \sum_{i=1}^{n} i \cdot x_i}{n \sum_{i=1}^{n} x_i} - \frac{n+1}{n},$$

where n is the number of units (e.g. persons) and x_i the value for the i-th unit sorted by x.

If the interview value y_i is observed instead of the accurate value x_i, the distribution of individual values is different, which has an impact on the Lorenz Curve and therefore on measures of inequality and poverty. The

---

[19] The Lorenz curve shows, for the bottom units (e.g., households), the total percentage of the total income (or other cumulative asset) they have. The percentage of units is plotted on the abscissa, the percentage of incomes on the ordinate. The Gini coefficient is the area between the line of perfect equality, where all units have the same share of income, and the actual Lorenz curve.

effect of rounding is related to the effect of grouping data.[20]

The following simulation demonstrates the hypothetical effect of rounding on the estimation of the Gini coefficient for the Fin-ECHP household data. Again, we used income data from the Finnish registers and subjected them to artificial rounding.[21]

We used a simulated rounding process which rounded each value at random to 1 or more significant digits with probabilities similar to the ones observed in the survey interview ($p = 0.56$ for rounding after the 1. digit, $p = 0.36, 0.05, 0.028$ for rounding after 2nd to 4th digit respectively). These probabilities, when applied to non-rounded data as a distribution over rounding after one or more digits, roughly result in data with a distribution of rounded data similar to the empirical frequency in the Fin-ECHP survey data.

Thus, a major partition of the data was rounded after the first digit. As we know from previous results, this has significant impact on the distribution of incomes and hence on measures of inequality and poverty.

Table 2.12: Simulation 8: Gini coefficient for rounded data

	sign. digits			all (no
	1	2	3	rounding)
Gini	0.24043	0.25326	0.25347	0.25348
discrepancy	-0.01305	-0.00022	-0.00001	–

In a bootstrap simulation, we applied the above rounding probabilities one hundred times to the same data and compared the resulting Gini coefficients of the simulated data to the value for the true data. The result in Figure 2.14 shows a bias and a random term of the Gini for rounded data. Clearly, rounding has reduced the observed income inequality for this data. The

---

[20] See Kakwani (1976), for an example. It is an idea to use methods from grouped data to improve the estimation of the Gini coefficient for rounded data.

[21] The data is annual disposable household income on personal level, OECD equivalence scale, see Sisto (2003).

Figure 2.14: Simulation 9: Gini coefficient of y_{ri} (rounded) compared to Gini coefficient of x_i (not rounded)

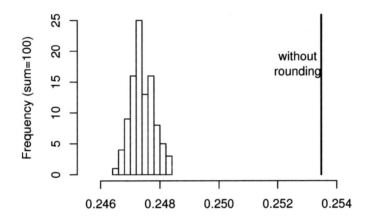

The histogram shows the empirical distribution of the Gini coefficients in the rounding simulations. The line shows the position of the Gini coefficient for the data prior to rounding.

Gini coefficient calculated using formula 2.2 is obviously smaller (and hence the distribution of incomes is less unequal) if data has been rounded.

2.7.2 Headcount ratio

In a similar fashion, the headcount ratio is measured inaccurately if rounding is present. The headcount ratio is defined as the ratio of units whose income is below the poverty line. A poverty line commonly used for European countries is a fraction α of the median income, for example half-median income. The headcount ratio is defined as (see e.g., Preston 1995, page 92):

$$(2.3) \qquad \pi_{\alpha\beta} = \frac{1}{N} \sum_{i=1}^{N} \mathbf{1}_{\{X_i \leq \alpha \cdot X_{(\beta)}\}}$$

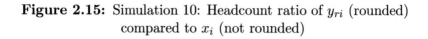

Figure 2.15: Simulation 10: Headcount ratio of y_{ri} (rounded) compared to x_i (not rounded)

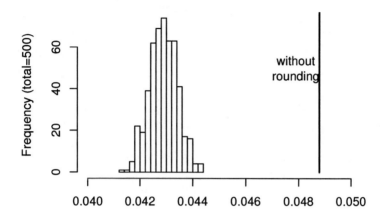

The histogram shows the empirical distribution of the headcount ratios in the rounding simulations. The line shows the position of the headcount ratio coefficient for the data prior to rounding.

with $\alpha = 0.5$, N the number of units in the population, X_i the income of unit i, $X_{(\beta)}$ the quantile of order β, and $\mathbf{1}_{\{v\}}$ is the indicator function taking the value 1 if v is true and 0 else. Since we are using a sample of size n with design weights w_i, we calculate a weighted estimator:

$$(2.4) \qquad \hat{\pi}_{\alpha\beta} = \frac{1}{\sum_i^n w_i} \sum_{i=1}^{n} w_i \mathbf{1}_{\{y_i \leq \alpha \cdot \hat{Y}_{(\beta)}\}}$$

For the purpose of the simulation, we use the income data sampled from registers for the Finnish sub-sample of the ECHP already used in the Gini simulation and apply simulated mixed rounding 500 times, each time estimating the poverty line and the headcount ratio. We use the poverty line $\alpha \cdot \hat{X}_{(\beta)} = 0.5 \cdot y_{(0.5)}$ estimated with rounded data, thus two error effects have an impact on the headcount: the estimation of the poverty line with rounded data, and units who move from one side to the other of the poverty line due to rounding.

Again, the measure calculated with rounded data is biased downwards, underestimating the true value. This result cannot be explained easily, it depends on the numerical distribution of incomes around the poverty line (altering the fraction of values below the poverty line) and around the median (altering the poverty line). If we would use a fixed poverty line, the bias would be somewhat smaller.

2.7.3 TIP Curve

The *TIP curve* (the name is an acronym for **T**hree '**I**'s of **P**overty) is a relatively new tool to analyze poverty. It simultaneously shows the *i*ntensity, *i*ncidence and *i*nequality dimensions of poverty and was introduced by Jenkins and Lambert (1997).

Basically, the TIP curve plots the ordered cumulated poverty gaps against the cumulated population share. A *poverty gap* is the difference between the current poverty line and his actual income. For a non-poor person, the poverty gap is equal to zero (he needs no more income to be non-poor).

Construction of the TIP curve

Given is the vector (x_i, w_i) of average incomes for groups $i \in \{1..n\}$, where x_i is the income and w_i is the weight (or population share) of group i. In our case, x_i is a single observation for a unit (household or person) and the design weight w_i is the inverse of the sampling probability for unit i. For the TIP curve, these vectors are ordered by the income level x_i, obtaining (x_j, w_j).

Let z be the poverty line. It has already been used in equation (2.3) to define the headcount ratio. The poverty gaps are defined by $g_{x,j} = max(z - x_j, 0)$. Often, not the actual poverty gaps are used, but a transformation, e.g., poverty gaps relative to the poverty line: $g_{x,j}/z$.

A TIP curve is generated by plotting the cumulated sum of (normalized) poverty gaps $g_{x,j}/z$ against the cumulated population share $N_k = \sum_j^k w_j$.

$$(2.5) \qquad \mathrm{TIP}(N_k) = \sum_{j=1}^{k} x_j$$

To calculate the poverty line and the TIP curve, I have implemented these construction in the statistical computing environment R, the source code for the program can be found in Appendix A.5.2.

In the Figure, the abscissa shows the share of the population, and the ordinate shows the cumulated relative poverty gap associated with this share. For example, to "fill" all poverty gaps in this population, additional social transfers with a volume of about 67000 times the amount of the poverty line were required. This is a useful interpretation for poverty analysis on an economic level.

Simulation 11: TIP curve for accurate and rounded data

Figure 2.16 shows the TIP curve for the net disposable equivalence household income in the Finnish (sub-sample of the ECHP) register data, the same data already used in Section 2.7.1.

In this example, the difference between the TIP curves for accurate data and (simulated) rounded data is rather small. For greater rounding, the difference is greater.[22]

Two explanations for differences in the TIP curve are obvious: The estimated median is shifted by rounding, and since the median is used to determine the relative poverty line, the latter is shifted by rounding, too. This has an effect on the incidence. The second effect is that some incomes close to the poverty line are rounded up or down and may cross the poverty line.

The effect is not always in the same direction. The impact of rounding on the TIP curve is related to the distance of the accurate median (and 50% median) to the next major rounding point. Figure 2.17 shows TIP curves for accurate values from 1995 and the same values with simulated rounding (the same simulated rounding procedure was used as in Section 2.7.1), and Figure 2.18 is a similar plot for incomes in 1999.

Obviously, in the first example (data from 1995) the TIP curve is not much different when either accurate or rounded values are used. In each of the ten simulation runs, the curve is very close to the accurate line. However,

---

[22] The TIP curve for the same data without using weights respectively using weights $w_i = 1 \, \forall i$ is shown in Figure A.2 in the Appendix A.2. Different from the TIP curve here, one curve for rounded data is above, the other below the curve for accurate data.

Figure 2.16: TIP curve for register data (1995)

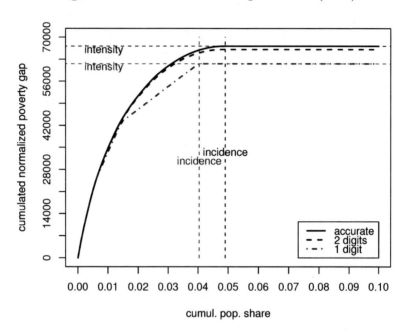

TIP curves based on register data (net disposable household equivalence income per capita in 1995) using design weights. The solid line is for accurate data, dotted and intersected lines are for simulated rounded data (rounding after 1 respectively 2 significant digits).

the situation could be very different when the estimated median would be shifted more away from the true one due to rounding. This is visible in the TIP curve for 1999. While the curves for rounded data are close to each other, they are all clearly under the line for accurate data. This illustrates how rounding has an impact on the comparison of different populations. If someone would compare TIP curves from 1995 and 1999, then he would observe a smaller change when using rounded data instead of accurate data.

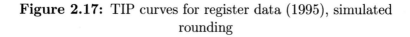

Figure 2.17: TIP curves for register data (1995), simulated rounding

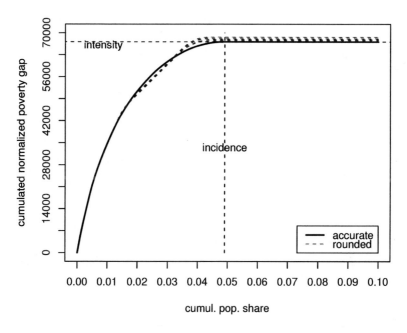

TIP curves based on register data (net disposable household equivalence income per capita in 1995) using design weights. The single dark solid line is for accurate data, the thinner, intersected lines are for data to which simulated rounding has been applied.

The main reason why the TIP curve is measured with rounding error is the estimation of the median. In 1995, the (weighted) median for accurate values was $\hat{x}_{0.5} = 74457.83$ and for rounded values it was $\hat{x}'_{0.5} = 74000$ which is a little bit smaller. The poverty line for rounded data slightly underestimated the accurate poverty line, but the difference did not have much impact on the TIP curve. According to this example, rounding does not seem to be the reason for the large differences between TIP curves for

Figure 2.18: TIP curves for register data (1999), simulated rounding

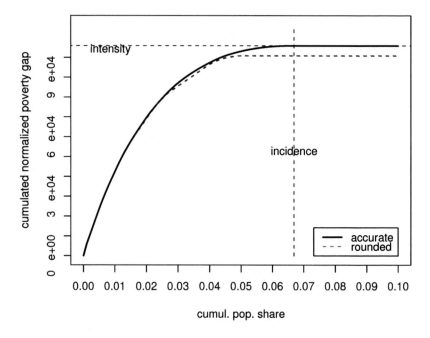

cumul. pop. share

TIP curves based on register data (net disposable household equivalence income per capita in 1999) using design weights. The single dark solid line is for accurate data, the thinner, intersected lines are for data to which simulated rounding has been applied.

income data from either register or interview data reported by Jäntti (2004). But for our 1999 data, the (weighted) median income for accurate data was $x_{0.5} = 82023.33$ and for rounded values $x_{0.5} = 80000$ in each iteration. Therefore, a smaller proportion of data was classified as "poor", and the poverty gap was systematically underestimated by more than 2000 (FIM). The average of incomes tends to change slowly over periods, most of the time rising. One can visualize the effect of rounding in the following way: When the accurate median income comes close to a major rounding point, the estimated median for rounded data tends to become attracted to the rounding point, clings to it for the following periods, and then starts rising again, causing an oscillating movement around the precise TIP curve. We demonstrate this phenomenon in a last simulation.

Simulation 12: TIP curve with increasing incomes

In this series of 8 experimental simulations $j = 1 \ldots 8$, all net disposable household income values $\mathbf{x_r} = \{x_{r,i}\}$, $i = 1 \ldots N$ with weights $\mathbf{w} = \{w_i\}$, $i = 1 \ldots N$ from the Finnish sub-sample of the ECHP are assumed to increase by 0%, 2%, 4%, ... up to 14% (the increase rate chosen here is $m_j = (j-1) \cdot 2\%$).

Once, for each unit i it is determined randomly whether the value is rounded after 1, 2, 3 or more significant digits (yielding the vector $\mathbf{b} = \{b_i\}$, $i = 1 \cdot N$). We use the same rounding probabilities used previously in Section 2.7.1.

Then, for each simulation run, two TIP curves are calculated, one using only accurate values and the other only with rounded values:

accurate: $\text{TIP}(m_j \cdot \mathbf{x_r}, \mathbf{w})$

rounded: $\text{TIP}(\text{Round}\,(m_j \cdot \mathbf{x_r}, \mathbf{b}), \mathbf{w})$

where $\text{Round}(x_i, b_i)$ is a function that returns the value x_i rounded after b_i significant digits.

The result is illustrative and shows how the TIP curve for rounded values is oscillating around the TIP curve for accurate incomes. The accurate TIP curve (solid line) is not changed when all values are increased by a constant factor – this is an axiomatic quality of all poverty measures based on Sen (1976) and Shorrocks (1995). However, the TIP curve for rounded data seems to violate this definition because rounding was applied *after* increasing the values.

Thus, rounding has to be taken into account in two situations: Firstly, when comparing TIP curves for data from sources with different level of rounding. If one data set is heavily affected by rounding (such as interview data) and the other is not (such as register data based on tax and employee accounts), then it is possible that differences are caused by rounding. Secondly, when comparing data of the same type (such as interview data from different panel waves), differences could be caused because the poverty line is jumping from rounding point to rounding point.

In both cases, a solution to improve the construction of the TIP curve is to use a poverty line based on non-rounded data, or at least to use a median estimator which takes the level of rounding into account. Another option would be to use the mean income $\bar{x}$, because the mean is less affected by rounding. If for example the TIP curve was constructed using rounded values but an accurate poverty line, the difference to the accurate TIP curve was very small and resembled random fluctuation.

Conclusion

Rounding potentially has an impact on the estimation of a relative poverty line and can cause individual values close to the poverty line change from poor to non-poor or vice versa, which has an impact on the estimation of the headcount ratio. Also, it changes the distribution of incomes and hence the Lorenz curve and the Gini coefficient as derived measures. Therefore, we expected the TIP curve to be effected in a similar way. The actual effect in empirical examples with Finnish household data was rather mixed and revealed an oscillating error which was related to the biased median estimation.

The analysis of poverty draws often on the estimation of quantiles and the median of an income distribution. However, these measures are heavily affected by rounding. Therefore, it is advisable to consider rounding as an additional cause for differences when discussing results from poverty analysis. In many cases, a simple simulation might give an idea about the possible effect of rounding in a specific situation.

This result applies not only to poverty analysis. Many other statistics in other fields of application make use of quantiles such as 90%/10% ratios or the median. These are likewise affected.

Figure 2.19: TIP curves for increasing income data

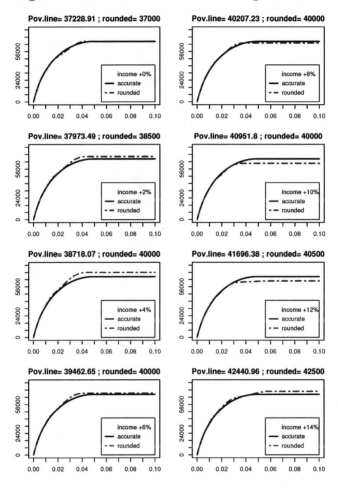

TIP curves for stepwise increased register data (net disposable household equivalence income per capita in 1995) using design weights and simulated (fixed) rounding. The solid TIP curve is for precise data, the intersected curve for data to which simulated rounding has been applied.

CHAPTER3

Rounding in Household Panels

It is the aim of this chapter to describe and compare the frequency of rounding in these panel surveys. The data were sampled with similar or even identical methods, but from different countries or different periods.

In this chapter we use data from national sub-samples from the German SOEP (GSOEP) and the ECHP, especially the German and Finnish sub-samples (G-ECHP and Fin-ECHP), but also the UK (UK-ECHP) and Luxembourgian (Lux-ECHP) sub-samples of the ECHP.

3.1 Overview

In the first sections of this chapter, two panel surveys are described: The German sub-sample of the European Community Household Panel (ECHP) and the German Socio-Economic Panel (GSOEP). In the following subsections, the ECHP and GSOEP are described in some more detail.

The *European Community Household Panel* (ECHP) is a survey on work and income, education, living conditions and health. It was intended to cover all EU member states on micro-level. The survey was conducted with *input-harmonized* questionnaires to allow for straight cross-country comparisons. The total duration of the ECHP was 8 years, from 1994 to 2001, with 12 countries participating from the first wave on. In the first wave, about 60,000 households were sampled to be interviewed each year on. For this thesis, data from the German, Finnish, Luxembourgian and United Kingdoms sub-samples were used – in particular from the Production Data Base (PDB) of the ECHP which contains the original survey data prior to imputation, anonymization and other transformation procedures.

The *German Socio-Economic Panel* (GSOEP) is a longitudinal study of private households on wide-ranging socio-economic aspects. It is similar to the ECHP. It was started 1984, conducted each year, and had about 15,000 adult participants in 1999 (including refreshment samples).

With regard to rounding, we use mainly the following income concepts: net disposable household income for households and personal gross wage and earnings for individuals. In the following sections, we introduce or define several concepts for this thesis, especially the household definition, income types and design weights.

3.1.1 The German Socio-Economic Panel

The German Socio-Economic Panel (GSOEP) is a representative household panel study for Germany. In Western Germany, it was started 1984, and 1990 in Eastern Germany (after reunification). The GSOEP today consists of multiple samples, which have been drawn to account for demographic changes and to refresh the sample. A list of the various sub-samples, with sample size, is shown in Table 3.1. More documentation for the GSOEP can be found in the "Introduction to the German Socio-Economic Panel" (Frick and Haisken-DeNew, 2002) and in articles of the SOEP-Group (2001).

Table 3.1: GSOEP sub-samples

Sample	Since	N	Note
A "West-German"	1984	4528	
B "Foreigners"	1984	1393	intentional over-sampling
C "East-Germans"	1990	2179	after re-unification
D "Immigrants"	1994	522	
E "Refreshment"	1998	1067	
F "Innovation"	2000	6962	new random sample of total pop.

Sample: Keycode and characterization of the sample. Since: Year of first wave. N: Number of participating households in first wave.

The panel contains micro-data on persons, families and household composition. Topics include various aspects on life and social and economical situation. The annual interviews contain both a core part (housing, income and earnings, education, employment, health, satisfaction with life and such) and topic modules with additional questions.

As a panel study, the GSOEP has several dimensions of time. The respondent is asked in retrospective questions concerning events and periods of time in the past year, questions on his current situation, and even questions regarding expectations and future prospects. Last not least, the interview is repeated annually, covering changes (or stability) in the life of the interviewees and changes in the household composition.

The interview methodology is in principle individual face-to-face interviews with all household members aged 16 and over. The basic interview is a paper-and-pencil interview. To gain information on family and household composition, a household interview with the "head of household" is done. If the usual method fails, self-administered interviews are proposed. In these cases, the interview data is checked by the data agency for inconsistencies.

Table 3.2: GSOEP: Interview modes in personal interview 1999

Interview mode	Percent
oral interview with interviewer present	43%
self-completed with interviewer present	28%
written interview	14%
self-completed without interviewer	5%
computer-aided personal interview (CAPI)	5%
part oral / part self-completed	4%
phone interview	< 0.1%
proxy interview	< 0.1%

Source: Frick and Haisken-DeNew (2003). "Written interview" is self-completed in written form and returned by postal mail.

The various instruments used include an address log with general information filled in by the interviewer, containing information on household size and housing area, on general information on individuals such as sex, year of birth, relation to head of household, and information on field work.

The most important instrument, of course, are the questionnaires. The interview includes different questionnaires for "new" and "old" or "moved" households, for temporary drop-outs, and – of course – different questionnaires for personal and household information.

The GSOEP has a follow-up concept, which means all households are to be surveyed in following years at the same address, or, if moved, anywhere else in Germany. This means the GSOEP is designed to describe regional mobility.

Persons are first interviewed at age 16. Persons in a GSOEP household who become 16 years old as well as persons who move into an existing household are interviewed and – since 1989 – also followed in case of leaving the household (thus forming a so-called split-off household).

Temporary drop-outs are followed as long as at least one member of the household is still responding or has been a respondent in the previous wave. To cover gaps, persons are asked to fill in a small questionnaire with central information on the time past upon re-entry.

Regarding data collection, two steps are relevant: Making successful contact with the household, and completing successful interviews. Different factors have an impact on the first and the second stage. While certain types of households are typically hard to contact, e.g., single person households, moving households and young persons who are starting to found their own household, other households are hard to interview, e.g., persons who distrust interviewers and their field agencies or persons who have trouble following the interview because of lingual or mental problems.

To increase the response rate, respondents receive a small gift and a ticket for a nationwide lottery. Also, a summary with some statistical results based on GSOEP data is send to all households.

To increase both the contact and the response rate, the SOEP tries to use the same interviewer in each wave. Thus, a personal relationship between interviewer and respondent is established which makes it easier for the respondent to participate. The success rate is very high: In 2001, after 18 waves, almost 48% of the initial respondents of 1984 have been successfully interviewed (Frick and Haisken-DeNew, 2003, p. 18).

When calculating population totals, the sample design, initial non-response, unit non-response and attrition (units leaving the panel because of loss of contact or refusal after the first wave) has to be taken into account. Therefore, the GSOEP data contains survey weights. The weights are calculated using the sampling probability and are corrected for external information. In addition to these wave 1 design weights, longitudinal weights are calculated based on the estimated probability of individuals to remain in the sample.

The weights base on predictions for contact and response probability (Frick and Haisken-DeNew, 2002, Section 5.3). The following factors had a significant impact on contact probability:

- household moved
- household was in a large city
- household size
- type of house
- split-off household

For the response probability, other variable came into play: The age and gender of the head of household, the household composition (and changes thereof), a change of interviewers (Rendtel, 1995), the number of interviews, head of household as a participant since first wave, change of marital status (separation of a couple), unemployment or expected job loss, occupational status, income and income types, reluctancy to report household income and assets, and migration background (East-West or immigrant). The number of factors seems large, but also the relevance across waves varies.

3.1.2 The European Community Household Panel

The European Community Household Panel (ECHP) is a representative cross-national household panel study for members of the European Community. An introduction and documentation can be found in Eurostat (1999a) and Eurostat (1999c). Currently, extensive documentation on the ECHP is also available online from the CIRCA (Communication & Information Resource Centre Administrator) user group:

http://forum.europa.eu.int/Public/irc/dsis/echpanel/home and
http://forum.europa.eu.int/irc/dsis/echpanel/info/data/information.html

The panel was started in 1994 in 12 EU member states, namely Belgium, Denmark, France, Germany, Greece, Ireland, Italy, Luxembourg, Portugal, Spain, The Netherlands and the United Kingdom, and it had been extended to two more, Austria in 1995 and Finland in 1996. The last and final wave of the ECHP was surveyed in 2001. Its role as the EU's main instrument to provide micro-level household information has been taken over by a new study, the EU Statistics on Income and Living Conditions, EU-SILC.

The main idea of the ECHP was to provide comparable data concerning the living conditions of private households, especially income and poverty, and also on housing, health, education, employment status, demographics and other social issues.

The cross-country design of the study was quite innovative and requires some comments. For most countries, the national data collection used the harmonized ECHP blueprint questionnaire, translated to national language. Also, some common procedures were shared, for example the definition of the target population for sampling, tracing rules in field work, classification and coding concepts. This approach is also called input harmonization, because – in theory – the data from all the various data providers are comparable in structure and quality when it is submitted to Eurostat. The operational details, however, were not necessarily identical, e.g., the exact sampling design was up to the national statistical institutes.

In some countries, the national institutes did not create new panels, instead they modified pre-existing national longitudinal surveys into ECHP format, namely Belgium and The Netherlands from 1994. In 1997, Germany, United Kingdom and Luxembourg converted national non-official surveys into ECHP format, using the previously mentioned GSOEP in Germany, the Panel socio-économique / Liewen zu Lëutzebuerg (PSELL) in Luxembourg and the British Household Panel Survey (BHPS) in United Kingdom. In Finland, part of the data was not sampled in interviews, but using existing administrative registers – official statistics on individual level. When using data from these countries and periods, users have to bear in mind that some items could be missing or were created by different methods than expected.

The raw data, which were very close to the values filled in the questionnaires, were submitted to the Statistical Office of the European Communities, Eurostat, where it was checked for errors and edited and put into so-called *Production Data Bases* (PDB), which were only available to the national statistical offices producing the data.

The PDB was then further processed by Eurostat: Units were weighted and anonymized, missing values were imputed and standardized data constructs were computed. Finally, a *User Data Base* was produced, which was made available to researchers under an ECHP research contract with Eurostat.

The UDB was not only more user-friendly than the PDB, it was usually the only way ECHP data was made available to data users outside the national statistical offices. For the purposes of our work, we wanted to analyze some points of interest, only raw and unprocessed data could provide. The User Databases contain only values which have been subject to data processing (i.e. imputation, aggregation) which remove or change the values which have been originally provided by respondents.

Thus, we had to use to the PDBs, which were made available to us by the Statistische Bundesamt for Germany 1994-1996, by Statistics Finland for 1996 and 2000 and by the PSELL for Luxembourg 1994-1996. In addition, the UK-PDB was made available, but due to technical problems it was used only sparsely in our work.

The ECHP is a cross-country study, and each country is providing a large number of units, both households and persons. The number of units per country was not equal or proportional to population, but roughly in-between: Samples from countries like Luxembourg were smaller than samples from France or Germany. The number of household units per sample is shown in Table 3.3.

In the ECHP, the same units were interviewed in each wave, both the households and the persons belonging to each household (the ECHP definition for *household* is in the next paragraph). Moving households were followed within countries, and persons entering or leaving households were interviewed, too. Therefore, the ECHP allows to analyze households, relationships and transition over time at micro level.

> **Household** "(German: Haushalt, French: Ménage). At community level, a household is defined in terms of shared residence and common arrangements, as comprising either one person living alone or a group of persons, not necessarily related, living at the same address with common house-keeping - i.e. sharing a meal on most days or sharing a living or sitting room. Not all countries adhere strictly to this EU definition. Persons currently residing in the household, persons temporarily institutionalized (health home, full-time education, military service) or absent for work or travel are included in all countries. However, in Denmark, persons in health homes are excluded."
> Source: Eurostat (1999c)

Table 3.3: ECHP: Number of interviewed households per country

country/panel	start	n	country/panel	start	n
B	1994	3490	LUX	1994	1011
DK	1994	3482	LUX/PSELL	1997	2978
GER	1994	4968	NL	1994	5187
GER/SOEP	1997	6207	A	1995	3380
GR	1994	5523	P	1994	4881
E	1994	7206	FIN	1996	4139
F	1994	7344	UK	1994	5779
IRL	1994	4048	UK/BHPS	1997	5124
I	1994	7115			

Total (EU in 1994): n=61273. B: Belgium, DK: Denmark, GER: Germany, GR: Greece, E: Spain, F: France, IRL: Ireland, I: Italy, LUX: Luxembourg, NL: The Netherlands, A: Austria, P: Portugal, FIN: Finland, UK: United Kingdom. Source: ECHP Newsletter.

3.1.3 The Finnish ECHP data for the CHINTEX project

Statistics Finland provided a special data base for use in the CHINTEX project. This data base included register and interview data on household and personal level. Since extensive use of this data base is made in this paper, it is necessary to explain several details.

The data have been used earlier e.g., in Nordberg et al. (2001); Hovi et al. (2001) and Sisto (2003), also in Neukirch (2003).

> **Sample structure** [...] The Finnish ECHP sample is based on the incoming rotation group of the Income Distribution Survey (IDS). The IDS has a rotating half-sample design, where every incoming panel is drawn, using systematic sampling, from a master sample drawn from the population register that has been stratified by income and socio-economic status. House-

holds are constructed around the sample persons using information on shared dwelling units. The procedure followed by Wave 3 of the ECHP is the same.
Source: (Jäntti, 2004, Section 2)

The initial sample consists of persons in selected dwelling units. Of course, the group of persons sharing a *dwelling unit*, e.g., a house, a flat, a small apartment or a unit in a large house, is just a proxy for *household*.

Some households are distributed across several dwelling units, e.g., when students have their own apartment or members are temporarily absent (military service, health institution). On the other hand, sometimes multiple households or members belonging to different households are sharing the same dwelling unit. Also, it is possible that persons are falsely registered as living in the same dwelling unit.

During the interview, the sample person will be asked a lot of questions and the true household composition will be defined. All persons belonging to a sample person's household form sample households and are part of the initial sample.

Other persons living in the same dwelling unit but not being household members are "not in household" and won't be interviewed. In those cases when no initial contact to the sample person could be established, however, or the person refused to be interviewed, information on all persons in this dwelling unit were drawn from registers. These information are not used in our paper, but several of the aforementioned authors made use of these information. This topic is important because differences in the composition of households based either on register or household data have consequences for the household income (either because the persons who contribute income to the household is different, or because the number of persons who share the income is different). A brief report on this issue was written by Sandström (2002).

Besides conceptual problems, a panel sample changes between periods. Each wave, some sample persons or households fail to respond. If contact cannot be regained in following waves, these are the *attriters*. Note that we do not discriminate between true refusals and nonvoluntary non-response, e.g., when a household moves and no contact could be established.

Non-sample persons are entering the household of a sample persons, and others are leaving the household. Babies are born and people die. By its very nature, a panel is permanently changing. In the best case, such changes reflect the change of population. In the worst case, the panel quickly deteriorates to a selective sub-sample which is not representative for the population.

The composition of the ECHP sample in wave 3 and 7 is shown in Figure 3.1 based on Figure 1 from Jäntti (2004).

Income values

After the sample composition, the most important detail is the calculation of income variables. In this paper, we use several income variables: *Household net disposable money income* which is the sum of all cash incomes, from labor and capital markets, social and private transfers, minus direct taxes and contributions to social insurance and pension (see ECHP questionnaire) and *personal gross wage and earnings*.

The household income variable is generated by two different ways. First, after Question 84 by asking the respondent directly about the monthly amount (Question 85) or – if the amount was not known – to chose from a number of income brackets (Question 86). Second, by asking each household member about the amount of all net disposable household income components in the previous year. These components are taken to calculate a sum to get the household income from interviews. Likewise, these components are taken from registers and summed for each household member (the household composition and identity of household members is asked in the interview) for the household income from registers.

Personal gross wage and earnings is asked in a similar fashion. The details have already been given in Section 2.2.

In some cases, we use the *disposable equivalence income*. Net disposable household income is a very important concept because it describes the amount of money the household as a whole can use for consumptions, savings and buying property without making debts. To compare the level of well-being in different households, it is necessary to take the number of persons and composition of a household into account by calculating the household net disposable equivalence income. Eurostat recommends a modified OECD scale that counts 1.0 for the head of the household, 0.5 for all the other adults and 0.3 for children younger than 14. The original OECD

Figure 3.1: Structure of the Finnish ECHP data

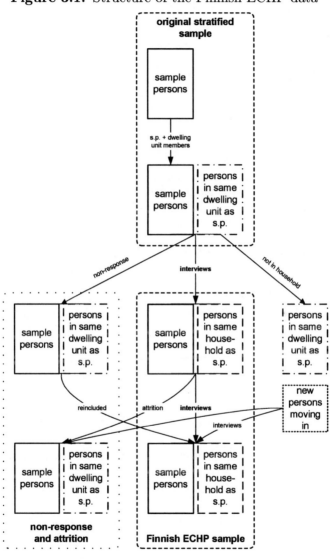

Source: (Jäntti, 2004, Figure 1).

scale counts 1.0 for the first adult, 0.7 for other adults and 0.5 for children.[1]
If equivalence income is used in this paper, the modified OECD scale was
used.

Sampling weights

The ECHP PDB offers *design weights* w_i. These are the inverse of the
selection probability. Design weights can be used to calculate population
estimates based on the sample that accommodate for individual sampling
probabilities.

3.2 Frequency of rounding in income variables

How many reported income values are rounded? Is the amount dependent
on survey techniques or is it constant across different surveys? By comparing
the same income variables across two different surveys, we want to get some
answers.

3.2.1 Comparison of rounding in two German household surveys

In the first part, we calculate the frequency of accurate (or rounded) values
by certain degrees among the respondents' answers to interview questions
regarding (a) household net disposable income and (b) personal gross wage
and earnings (see Table 3.4).

Both samples have relatively low fractions of exact data (non-rounded data)
in 1994-1996: between 12.6%, 14.5% and 13.3% in the G-ECHP, and 17%,
18.1% and 16.5% in the GSOEP. Across waves, the frequency of rounding
changes, although we do not see an apparent upward or downward trend.
Remarkably, the difference between GSOEP and G-ECHP stays approximately at 3.5 percentage points. The SOEP has started 12 years earlier,
thus the difference either indicates that people tend to tell exact numbers
more likely when panel participation duration increases, or that the difference is caused by survey design and interview techniques. An analysis in a
later chapter will shed some light on this point.

A remark on the number of valid observations: The total number dropped
in the G-ECHP by 136 in the second wave, and by 89 in the third. At

---

[1] Cf. Sisto (2003); OECD (1982); Atkinson et al. (2002).

Table 3.4: Rounding of Net Disposable Household Income

| | rounding 1994 | | rounding 1995 | | rounding 1996 | |
rounded	GECHP	GSOEP	GECHP	GSOEP	GECHP	GSOEP
no	12.6%	17.0%	14.5%	18.1%	13.3%	16.5%
by 100	60.2%	57.6%	59.5%	57.4%	61.2%	57.5%
by 1000	27.3%	25.4%	29.0%	24.5%	25.4%	26.0%
Total N	4038	5316	3902	5189	3813	5171

Unweighted relative frequency of "round" net disposable household income values in G-ECHP and GSOEP data. "yes, 100": value is a multiples of 100, but not of 1000. "yes, 1000": a multiple of 1000. "no": not a multiple of 1000.

the same time, the numbers in the GSOEP dropped by 147 respectively 28. The reason for this is that persons are leaving and others are joining the survey. In addition, some switch to or from item non-response and bracket response. We have to keep this in mind when drawing conclusions.

Also the mixture of rounding types is similar. About 70% of the rounded values are multiples of 100 but not 1000, and 30% are multiples of 1000. Rounding to multiples of 1000 yields larger measurement errors, so the mere frequency of rounding is not a sufficient measure for relative error due to rounding.

3.2.2 Comparison of rounding for the personal data

The values are most often rounded to multiples of 100. One out of five rounded answers is a multiple of 1000, both in the G-ECHP and GSOEP. For household data, rounding to multiples of 1000 was more frequently found. We can conclude that the rounding error is smaller for personal data than for household data. This is plausible because individual wages are better known to a respondent and do not require additional calculations like total net disposable cash household income does.

The difference between GSOEP and G-ECHP for individual wages (see Table 3.5) is much bigger than for the household data. In the G-ECHP of

Table 3.5: Rounding of personal gross wage and earnings

rounding	rounding 1994		rounding 1995		rounding 1996	
	GECHP	GSOEP	GECHP	GSOEP	GECHP	GSOEP
no	16.5%	31.8%	19.7%	31.5%	17.3%	31.6 %
yes, 100	66.5%	55.1%	64.9%	55.2%	66.2%	54.9%
yes, 1000	17.1%	13.1%	15.3%	13.3%	16.5%	13.5%
Total N=	3695	7247	3843	7488	3738	7286

Data: G-ECHP and GSOEP, personal gross wage and earnings.

1994, 16.5% of valid observations are non-rounded values, and 31.8% in the GSOEP. However, the level does not seem to be stable in the G-ECHP. In the first three waves, we see no clear trend that rounding error decreases (or increases) with longer panel participation duration. The fraction of non-rounded values seems to rise slightly in the G-ECHP, from 16.5% in 1994 to 19.7% in 1995, then it drops to 17.3% in 1996. In the G-SOEP, no such change between waves is observed.

The results seem to be in accordance with our a priori hypothesis of a more precise measurement in long-running panels (the GSOEP started ten years earlier). But one has to admit that the trend is not apparent *during* the first three waves of the G-ECHP. Therefore either the assumed panel conditioning is working very slowly, or not at all and the difference is caused by other effects.

An alternative explanation for this trend is self-selection: Persons who provide exact values are more cooperative and also have a higher propensity to stay in the panel. If more persons who initially provided rounded values tend to leave the panel, then the relative percentage of accurate values would automatically rise.

But this would not be a panel conditioning effect. Panel conditioning happens when the respondents get more familiar with the interviewer, the aims of the survey and the questionnaire. Or, when they remember their last wave response. These factors could motivate the interviewees to be even more cooperative than in previous waves. More cooperation implies a higher quality of response, e.g., providing more significant digits (even when the absolute number of digits stays the same), or a switch from non-response or bracket usage to income values. An answer to these hypotheses must be found in an analysis of individual rounding behavior, e.g., in Chapter 6 of this thesis.

3.2.3 Rounding in the Lux-ECHP

The Luxembourgian sub-sample of the ECHP is quite interesting with regard to household income. The fraction of rounded values is relatively large (see Table 3.6), compared to other sub-samples.

Table 3.6: Table of Frequencies

rounded	1994		1995		1996	
	N	(%)	N	(%)	N	(%)
no or by 10	26	5.0	43	8.2	55	9.2
by 100	43	8.2	28	5.3	69	11.6
by 1000	267	51.1	279	53.0	290	48.6
by 10000	187	35.8	176	33.4	183	30.7
total	523	100.0	526	100.0	597	100.0

Accuracy of response type, data Lux-ECHP wave 1-3 net disposable household income. 40 LUF ≈ 1 Euro. Rounding by 10000 includes rounding by 100000.

Most values are rounded by 1000, while the most common rounding unit in the G-ECHP was 100. This might be explainable by the different numeraire – one DEM had approximately the same worth as forty LUF. In addition, the average real income level in Luxembourg is the highest in the European Union, which could also play a role.

In the Lux-ECHP, some improvement with respect to accuracy can be seen – the frequency (both in absolute and relative numbers) of values which are not or moderately rounded increases constantly, while the frequency of values which are highly rounded drops. Here, we can see an indicator for positive panel conditioning.

Rounding and bracket usage in the Lux-ECHP will be further discussed in

Section 4.2.

3.2.4 Other national sub-samples

Tables with the frequency for rounding of the net disposable household income in the Finnish, German and Luxembourgian sub-samples of the ECHP are listed in the Appendix Section A.2.3.

It would be interesting to compare the level of rounding across all nations participating in the ECHP. Unfortunately, because of technical reasons we could analyze only a few sub-samples. Only the Production Data Base (PDB) files contained the original values sampled in interviews, the User Data Base files contained only edited values which no longer were guaranteed to contain sufficient information on the rounding in the reported value.

The UK-ECHP PDB was available to us, but was odd in a peculiar respect: Obviously, people in the UK are used to receive weekly wages, and thus the majority of reporters told the interviewer their weekly averages. However, because the blueprint questionnaire did not contain a field for weekly figures, the fieldwork institute responsible for data collection multiplied these weekly averages by some unknown factors to a monthly income. We did not manage to find out the precise factors, which seemed to be around but not always exactly to 4.345, which is equal to $365/(12 \cdot 7)$.

The UK-PDB personal gross wage and earnings data is an interesting example for values which are rounded, but not such that the resulting values are multiples of some decimal base like 10 or 100.

3.3 Rounding as a sequential process: Digit by digit

We show several examples of sequential rounding for the Luxembourgian sub-sample of the ECHP, and calculate conditional probabilities or ratios (but not odds ratios) $h(B > i)/h(B \geq i)$. Luxembourg is a good example because the numeraire, Luxembourgian Francs, has a relatively low base value, and thus incomes have 5-6 digits. In the following section, the results for Luxembourg are discussed. Tables for Germany (GSOEP and G-ECHP) and Finland (Fin-ECHP) can be found in the Appendix, Section A.2.3. A slightly different approach, using an indicator for the number of significant digits, counted absolutely, is foundin the Appendix, Section A.4.2.

3.3.1 Empirical results for sequential rounding of household income in the Lux-ECHP

Table 3.7: Absolute frequency for the number of leading digits $b = i$

i	Wave 1		Wave 2		Wave 3	
1	105	20%	82	16%	91	15%
2	240	46%	262	50%	236	40%
3	138	26%	136	26%	179	30%
4	16	3%	6	1%	41	7%
5	18	3%	23	4%	27	5%
6	6	1%	17	3%	23	4%
	523	100%	526	100%	597	100%

Absolute frequencies of $b = i$ (index of last non-rounded digit)least i non-rounded digits) in the right. Data: Luxembourgian sub-sample of ECHP, 1994-1996, net disposable household income.

Table 3.8: Ratios $h(B > i)/h(B \geq i)$ (household income)

i	Wave 1	Wave 2	Wave 3
1	79.9%	84.4%	84.8%
2	42.6%	41.0%	53.4%
3	22.5%	25.3%	33.7%
4	60.0%	87.0%	54.9%
5	25.0%	42.5%	46.0%

Ratios $h(b > i)/h(b \geq i)$ (the relative frequency of values where the $(i+1) - th$ digit is not rounded conditional that the i-th digit is not rounded). Data: Luxembourgian sub-sample of ECHP, 1994-1996, net disposable household income.

Figure 3.2: Ratios $h(b \geq i+1)/h(b \geq i)$ (household income)

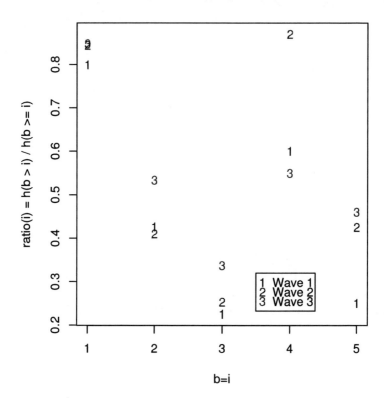

Data: Luxembourgian sub-sample of ECHP, 1994-1996, net disposable household income.

According to the table of frequencies, only a few digits play a role in response behavior of Luxembourgian data. Values with four or more significant digits are very rare. Thus, only the first two or three ratios are of relevance. And these three ratios show a clear downward trend, which means the propensity to report additional digits decreases after each of the first three digits.

It is easy to see that most people edit only the first two digits of their household income value and round the remaining digits. In the first two waves, the ratios of persons who tell subsequent digits after the second or third digit are around 40% respectively 25%. A trend towards higher ratios is visible in wave two, indicating improvement in data quality. But in the third wave we see a major improvement of the second and third ratio.

3.3.2 Empirical results for sequential rounding of personal income in the Lux-ECHP

Table 3.9: Table of Frequencies for $b = i$ and $b \geq i$, individuals

Absolute frequencies of $b = i$				Absolute frequency of $b \geq i$			
i	Wave 1	Wave 2	Wave 3	i	Wave 1	Wave 2	Wave 3
1	109	78	55	1	542	466	385
2	288	234	197	2	433	388	330
3	99	89	82	3	145	154	133
4	9	15	9	4	46	65	51
5	22	33	26	5	37	50	42
6	15	17	16	6	15	17	16

Data: Luxembourgian sub-sample of ECHP, 1994-1996, personal income from wage and earnings.

Most responders edited more than one digit (79.9% in the first wave, 85.7% in the third), but only a few who had edited two digits continued with a third digit (33.5% in the first wave, and around 40% in the second and third). Thus, the first two or three ratios are of relevance, the others have been reported on a few persons only.

An improvement in data quality, expressed in an increase of the ratio, occurs from wave 1 to wave 2. In the personal interview, there is no obvious improvement from wave 2 to wave 3. Instead, the absolute number of observation decreases, which means more people are switching from response to non-response, than vice versa. Regardless of changes in rounding behavior, this decreases the overall accuracy of data.

Table 3.10: Ratios $h(b \geq i + 1)/h(b \geq i)$ (wage and earnings)

i	Wave 1	Wave 2	Wave 3
1	79.9%	83.2%	85.7%
2	33.5%	39.6%	40.3%
3	31.7%	42.2%	38.4%
4	80.4%	76.9%	82.4%
5	40.5%	34.0%	38.1%

Ratios $h(b \geq i + 1)/h(b \geq i)$ (the relative frequency of values where the $(i + 1) - th$ digit is not rounded conditional that the i-th digit is not rounded). Data: Luxembourgian sub-sample of ECHP, 1994-1996, personal income from wage and earnings.

3.3.3 Conclusion for Luxembourgian data

The analysis of sequential rounding in the Luxembourgian sub-sample of the ECHP shows clear signs for an improvement of the quality of income data with respect to level rounding in both the second panel wave (improvement in personal income) and the third wave (improvement in household income). Despite improvement in data quality, most persons tell the two or three leading digits of income data and round off the figure, thus turning the remaining digits to zeros.

3.3.4 Frequency of sequential rounding in the GSOEP and four national sub-samples of the ECHP

For this section, we calculated the ratios for rounding in the sequential process for several panels: For the German, Finnish and Luxembourgian sub-samples of the ECHP, and for the German Socio-Economic Panel. The results are given in Table 3.11.

The individual values are different across countries, but some similarities can be discerned.

In all samples except for the Fin-ECHP, the first ratio is relatively high. This means that many respondents edit at least two values.

The next second ratio, for editing more than two values, is much smaller.

Figure 3.3: Ratios $h(b \geq i + 1)/h(b \geq i)$ (wage and earnings)

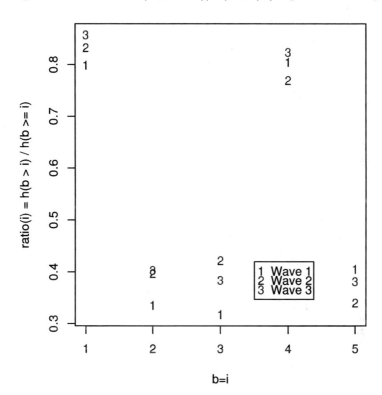

Data: Luxembourgian sub-sample of ECHP, waves 1, 2 and 3, personal income from wage and earnings.

The exception is the UK, but technical reasons throw some doubt on the assumption that the UK income values are the original interview values (see Section 3.2.4).

The ratios in the G-ECHP and GSOEP are very similar. This is interesting because both panels are different with respect to the samples, the interviewers, the statistical institute processing the data and the interview

Table 3.11: Sequential rounding of household income

G-ECHP

digits	1993	1994	1995
1	0.7263	0.7404	0.7492
2	0.1640	0.1907	0.1969
3	0.3160	0.3285	0.3380
N=	4038	3902	3891

G-SOEP

digits	1993	1994	1995
1	0.7407	0.7455	0.7353
2	0.2218	0.2362	0.2139
3	0.3262	0.3219	0.3579
N=	6530	6617	6554

Lux-ECHP

digits	1993	1994	1995
1	0.7992	0.8441	0.8475
2	0.4258	0.4099	0.5335
3	0.2247	0.2527	0.3370
4	0.6000	0.8695	0.5494
5	0.2500	0.4250	0.4600
N=	523	526	597

Fin-ECHP

digits	1995	1999
1	0.3973	0.3496
2	0.1425	0.0767
3	0.3213	0.1375
4	0.0704	0.0909
N=	3904	2983

UK-ECHP

digits	1993	1994	1995
1	0.8615	0.8564	0.8469
2	0.5938	0.5710	0.5635
3	0.1982	0.2072	0.2236
N=	5299	4026	3417

Relative frequencies of respondents who filled in the following digit of the "net disposable household income" question, conditional on the fact that he has already filled in the current one.

questionnaire. On the other hand, the Lux-ECHP has different ratios from the G-ECHP, and the ratios for incomes from the Fin-ECHP are very much different from both G-ECHP and Lux-ECHP data.

This similarity between the two German samples gives grounds for the hypothesis that rounding behavior can be related to some common factors which are similar in both samples.

But it also shows that differences between countries can have a greater effect on quality than differences between panel designs. The difference between the three ECHP sub-samples is an argument for the assumption that an input-harmonized approach cannot guarantee similarity in all dimensions of quality. The accuracy of household income data, expressed as the number of digits reported, is very different across various sub-samples.

The temporal change is small and does not seem to follow an obvious law. In some samples, G-ECHP and Lux-ECHP, a small upward trend in the first ratio is visible, and in the others a downward trend can be seen.

An analysis of personal gross wage and earnings, the results are shown in Table 3.13, leads to similar results. Compared to household income, the results for both German panels and especially for Finland show a relatively higher accuracy of reporting. However, all three panels do not have a noticeable improvement in accuracy from wave 1 to wave 3.

An exception is Luxembourg. Here, we have an improvement in accuracy, but the accuracy of earnings is lower than the accuracy for household incomes (Table 3.11). The reason for this is probably based on the fact that most Luxembourgians know their net wage and earnings but not the gross values. Table 3.12 shows how frequently interviewees reported net and gross wage and earnings (or both), and how often they did not respond a value despite the fact they previously stated they were receivers of wage or earnings.

A plausible explanation for the difference between household income and gross wage and earnings is that persons might find the concept of a household income unfamiliar at first, but become more accustomed to it. Maybe they spend some time to calculate a better estimate.

3.4 Comparison of final digit distribution

The distribution of single digits, especially the final digits, can be analyzed with respect to the theoretical distribution of these digits.

Table 3.12: Frequencies of non-response and responses by 1 or more significant digits in the Lux-ECHP wage and earnings question

digits	wage and earnings	
	gross	net
non-resp.	60.7%	10.7%
1	3.7%	18.3%
2	20.1%	50.2%
3	8.4%	12.4%
4	0.9%	0.8%
>4	6.2%	7.7%
n total	979 (100%)	

Final digit distribution in the German panels

A very illustrative way to visualize the numerical distribution of digits is the histogram of final digits. Figure 3.4 shows the distribution of the final digits of net household disposable in the G-ECHP and the GSOEP by applying the modulo operator to base 10, 100 or 1000 and calculating histograms with certain bin size.

The first histogram (upper left) has bins of width 100, so the histogram is determined by the distribution of the second digit. It is easy to see that the first bin has a very high density, followed by the medium bin (around 500). All the ten bins at 0, 100 ... 900 have high densities. This is an indication for rounding to next multiple of 100.

A second important observation is a certain shape of the distribution. Intuitively, income is a continuous variable whose final digits should be roughly rectangularly distributed. The extreme peaks at zero dwarf all other peaks. Therefore, we omit zero digits in Figure 3.5.

Instead, the distribution looks wave-like, interrupted by distinct peaks. Close to rounding points, the density drops even more. This phenomenon can be seen for any number of final digits, either the last digit only, 2 digits, or even 3 digits (see Figure 3.5).

The different histograms bear remarkable similarities which can also be found in the corresponding histograms for the Lux-ECHP (Figure A.4). One

Table 3.13: Frequencies in sequential rounding of personal gross
wage and earnings

G-ECHP

digit	1993	1994	1995
1	0.8027	0.8173	0.8127
2	0.1612	0.1792	0.1600
3	0.3619	0.3215	0.3107
N	3695	3843	3738

G-SOEP

digit	1993	1994	1995
1	0.8543	0.8580	0.8562
2	0.3582	0.3528	0.3571
3	0.5406	0.5530	0.5716
N	5641	5646	5527

Lux-ECHP

digit	1993	1994	1995
1	0.7989	0.8326	0.8571
2	0.3349	0.3969	0.4030
3	0.3172	0.4221	0.3835
4	0.8043	0.7692	0.8235
5	0.4054	0.3400	0.3810
N	542	466	385

Fin-ECHP

digit	1995	1999
1	0.6853	0.6922
2	0.3069	0.2971
3	0.2787	0.2114
4	0.2346	0.3796
N	4436	3151

Frequencies of respondents who filled in the following digit of the
"personal gross wage and earnings" question, conditional on the
fact that he has already filled out the current one (minimum 1).

reason for this is sequential rounding, which has been explored in Section
3.3.

3.5 Rounding of all income variables in the Fin-ECHP

The Finnish sub-sample contains a lot of different income variables, and
all of them are more or less affected by rounding. To commemorate some
results, Table 3.14 shows the frequency of values rounded after b significant
digits in response to the questions on the average personal gross wage and
earnings from main job (left), and the net cash disposable household income

Figure 3.4: Histograms of final digits of income values

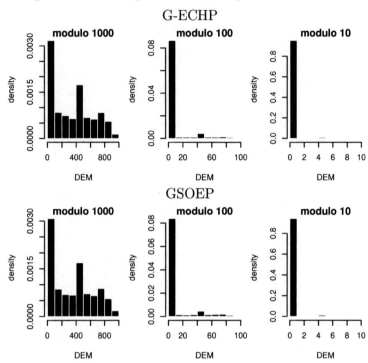

Histograms of final digits of income values (bin size 100, 10 and 1). Data: G-ECHP wave 1-3 (pooled), and G-SOEP, 1994-1996.

(right).

The rather abstract income concept "net disposable cash household income" is usually reported with one digit only (1996: 60.3%), and the more familiar "personal gross wage and earnings" is often reported with two (1996: 47.5%) or more digits.

The ECHP interview covered about 60 income-related questions that had to be answered with a money amount. Table A.13 in Section A.2.6 of the Appendix shows the amount of rounding in these questions. One of the

Figure 3.5: Histograms of final digits (excluding zero) of income values

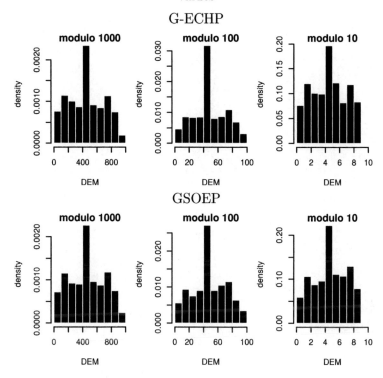

Histograms of final digits of income values (bin size 100, 10 and 1). Data: G-ECHP wave 1-3 (pooled), and G-SOEP, waves of 1994-1996. Zero digits were omitted.

highest relative amounts of rounding was observed in the question about the minimum net monthly income an unemployed person would accept to work (P031000). In 1996, 69.8% responses were rounded after the first digit, and 29.7% after the second. This high level of rounding is plausible because the answer to this question is always based on estimation. On the other hand, a variable with the relatively low amount of rounding was the

Table 3.14: Frequency of rounded income values in the Fin-ECHP.

Personal gross wage and earning			Net disposable household income		
digits	1996	2000	digits	1996	2000
$b = 1$	31.5%	30.8%	$b = 1$	60.3%	65.0%
$b = 2$	47.5%	48.7%	$b = 2$	34.1%	32.3%
$b = 3$	15.2%	16.2%	$b = 3$	3.8%	2.3%
$b = 4$	4.5%	2.7%	$b = 4$	1.7%	0.3%
$b = 5$	1.4%	1.7%	$b = 5$	0.1%	0.0%
n (100%)	4436	3151	n (100%)	3904	2983

Percent of reported values reported with b significant digits. Data: Fin-ECHP, waves of 1996 and 2000, gross wage and earnings from main job respectively net disposable household income, available cases analysis.

question on average monthly child allowance paid to mothers (P032860). Only 8.0% values were rounded after the first digit, 42.3% after the second, 35.3% after the third and 16.3% of the responses had four or more digits. The reason for this high accuracy is probably that the amount of child allowance – once fixed – rarely varies and is an important income source for mothers. Compared to these two extremes, interview data on the variable personal gross wage and earnings from main job contain a medium amount of rounded values.

To illustrate the differences in the average precision in income reports, Figure 3.6 shows the average precision or rounding level of each and every money-related question in the Fin-ECHP personal interview questionnaire. This includes questions on earnings and wage, social assistance payments, contribution to pension schemes, child benefits, early retirement scheme, and so on. The center of each circle indicates mean precision by mean income level of all responses to one specific question. Because both the number of persons eligible for the questions and the response rates differ,

Figure 3.6: Average precision of income variables in the Fin-ECHP

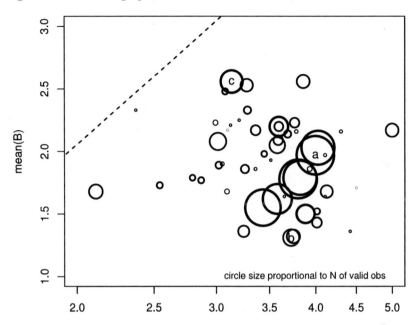

The centers of the circles indicate the average number of digits reported in response to the question on one specific income component on the ordinate, and the mean amount (as the logarithm to the base of 10) defines the coordinate along the abscissa. No observations are possible above the slashed line. Data: Income questions in Finnish ECHP personal interview 1996. **a**: personal gross wage and earnings. **b**: minimum net monthly income an unemployed person would accept to work. **c**: average monthly child allowance.

the size of the circles indicates the number of valid responses. One axis of
the plot marks the average precision, calculated as $\sum b \cdot \hat{Pr}(b)$ the other
axis is for the average value for the variable, transformed by $\log_{10}$. This is
a natural upper bound for b. For reference, the average precision level b for
personal gross wage and earnings is 1.967, and the average $\log_{10}$ earnings
level is 3.996.

The figure shows that the average precision in answers is scattered around
$b = 2$. Three important things can be read from this figure of a relatively
random scattering of circles: (1) The "big" questions, ones that have been
asked and answered by thousands respondents, are not better or worse with
respect to rounding than "small" questions with small number of responses.
The average precision seems to be between 1.5 and 2.5 digits. (2) The
relative precision – as measured by $mean(b)$ – does not seem to increase
much with the average amount of money in question. Therefore, neither
small values nor big ones are reported with higher relative precision. And
(3) almost each ECHP interview question related to amounts of money has
a high propensity of being answered with a rounded value.

Three circles are marked with letters in the middle. These are: **a**. gross
wage and earnings from main activity, **b**. the minimum net monthly income an unemployed person would accept to work, and **c**. average monthly
child allowance (paid to mothers). **b** is always a guess and therefore it is
reasonable that this variable has among the highest rates of rounding. On
the other hand, **c** is a very specific variable which rarely varies, which is
probably the reason why it is least affected by rounding. The variable of
interest, gross wage and earnings, is in the middle of these extremes.

Rounding of all incomes for G-ECHP and Lux-ECHP

We have computed similar Figures like Figure 3.6 for G-ECHP and Lux-
ECHP data. The results are displayed in Figures 3.7 and 3.8.

Obviously, the figures for the three national surveys look quite different.
The Finnish and the Luxembourgian data seems somewhat similar, but the
German data is very different with a number of "big" variables reported
with high precision.

The simple reason for this is ex-post anonymization of values. Germany's
statistical office responsible for ECHP data collection changed income values
and thereby masked the effect of rounding. In the data delivered to Euro-

Figure 3.7: Average precision of income variables in the Lux-ECHP

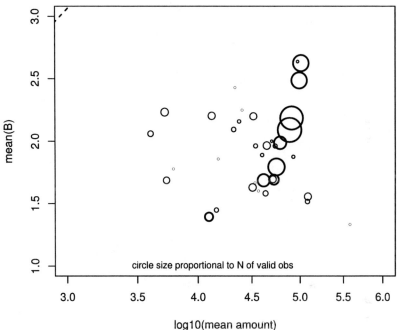

Circles indicate the average number of digits used in reports on specific income components on the ordinate, and the mean amount (as the logarithm to the base of 10) along the abscissa.

stat, the information about the relative precision (number of significant digits) of individual digits was no longer available in G-ECHP data.

Figure 3.8: Average precision of income variables in the G-ECHP

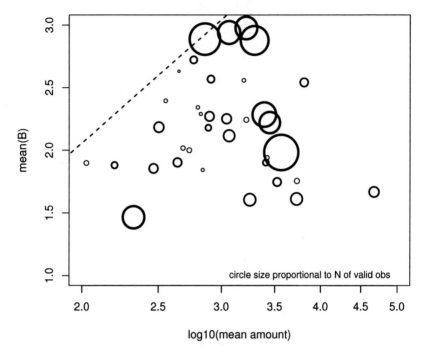

Circles indicate the average number of digits used in reports on specific income components on the ordinate, and the mean amount (as the logarithm to the base of 10) along the abscissa.

CHAPTER4

Income brackets

In this chapter, we first explain what income brackets are and how they are used in the ECHP interview to measure income. Using the LUX-ECHP, we analyze the frequency of income brackets compared to the frequency count of income values and item non-response. Then the empirical cumulative distribution functions of income values and income brackets are compared from two different points of view:

- the marginal frequency,
- the distribution within brackets.

In the fourth section of this chapter, two sources of data for the same population are analyzed to find differences and similarities with respect to brackets. Finally, a simple yet intuitive approach to improve the quality of data with respect to the design of brackets is suggested.

4.1 Introduction

It is not a simple task to report the quantities of income components: Often, the respondent knows specific components only with some uncertainty or inaccuracy and is reluctant to provide an answer. *Income brackets* are an alternative to open-end questions format where the respondent is asked to report a numeric value. Instead, he is given range cards with categorized income brackets and asked to chose one card. In the ECHP, this option is used several times in the household questionnaire, especially in questions about household income components.

In the ECHP blue-print questionnaire, income brackets are only used when the person refused to tell an exact value when asked for the amount of net disposable household income. Thus, for each household in the survey we have either a value, or an income bracket, or item or unit non-response.

Table 4.1: Coding for income brackets in the ECHP

range of values	code
less than 500 EUR	01
500 to under 1000 EUR	02
1000 to under 1500 EUR	03
1500 to under 2000 EUR	04
2000 to under 2500 EUR	05
2500 to under 3000 EUR	06
3000 to under 5000 EUR	07
5000 EUR or more per month	08

The income brackets (and coding) is shown in Table 4.1. Only brackets 2 to 6 each have the same width of 500 Euro. The first and the last bracket are open-ended (the first could possibly include negative household incomes, and the last includes all values greater or equal 5000). The seventh bracket is from 3000 to under 5000, a width of 2000, four times that of brackets 2 to 6. All bracket limits are multiples of 500 Euro, and thus close to rounding points if income was asked for in Euro.

In the country specific questionnaires, these ranges were translated into national currencies and roughly rounded to "even" numbers. For example, 500 EUR is the equivalent of 977.92 DEM, but in the German questionnaire 1000 DEM is used as the bracket limit. The bracket ranges in different national interviews are therefore not fully comparable.

There are several questions with respect to income brackets:

a) Is the income distribution for persons who used values in their response different from the persons who used income brackets?

b) What is the distribution of values within income brackets?

c) Can the design of income brackets be improved?

We analyze values and income brackets in the Luxembourgian, Finnish and German sub-samples of the ECHP using descriptive and visual methods.

4.2 Bracket usage in the Lux-ECHP

4.2.1 Empirical frequency of bracket usage

The Luxembourgian sub-sample of the ECHP – though small when compared to other national sub-samples – is suited well for empirical analysis. When asked about their net household income during the household interview, a relatively high number of persons (almost 50% of respondents) refused to provide a value, but agreed to choose an income bracket.

Table 4.2: Empirical frequency of response types, Lux-ECHP

response type	wave 1 Count	Prc.	wave 2 Count	Prc.	wave 3 Count	Prc.
value	523	51.7%	531	55.2%	597	64.0%
bracket	473	46.8%	403	41.9%	312	33.4%
non-response	15	1.5%	28	2.9%	24	2.6%

Absolute and relative frequency of response types to question regarding the amount of net disposable household income. Data: Lux-ECHP, wave 1-3.

In the first wave, about half of the persons (51.7%) in the household interview reported the net disposable household income as a (more or less rounded) value, and almost all the others (46.8%) chose an income bracket. Only a few interviewees (1.5%) did not answer the question.

In consecutive waves, the number of people who answered the question with a value increased, both absolutely (from 523 to 597) and relatively (from 51.7% to 64.0%). This is an indication of a panel effect, this would imply that the quality of data in the Luxembourgian sub-sample of the ECHP improves after the first wave.

4.2.2 Comparison of value and bracket usage

If so many persons refused to report a value and used brackets instead, then the question arises whether the type of response is correlated with certain factors, and especially with the amount of income value which was asked for. It could be assumed that higher income implies more rounding.

In Figure 4.1 and Table 4.3, the empirical frequency of values and bracket usage at different income levels is shown. For simplicity, 1 EUR $\approx$ 40 LUF in this section.

If the set of persons with value response was similar to the set of persons with brackets, then the distribution and cumulative distribution of incomes would be similar. If the distribution was different, then a gap between the two would be visible.

Figure 4.1: Cumulative frequency of values and bracket usage by different income levels

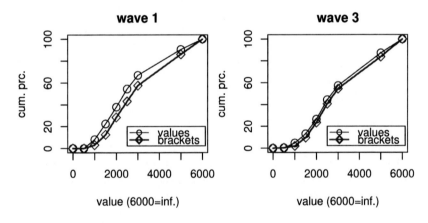

Cumulative frequency of values and bracket usage on different income levels. The rightmost bracket is open, higher values have been censored to 6000. Data: Lux-ECHP wave 1-3, unweighted.

In the first wave, persons with low income levels (less than 1500 EUR) were more likely to tell values, while persons with higher income (2500 EUR and more) preferred brackets. Thus the two groups of persons (value and bracket users) are different on the average with respect to household income. The marginal income distribution of value and bracket users is different.

Two years later, in wave 3, the difference is much smaller, and the two curves of cumulative empirical distribution are almost identical. The reason for this is that many persons (in absolute and relative terms) have switched from brackets to values.

The relative frequency of the ratio of bracket users to value users in each income group approximates one (see Table 4.3).

We conclude that the quality of household income data with respect to bracket usage at different income levels has improved. This effect can possibly be contributed to *panel conditioning*. The interviewer gained the trust of respondents who were initially reluctant and used brackets, but switched to values in later waves.

4.2.3 Distribution of values in brackets

While the marginal income distribution of value and bracket responses are different, it is not known whether the distribution of the (accurate) values *within* bracket limits is different, too.

The question is whether the conditional distribution of values $X : x_l^* \leq X < x_u^*$, where x_l^* is the lower limit and x_u^* the upper limit of a certain bracket (respectively, the lower limit of the next greater bracket) is similar for the two groups of persons who choose either values or brackets in the interview, or is it different?

In the data from the survey interview, the information about the distribution of income values (here: net disposable household income) within income brackets is missing. Income brackets are only incomplete information. [1]

For a first visual analysis, we calculate the cross-sectional empirical distribution of values within the range of income brackets. Instead of using

---

[1] Our first plan was to use the Finnish ECHP data to compare the register incomes for person who reported values with the register incomes for persons who reported income brackets. However, the number of persons who used income brackets is extremely low compared to Luxembourg or Germany and it was not meaningful to carry out that plan. Also, income brackets were offered as a follow-up question for wage and earnings in Germany, but not in Finland and thus not available.

Table 4.3: Frequencies of value and bracket usage in Lux-ECHP

wave 1	values			income brackets			ratio
	N	%	Cum.	N	%	Cum.	
<500 EUR	0	0.0	0.0	0	0.0	0.0	–
500- 999 EUR	42	8.0	8.0	14	3.0	3.0	0.37
1000-1499 EUR	75	14.3	22.4	45	9.5	12.5	0.66
1500-1999 EUR	81	15.5	37.9	75	15.9	28.3	1.02
2000-2499 EUR	87	16.6	54.5	70	14.8	43.1	0.89
2500-2999 EUR	65	12.4	66.9	68	14.4	57.5	1.16
3000-4999 EUR	123	23.5	90.4	135	28.5	86.0	1.21
≥5000 EUR	50	9.6	100.0	66	14.0	100.0	1.46
wave 2	N	%	Cum.	N	%	Cum.	ratio
<500 EUR	1	0.2	0.2	0	0.0	0.0	0.00
500- 999 EUR	32	6.0	6.2	12	2.9	2.9	0.49
1000-1499 EUR	60	11.3	17.5	37	9.1	12.0	0.80
1500-1999 EUR	95	17.9	35.4	50	12.3	24.3	0.68
2000-2499 EUR	82	15.4	50.8	71	17.4	41.7	1.13
2500-2999 EUR	61	11.5	62.3	55	13.5	55.1	1.17
3000-4999 EUR	149	28.1	90.4	119	29.2	84.3	1.04
≥5000 EUR	51	9.6	100.0	64	15.7	100.0	1.63
wave 3	N	%	Cum.	N	%	Cum.	ratio
<500 EUR	2	0.3	0.3	1	0.3	0.3	0.96
500 - 999 EUR	26	4.4	4.7	5	1.6	1.9	0.37
1000-1499 EUR	50	8.4	13.1	24	7.7	9.6	0.92
1500-1999 EUR	80	13.4	26.5	43	13.8	23.4	1.03
2000-2499 EUR	107	17.9	44.4	54	17.3	40.7	0.97
2500-2999 EUR	77	12.9	57.3	43	13.8	54.5	1.07
3000-4999 EUR	178	29.8	87.1	91	29.2	83.7	0.98
≥5000 EUR	77	12.9	100.0	51	16.3	100.0	1.27

Bracket and usage in response to question about level of net disposable household income. Data: Lux-ECHP wave 1-3. N: Number of persons in the income group using this response mode. %: Relative frequency of responders in this income group relative to the total number of persons using this response mode. Cum.: Cumulative Percent. Ratio: Prc(income brackets) / Prc(grouped values) income brackets only, we use data from persons who did respond values, and calculate which income bracket this income value belongs to.

Figure 4.2 shows separate histograms for individual income bracket range. The group labels are counted from low incomes (grp 2) to high incomes (grp 8). Group 9 (above 400,000 LUF) and group 1 (below 20,000 LUF) were not included because only a few persons are in these groups. These group labels corresponds to the coding in the data base.

Figure 4.2: Histograms of values in separate income bracket ranges

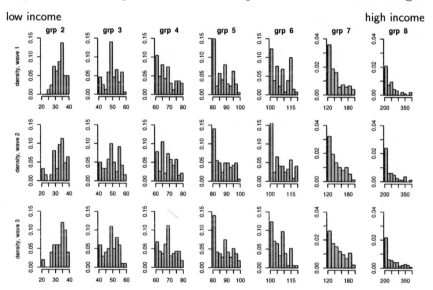

Data: Lux-ECHP wave 1-3. Units: 1000 LUF.

At the lower end of brackets labelled group 5 to 7 are always peaks, and several smaller peaks are in the brackets 3 and 4. For peaks at the lower end, two reasons are possible:

(I)   More values are near the lower limit creating a skewed distribution.

(II) The left border of the bracket is equal or close to a major rounding point.

If (I) was true, then the distribution within brackets would perhaps look more like a triangle or trapezoid (as seen in grp 7, w 3), and not roughly rectangular with a single peak (as seen best in grp 4, w 3) but more like a triangle or trapezoid (as seen in grp 3, w 3).

Regarding (II), all brackets in the questionnaire start with round values like 20000 and end with irregular values like 39999. But 20000 is a major rounding point, a value with one significant digit, which is also a multiple of 10000. This is an explanation for peaks at lower boundaries where rounded data causes data heaping.

In all brackets, heaping (rounding) accounts for the shape of the distribution within brackets. And in some brackets, the skewness of the income distribution also plays a role. The pattern in groups 2 and 3 is skewed, while the pattern in group 4 and 5 is not skewed.

4.2.4 Distribution of final digits in brackets

All the bracket limits used in the questionnaire are multiples of 20000 LUF (roughly 500 EUR). After analyzing the brackets one by one in the previous section, in this section the distribution of the final digits is analyzed. The main result is that certain final digits (especially 0 and 5) are observed more frequently than the others.

For the next calculation the *Modulo* division is used, which finds the remainder after an integer division (e.g. 17 mod 10 = 7, 20 mod 10 = 0). By pooling data from all waves and brackets, the distribution of the last digit(s) is analyzed in the next step.

Figure 4.3 shows the resulting distribution of the income values after Modulo division. The first histogram (upper left) with the smallest bin size shows a ragged and almost symmetrical distribution, except for the heap at the left limit. Peak densities are at 0 and 10000, smaller peaks at 5000 and 15000, and even smaller peaks are at other multiples of 1000. The regions between these bins have only sparse densities. With increasing bin size in histograms 2 (upper right) and 3 (lower left), the distribution gets more even but retains its general shape. Histograms with carefully chosen bin width seem to be a useful tool to display the frequency of data containing rounded values. The bins should be centered around rounding points and the bin width should be large enough to cover the most common rounding intervals.

Figure 4.3: Density of household income in brackets

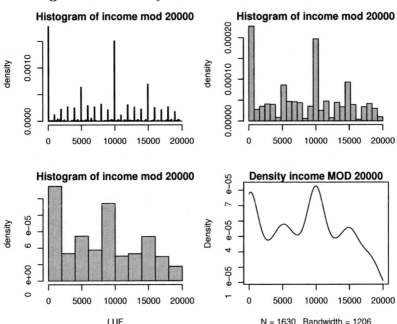

Three histograms (bin size 100, 800 and 2000 LUF) and a kernel density estimator of the net household disposable income value modulo 20000 LUF ($\approx$ 1000 DM). Data: Lux-ECHP wave 1-3 pooled.

The explanation is that the values are rounded by different degree. most values are rounded by 1000 or 10000, and a few are not rounded or rounded by small amounts much.

The distribution seems to follow a particular pattern. With a keen eye, an interesting detail can be discerned: The direct neighborhood to prominent rounding points (zero, 10000 and to a lesser amount 5000 and 15000) has less density than more remote areas. It seems as if the major rounding points have "attracted" their density, i.e., persons with incomes close to rounding points are more likely to round up or down than persons whose income is farer away from the rounding point, even if their income would be rounded to the same rounding point.

Therefore, there are reasons for the assumption that the propensity to round income values is somehow dependent on the absolute distance to neighboring rounding points. However, without suitable data this hypothesis cannot be tested here.

4.3 Bracket usage in the G-ECHP

This section shows results from the German sub-sample of the ECHP (G-ECHP). When the structure of this section is similar to the previous section, the explanations are kept shorter than in the previous section.

4.3.1 Empirical frequency of bracket usage

The number of persons in the German sub-sample of the ECHP who – when asked about net disposable household income – refused to provide an open-format value but chose one of several income brackets offered to them is rather low: About 852 ($\approx 16.9\%$) of 5053 household interviews in the first wave of the panel.

Table 4.4: Empirical frequency of response types

	wave 1		wave 2		wave 3	
response type	Count	Prc.	Count	Prc.	Count	Prc.
value	4038	79.9%	3902	82.1%	3891	83.6%
bracket	852	16.9%	682	14.9%	605	13.0%
item non-response	163	3.2%	169	3.6%	158	3.4%

Absolute and relative frequency of response types to question on the amount of net disposable household income. Data: G-ECHP, wave 1-3, respondents.

The number of values and brackets decreases in wave 2 and 3, but the relative frequency of brackets drops faster. This is an indication for a panel conditioning effect, i.e., the quality of data (for units that stay in the panel) improves with panel participation. A similar though much stronger effect can be observed in the Lux-ECHP (see section 4.2).

The number of persons who returned a value increased in relative terms (79.9% to 83.6%), but the absolute number dropped. It is not sure whether the relative reduction in bracket usage is really due to panel conditioning (persons switching from bracket to value), or because of attrition (bracket users more likely to leave the panel).

4.3.2 Switches between response types

In this section, some results for the analysis of rounding and income brackets are combined. The question is, if the quality of data with respect to use of values or income brackets improves, what is the nature of the change? How many who have participated in one panel switch to the response type with the next higher level of data?

Figure 4.4 shows the response type of respondents in the first wave of the German ECHP. In addition, it shows how many switched the type of response in the second wave, and which new type they chose. The circles symbolize the different response types (with N being the number of observations), and arrows show N of units switching from one response type to another. The size of arrows and circles roughly corresponds to the number N of observations.

Considerable switches (both relatively and absolutely) are between "value" and "rounded value" and "other" (non-response and no income). Many persons switch between bracket and rounded value, but very rarely between bracket and (non-rounded) value. This could also indicate that choosing rounded values and brackets is influenced by an uncertainty about the true value. Interestingly, more persons are switching from brackets to other response types than vice versa, indicating that brackets are a good option for first-time respondents who were reluctant to disclose their income.

A flow from a response type to another one with a higher level of accuracy (the levels of accuracy are: Value $\succ$ Rounded value $\succeq$ Income bracket $\succ$ Other) is interpreted as an improvement, and a flow in the opposite direction is a decrease of quality or accuracy. For each pair of response types, one flow is an improvement, the other a reduction. The balance of the two is an indicator for overall change. In this example, quality increases for all response types except for the flow between "Income bracket" and "Other"

Figure 4.4: Response type in consecutive waves

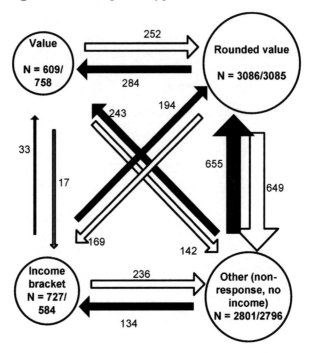

Data: G-ECHP wave 1 and 2, personal data, gross wage and earnings.

$(+134 - 236 = -102)$. Summing up all flows, the overall change of quality is a small improvement.[2]

The following Tables 4.5 and 4.6 show switches between response types for household income in the German SOEP.

Clearly, the results for the household data are similar to the results for the personal data. Interviewees have a high (and from wave to wave even increasing) propensity to stay at a certain response type. And if they switch,

---

[2] In figures: $+284+655+134+33+243+194-252-649-236-17-142-169 = +78$.

Table 4.5: Transition between response types wave 1→2

wave 1	wave 2 bracket	1-2 digits	3+ digits
bracket	444	432	39
	48.5%	47.2%	4.3%
1-2 digits	365	2597	347
	11.0%	78.5%	10.5%
3+ digits	25	258	159
	5.7%	58.4%	36.0%
Total	834	3287	545
	17.9%	70.4%	11.7%

Data: G-ECHP wave 1 and 2, household data, net disposable household income. Persons with missing values in wave 1 or 2 are excluded.

they more likely switch to an adjacent response type (brackets are adjacent to rounded values and rounded values are adjacent to non-rounded values). The number of persons who are switching from brackets to values is higher than the number of persons who are switching from values to brackets. Therefore, on the average the accuracy of data increases.

4.3.3 Comparison of value and bracket usage

In this section, we do not work with bracket usage for household income data only. In the German ECHP, the national questionnaire offered brackets in the question on personal wage and earning, too. However, because this was a deviation from the blueprint questionnaire, it was not used by Eurostat in the ECHP.

We compare the empirical frequency of values and bracket usage at different income levels (see Figure 4.5. For simplicity, we use the approximation 1 EUR $\approx$ 2 DEM in this section.

In both waves, interviewees with low income levels (less than 1500 EUR) were more likely to report values, while interviewees with higher income

Table 4.6: Transition between response types wave 2→3

| | wave 2 | | |
wave 1	bracket	1-2 digits	3+ digits
bracket	445	317	33
	56.0%	39.9%	4.2%
1-2 digits	277	2590	338
	8.6%	80.8%	10.5%
3+ digits	25	309	187
	4.8%	59.3%	35.9%
Total	747	3216	558
	16.5%	71.1%	12.3%

Data: G-ECHP wave 1 and 2, household data, net disposable household income. Persons with missing values in wave 2 or 3 are excluded from this table.

(3000 EUR and more) preferred brackets. The difference is smaller than in the Lux-ECHP, and we do not see an improvement from wave 1 to 3.

4.4 Comparison of Bracket Usage in the G-ECHP and GSOEP

The German ECHP and the German Socio-Economic Panel (SOEP) are two different household panels with respect to sample, questionnaire and field-work. But they basically cover the same population. In the years 1994 to 1996, both survey have been conducted independently. This situation can be utilized to compare the marginal distribution of income data in both panels.

4.4.1 Comparison of G-ECHP and GSOEP

When one survey does no offer brackets, like the GSOEP, and is conducted at the same time like a survey that offers interviewees both ways to report incomes (incomes as a value or by choosing a bracket), like the G-ECHP, then it is possible to compare the two distributions for each bracket. If there

Figure 4.5: Cumulative Frequency of Values and Bracket Usage

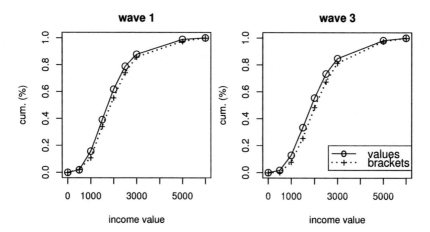

Cumulative frequency of values and bracket usage at different income levels. The rightmost bracket is open, i.e. 6000 stands for "maximum value". Data: G-ECHP wave 1 to 3, unweighted.

are no differences, we could conclude – with caution – that the unobserved information for bracket users does not change the entire distribution for all persons (Rendtel et al., 2004).

Though the sample design is different, we decide to use unweighted distributions because population estimates are unimportant here. Instead, we focus on distribution of values within brackets and distribution of final digits.

The histograms in Figure 4.6 show remarkable similar patterns across time and surveys (column-wise). The distribution of values within brackets is quite stable across waves and even across the two panels. Row-wise, the distribution is different, though most groups show a distinct peak at the left end (at 2, 3, 4, 5, 6 and 10 thousand DEM) and in the middle (at 2.5, 3.5, 4.5 and 5.5 thousand DEM). In any case, the distribution is different from an uniform or normal distribution.

An explanation is that the psychological process of rounding in an interview situation is similar for groups of persons from the same population, even

Figure 4.6: Distribution of values in bracket limits

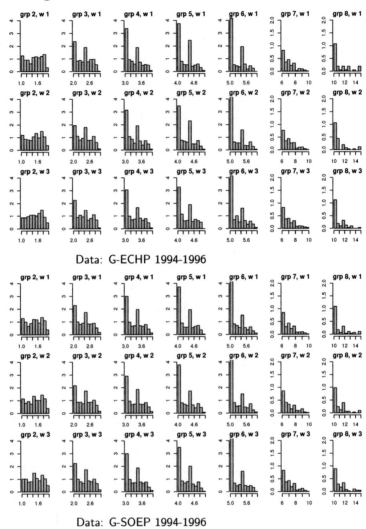

Histograms of values conditional on wave (top to bottom) and income group (left to right, codes according to Table 4.1).

though two samples are different with respect to the sample of persons, the fieldwork and questionnaire design, and one panel uses brackets and the other does not.

Further evidence for this hypothesis can be found in a quantile-quantile plot (bracket-wise) of the distribution in the two panels. A comparison of the within bracket distributions by Quantile-Quantile plots in Figure 4.7 reveals no systematic differences, as all pairs of quantils are near to the diagonal. Furthermore a formal Kolmogorov-Smirnov test of in-equality for the ECHP and the GSOEP does not reject the null-hypothesis of no differences. The corresponding p-values are displayed in the plots. This is even more remarkably as we did not use design weights to adjust for different household selection probabilities.

4.4.2 Distribution of values within income brackets

As we have seen in the previous section, the distribution of reported values within bracket limits is similar in both panels, regardless whether brackets have been offered or not.

If we look for an imputation strategy, the very simple and crude interval halving is not as bad as might be expected. This is displayed in Figure 4.8 which shows the bracket limits (thin long lines) and the means within the brackets (thick short lines) for the G-ECHP. The means are always close to the middle of the brackets. However, since the range of the income brackets is quite large, the resulting data would have less variation than accurate data, with similar consequences as for rounded values.

A more advanced strategy, which can be applied in the case of the ECHP, is to re-sample from the observations that give explicit values within the bracket. Here the question arises, whether the unobserved distribution of those who use brackets and the observed distribution of those who do not use them are equal.

Figure 4.8 shows a histogram of values (censored at 15,000 DEM) for waves 1 to 3 of the G-ECHP. The empirical distribution is skewed and has a long tail at the right end. Most values are in the range of 1000-5000 DEM ($\approx$ 500-2500 EUR). The peaks – which are characteristical for data containing highly rounded values – are often distant to the group means (thin lines).

For convenience, Table 4.7 shows the middle and mean value for each bracket in the ECHP. With the exception of the first closed bracket (1000-2000

Figure 4.7: Quantile-Quantile plots of the household income
values in G-ECHP and G-SOEP

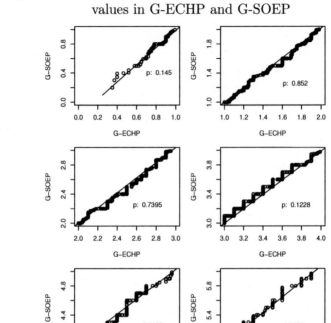

Data: G-ECHP (abscissa) and GSOEP (ordinate) from 1994. Plots are
by respective income group. p-values are for Kolmogorov-Smirnov test of
equality of the marginal distribution. Labels on axis are by a magnitude
of 1000 DEM.

Figure 4.8: Histograms of income values and bracket limits

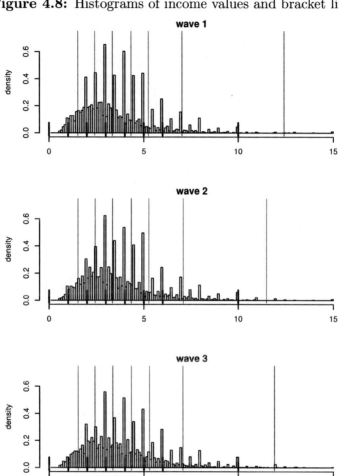

Bars are the density, the short lines are at the borders of income brackets, and the long thin lines indicate average within groups. Data: G-ECHP wave 1 (1994) to 3 (1996).

DEM), the middle of the bracket is always greater than the actual mean of values within brackets. Of course, the expected mean for a non-uniform distribution is usually different from the middle, but for the data at hand, the difference is quite unexpected. As a reference, the column titled "mean approx" shows an approximate mean for values within the respective bracket limits. The mean has been calculated by fitting the incomes in the German ECHP data to a Singh-Maddala distribution (Singh and Maddala, 1976), which can quite successfully mimic observed income distributions in various countries, as shown by Brachmann et al. (1996).[3] Here, the Singh-Maddala distribution is used to give better estimates for the mean of values within brackets. Though the values predicted by the theoretical distribution are different from the middles of the brackets, they are far away from the actual means in the data.

Table 4.7: Middle and mean value of income brackets.

bracket (DEM)	middle of bracket	approx. mean	mean wave 1	mean wave 2	mean wave 3
< 1000	–	322	814.0	826.6	809.4
1000-2000	1500	1431	1517.8	1517.8	1526.0
2000-2999	2500	2451	2414.4	2430.8	2421.0
3000-3999	3500	3460	3339.8	3348.0	3363.6
4000-4999	4500	4470	4321.0	4335.9	4342.3
5000-5999	5500	5475	5244.4	5262.2	5293.6
6000-9999	8000	7692	7024.1	7085.5	7070.6
≥ 10000	–	>20000	11283.7	10991.2	10915.5

The first column shows the bracket limits (DEM) in the German ECHP questionnaire. "middle of bracket" is the arithmetic average of upper and lower limit. "approx. mean" is the approximated mean for a fitted Singh-Maddala-Distribution. "mean wave 1" to "mean wave 3" is the (unweighted) mean of values in each bracket in the respective wave. Data: G-ECHP, 1994-1996.

---

[3] A log-normal distribution could have been used, too.

4.5 The design of income brackets

Income brackets were offered to the respondents in order to reduce the item non-response. This method worked with good success as the item non-response for the household income is as low as 2.5 % in Luxembourg or 3.5 % in Germany.[4]

4.5.1 The trade-off between precision and response

In order to gain additional information instead of non-response, a reduced level of information has to be accepted, due to the lower accuracy of measurement. Assuming the respondent choose the correct bracket, the exact location within the bracket is unknown. Here we take the within-bracket variance as a measure of this loss.

Of course, by shortening the width of the bracket intervals one could reduce this variance. Shortening the bracket width increases the absolute number of brackets and therefore increases the interview burden. This would lead to a degenerate solution, namely to use no bracket. Therefore, the bracket design involves a trade-off between the precision and response rate for the question.

A good choice of limits for the income bracket should consider these conditions:

- stimulate as much persons as possible to answer the question,
- yield useful information about the value (small bracket width is better),
- and maximize observed variance between brackets (see below).

We put the focus of our work on the third point, maximization of variance. What we investigate here, is not the bracket width, but instead a different parameter: The lower limit of each bracket can be shifted by a constant factor. The reason for this approach is motivated by the rounding behavior. Because the values are not evenly distributed across the scale, but have peaks on the rounding lattice, a shifting of the bracket limits has an effect on the variance of values within brackets as the number and the location of the rounding points within a bracket have a large impact on this measure.

---

[4] However, the baseline is a survey where the option of brackets is not offered, like the GSOEP. Here, the item non-response is not much larger (about 5 % in 1996).

4.5.2 Variance within simulated bracket limits

The exact bracket location affects the within-bracket variances, as the number and the position of the rounding points within a bracket have a large impact on this measure. If s_k^2 is the empirical within variance of bracket k, we try to reduce the mean value of the within variances:

$$(4.1) \qquad\qquad MSS_{\text{within}} = \sum_{k=1}^{K} h_k s_k^2$$

where h_k is the frequency of observations in bracket k, and s_k^2 is the empirical variance of values within bracket k.

In the following simulation study we estimate the unknown value of s_k^2 by the empirical variance of the un-grouped observed values that fall into the bracket k.

$$(4.2) \qquad s_k^2 \;=\; \frac{1}{n_k} \sum_{i \in \mathbb{X}_k} (x_i - \bar{x}_k)^2 = \frac{1}{n_k} \sum_{i \in \mathbb{X}_k} x_i^2 - (\bar{x}_k)^2$$

where $i \in \mathbb{X}_k$ are the interviewees with income values within the limits of bracket k, n_k is the number of observations in $\mathbb{X}_k$ and $\bar{x}_k$ is the mean of values in bracket k.

As the results of the previous section indicated there are no substantial differences between the observed and the unobserved distribution within the bracket. For the bracket length we used the 500 Euro interval from the blueprint questionnaire and rounded this value to the nearest even number in the respective national currency. This procedure resulted in 20.000 LUF (Luxembourg), 1.000 DEM (Germany) and 3.000 or 4.000 FIM (Finland).

4.5.3 Empirical results

A simulation shall give some insight about how well chosen the current bracket limits are, and whether a different choice would be better.

The lower bracket limits will be given by $x_{j,l} = x_o + k \cdot j$, where $j \in \mathbb{N}$ is the bracket number and k is the (fixed) bracket width. The upper bracket limits are equal $x_{j,u} = x_{j,l} + k$. Assume that left of the bracket $j = 1$ is the "zero" bracket starting at zero, but it does not necessarily end at k. Instead, it is shifted by the value x_o. All brackets have constant width of k.

For different values of x_o we can estimate MSS_{within}. The result is shown in Figures 4.9 to 4.11.

Figure 4.9: Sum of squares within simulated brackets (Lux-ECHP 1994)

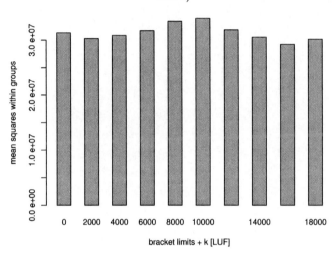

Bar chart for the sum of squares within values grouped into simulated income brackets with starting with different offset value. Data: Lux-ECHP 1994.

Figure 4.9 for LUX-ECHP shows a function with a distinct peak in the middle and smaller peaks near the lower and upper limits. Between these peaks are regions with smaller variances.

Figure 4.10 for FIN-ECHP has a small peak at the lower limit and no distinctive peaks elsewhere. It seems as if the differences in the height of the bars are more or less random.

Figures 4.11 for GSOEP and G-ECHP values are similarly shaped with relatively high peaks at the limits and a smaller peak in the middle. In fact, both figures seem so similar as if they were computed not only for the same population, but the same data set.

Figure 4.10: Sum of squares within simulated brackets
(Fin-ECHP 1996)

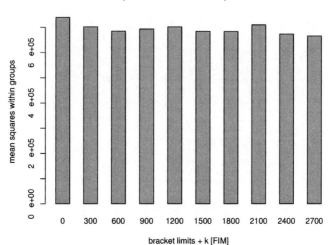

Bar chart for the sum of squares within values grouped into simulated income brackets with starting with different offset value.
Data: Fin-ECHP 1996.

The results suggest that the offset value x_o should be different from an
even value, which is a rounding point in the national currency. Within the
original bracket limits, there are 2 rounding points (1.000 and 2.000 FIM) in
the Finnish sample, while there is only one rounding point (10.000 LUF and
500 DM) in the two other countries. In all countries an amount of about
100 EUR (ca. 4.000 LUF, 600 FIM, 200 DEM) yields an improvement of
the solution used in the ECHP.

The Finnish survey is different from the other three because the bracket
boundaries used in the survey (4000, 7000, 11000, 14000, 18000, 22000,
26000) were not as close to distinct rounding points as in other national
surveys, and neither equidistantly spaced. This might be an explanation
why varying the value of x_o does not change the variance within brackets

Figure 4.11: Sums of squares within simulated brackets (G, 1994)

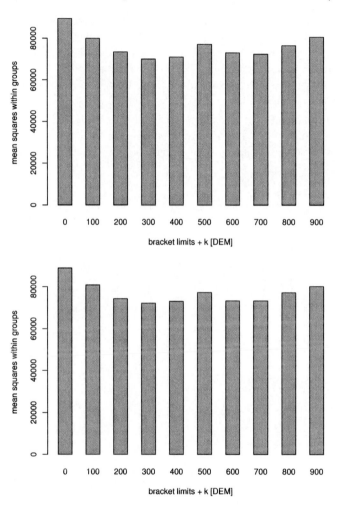

Bar chart for the sum of squares within values grouped into simulated income brackets with starting with different offset value. Data: G-ECHP (upper bar chart) and G-SOEP (lower bar chart) 1994.

for the Fin-ECHP data as much as for other national samples.

The minimum values were achieved at: 3.000 LUF (ca. 75 EUR), 2.700 FIM (ca. 450 EUR) and 350 DM (ca. 175 EUR). Of course, this result is partly caused by the large number of rounded responses and the fact that bracket limits were put close to prominent rounding points. Here, an interaction between the problem of rounded values and income brackets happens. Putting bracket limits more away from rounding points reduces the problem.

In contrast to these four examples with real interview data, Figure 4.12 shows the results for pseudo-random values without rounding. Neither peaks nor a trend is visible, each design of bracket limits is as good as any other.

Figure 4.12: Sum of squares within simulated brackets (random data)

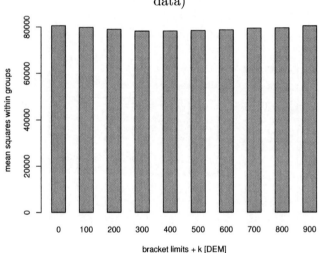

Bar chart for the sum of squares within values grouped into simulated income brackets with starting with different offset value. Data: Random sample from a non-rounded log-normal distribution fitted to GSOEP data.

4.5.4 Other approaches to the design of income brackets

As an alternative to using one set of more or less equidistant ranges, researchers have recently started to use different approaches. One procedure is called *unfolding brackets*. The idea is that the interviewer starts with a limit, e.g. whether a certain income item exceeds $25000 (Health and Retirement Study), and if the answer is "yes", then they are asked if it exceeds $50000. If the answer was "no", then they are asked whether it exceeds a lower limit. Several sequential limits could be asked consecutively, resulting in increased precision. While this procedure seems appealing, it has drawbacks. It increases the burden of work on interviewer and interviewee. And much worse, it has been shown in an experimental study by Hurd et al. (1998) that the initial bid has an effect on the response (even on following questions). This is known as *anchoring bias* and has been widely neglected in economics literature (Winter, 2002).

A different and experimental procedure using *implicit brackets* has been tested by the US Bureau of the Census. Instead of asking for the income range in one question, and for an income bracket in a follow-up question if income range was not answered, income range and bracket are merged into one two-step question. "In essence, the implicit bracket approach first asks whether the amount exceeds some minimum threshold (...), and then, if yes, asks for a report of the income amount "to the nearest X dollars", with X (...) depending on the type of asset." (Moore and Loomis, 2001)

4.6 Conclusions and recommendations

The distribution of net household incomes within bracket-like income groups is very peculiar. With respect to the frequency of final digits, the data seem to follow similar rules in different national surveys and panel waves. Observed data are composed of values rounded by different degrees. The propensity of rounding values increases in the vicinity of so-called "rounding points". This has to be kept in mind when using observed values, for example in (multiple) imputation.

Regarding the choice of bracket boundaries, we have illustrated that the bracket limits used in the ECHP survey coincide with major rounding points for three of four countries. This causes unnecessarily great variances of values within brackets. It would be better if all limits would be shifted by some amount of, for example, 100 EUR. Following this result, we would suggest to use something like the following bracket limits (units: EUR) instead of the ones currently used:

up to 599,   600-1.099,   1.100-1.599,   1.600-2.099,   2.100-2.599,
2.600-3.099,   3.100-3.599,   3.600-4.099,   4.100-5.099, $\geq$5.100

We hope to gain two positive effects from using these limits: Firstly, an imputation of values for people who used income brackets is more exact, because the observed values used for imputation (e.g. grouped mean imputation, multiple imputation) are more informative. Secondly, we expect the psychological effect that respondents have a higher stimulus for choosing the correct bracket.

For future surveys, we suggest that bracket limits should avoid the major rounding points (individual values which are reported very frequently) in questionnaire design.

CHAPTER 5

Comparison of Register and Survey Data

5.1 Introduction: Register vs. survey data

Register and interview-based survey data contain values for the same characteristics of the same units, but both sources can provide different values. The differences can be random variations, for example, caused by measurement error, but also the data are generated through specific procedures and are often based on different income concepts.

Registers contain various information related to persons. In Finland, various registers are maintained for various administrative purposes, which have usually other requirements than social surveys. Using these register data for the ECHP is only a secondary usage. As a consequence, while the data perhaps meets the formal requirements, e.g., those of the revenue authorities, these might be quite different from the data concepts a statistician wants to use. Moreover, since registers have very specific purposes, it is very likely that some information required in a survey (for example, attitudes and general statements) are not available from registers.

Survey data from interviews are collected with the aim to gain specific information. Register data, on the other hand, are to be sampled, transformed and edited before it can be put into a survey data base. Therefore, differences and complications are possible when using register information instead of interview data.

One example where discrepancies appear is the concept of a "household". This is of minor importance for taxation, and thus a household unit constructed from information in registers might be different from the household composition reported by someone who is actually living in that household. Another difference is in the operationalization of survey questions. In a survey interview, the wording of questions, the sequence of questions, the questionnaire form design, interviewer training, interview situation and additional questions can either be arranged as desired (within certain restrictions, of course), or at least be observed and registered. But the circumstances and methods by which register information is measured is usually fixed and cannot be customized for survey purposes. Therefore, because the interview situation is more flexible, we would expect register information to be of inferior quality compared to interview data.

On the other hand, the artificial and unfamiliar situation of being interviewed, often by a representative of the government or some agency working for the government, could have an adverse effect on the interviewee. He could not be motivated enough to provide certain information, and perhaps does not want to be interviewed at all. In that case, the person would not disclose information to an interviewee while he would be oblieged to disclose this information to official registers.

With regard to the sample definition, register-based samples often have an important advantage over interview-based samples: Many registers contain information for the total population, while surveys cover only a more or less random sample. In Finland, for example, practically every person can be found in the registers, and even many homeless persons are registered. Interview-based samples, however, are often the product of several prior actions: An approach must be found that samples units from the population, the interviewer must establish contact, and last but not least the individual must be able and willing to participate in the survey.

The *Finnish sample of the European Community Household Panel* (Fin-ECHP) is of particular interest for the study of measurement errors. As mentioned in Section 3.1.3, income data in the Fin-ECHP was sampled in 1996 by a interviewer-based survey and – in addition – from various registers: tax files, unemployment records, and other administrative sources. Thus, for survey participants, information on wage and earnings and on household income is available from two sources. This approach was repeated three waves later, in 2000.

Within the CHINTEX project, another team of researchers analyzed the discrepancies between register or survey interview data, see Hovi et al. (2001). In this chapter of our thesis, we are concerned with the question whether there is a difference in cross-county comparisons when either register information is used, or data from questionnaires. For this aim, we compare interview and register data from the Finnish sub-sample of the ECHP with respect to differences in precision due of rounding.

5.2 Distribution of the rounding error

If rounding was the only measurement error in interviews, then the rounding error would simply be the difference between the responded value and the register value. The data sampled from registers should be the "true" income,[1] or, at least an accurate, non-rounded value. In that case, non-rounded responses would be equal to the register values, but as we will see shortly, this is not the case.

However, it is possible to calculate the difference between survey interview value and a register-based reference value (defined in the following section) at different levels of rounding of the interview value.

This section focuses on the "personal gross wage and earning". This income type should be known to all employees, and should also be easily extractable from registers.

5.2.1 A reference value based on annual register data

Though register data has been processed with great care by Statistics Finland (Tilastokeskus) to be comparable with the survey variable, some conceptual differences between the survey and the register variable still remain. For example, while the interviewer primarily asks for *monthly* gross earnings, register values are *annual* wages and earnings.

Let x_a be the value for annual gross wage and earnings based on register data, x_{reg} be a register-based value for monthly gross wage and earnings, x_{ref} be an improved reference value based on registers and other information, and y the income value from the ECHP survey interview.

---

[1] Recently, the data has been examined with results that throw some doubt on the assumption that registers measure the true income, see Nordberg et al. (2001). Both the registers and survey measure only values which are correlated with the true income, and registers are closer to the true income than surveys.

In order to compare incomes per month and incomes per annum, we construct a reference value x_{ref} for gross wage and earnings per month. This value is primarily based on the register income per annum x_a.

To compute this reference value, we tried several approaches and decided upon the one which seemed to yield the best results.

A) A naive approach is to divide annual income by 12, the number of working month.

B) People often forget income components when reporting the average monthly figure. We could choose a conversion factor different from $1/12$ to correct this, e.g. the OLS estimate $\hat{\alpha}$ for $y_i = \alpha \cdot x_{a,i} + \epsilon_i$.

C) A more sophisticated method is to estimate a linear regression with several independent variables and factors and an adjusted income variable.

Approaches A) and B) are quite simple and assume that there is a linear relation between monthly and annual earnings and a linear error. In the following section, we present empirical results for these models before going to the final approach.

5.2.2 Approach A) - a direct comparison of register and survey earnings

Personal gross wage and earnings x according to registers and self-reported gross wage and earnings y can be compared directly. We computed the ratio y/x, the results are shown in Table 5.1 and Figure 5.1.

The mean and the median value are very different from each other. The explanation for this is a small number of extreme values in the sample. Most values (including the first and third quartile) are in a range from 0.07 to 0.09, which is acceptable for persons who receive 12-13 monthly wages per annum. However, the mean value 0.1224 is outside this range. This is a distribution with very high skewness and kurtosis.

5.2.3 Approach B) - predicting reported earnings from register earnings using a conversion factor

The regression Models 1a and 1b predict the personal gross wage and earnings value provided by respondents, given the gross wage and earnings from

Table 5.1: Statistics for the ratio $c = y/x$

statistic	estimate	std. error of the estimate
valid n	3430	
mean ($\bar{c}$)	0.1224	0.0064
Q1 ($c_{.25}$)	0.0751	
median ($c_{.50}$)	0.0810	
Q3 ($c_{.75}$)	0.0907	
variance (s_c^2)	0.1421	
skewness	43.5120	0.0420
kurtosis	2260.0580	0.0840

registers. When reading the results, please note that the models are without a constant, thus the regression line is going through the origin. Therefore, the R^2 model fitness parameters are not the same as the usual R^2 values in OLS regression analysis.

For Model 1a, all wage earners were included, and for Model 1b only wage earners who did not receive income from self-employment. The best estimate for approach B) was $\hat{b} \approx 1/13$, which is a plausible result considering that a typical wage earner gains wage for 12 month, plus 13th salary and other bonus payments.

Regression 1a: Survey income given register income

dependent:	y :=P031880
predictor:	x :=P031910R
model:	$y = \beta_1 x + \epsilon$
sample:	sample persons, wage earners

Coefficients:

predictor	coefficient	Std. Err.	t-value	p-value
x	0.07689	< 0.001	230.604	< 0.001

Figure 5.1: Histogram for y/x

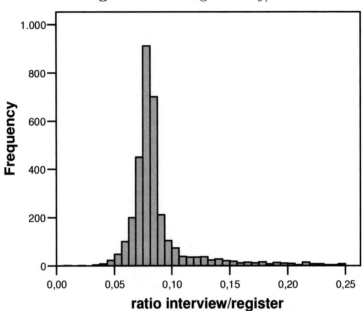

The p-value is the probability that the true value of the coefficient is equal to zero under H_0.

Model Summary:

Model	R	R^2	Adj. R^2	$\hat{\sigma}_\epsilon$
1a	0.969	0.939	0.939	2980.731

For regression through the origin, R^2 is the proportion of the variability in the dependent variable about the origin explained by regression. This CANNOT be compared to R^2 for models which include an intercept.

ANOVA:

Model	Sum of Sq.	df	Mean Square	F	sig.
Regression	4.7247e11	1	4.7247e11	53178.120	< 0.001
Residual	3.0465e10	3429	8.8848e06		
Total	5.0294e11	3430			

The total sum of squares is not corrected for the constant because the constant is zero for regression through the origin.

Regression 1b: Survey income given register income

The previous regression (Model 1a) was potentially biased because of the following reason: Some wage-earners have additional income from self-employment, see Table 5.2. Here, a high level of misreporting was observed: 498 persons with income from self-employment neglected to report this income in the interview (e.g., because it was only part-time income), and a small number of 31 persons did report such income in the interview though no trace of this was found in registers.

Table 5.2: Income from self-employment according to registers or interviews

		income according to interview		
		no	yes	Total
income	no	4841	31	4872
according	yes	498	54	552
to registers	Total	5339	85	5424

We decided to estimate a separate regression without persons with income from self-employment either according to registers, interview, or both.

Model:

dependent:	$y :=$P031880 (monthly survey earnings, self-reported)
predictor:	$x :=$P031910R (annual register earnings)
model:	$y = \beta_1 x + \epsilon$
sample:	wage earners, no income from self-employment

Coefficients:

predictor	coefficient	Std. Err.	t-value	p-value
x	0.07686	< 0.001	221.338	< 0.001

The p-value is the probability that the true value of the coefficient is equal to zero under H_0.

Model Summary:

Model	R	R^2	Adj. R^2	$\hat{\sigma}_\epsilon$
1b	0.970	0.941	0.941	2924.275

For regression through the origin, R^2 is the proportion of the variability in the dependent variable about the origin explained by regression. This CANNOT be compared to R^2 for models which include an intercept.

Analysis of Variance:

Model	Sum of Sq.	df	Mean Square	F	Sig.
Regression	4.1739e11	1	4.174e11	48990.571	< 0.001
Residual	2.6198e10	3075	8.5198e06		
Total	4.4359e11	3076			

The total sum of squares is not corrected for the constant because the constant is zero for regression through the origin.

5.2.4 Discussion

The difference between Regression Model 1a and 1b is very small. Though the fit of the model (expressed as the ratio of sum of squares "explained" by the regression compared to the total sum of squares) increases, this is accompanied by a decrease in residual df (3429 to 3119).

The two slope coefficients are very similar: 0.07689 and 0.07686, both ≈ 1/13. We conclude that the amount[2] of self-employed income does not

---

[2] When using a dummy variable for "self-employed income > 0" instead of the amount, the coefficient was not significantly different from zero.

seem to have a relevant effect on the reporting of income from wage and earning.

On the average, the residual differences between *interview and reference value* were too huge to be plausible, with very large extremes. The average absolute difference was A) 1813 respectively B) 1728 FIM, the maximum was 39390 respectively 46956 FIM. For an analysis of rounding error, these residual errors are too high compared to the rounding error we would expect for the observed rounding frequencies. This could have reasonable causes:

(i) Some persons receive less than twelve salaries per year, or special lump-sum payments. This results in inaccuracies unrelated to rounding.

(ii) Unemployment, change of main activity and unusual income components are not covered in the model. Systematic over- or underreporting would only be accounted for, when it was proportional to income level. [3]

The question is, which range would be acceptable? In the Finnish subsample of the ECHP, personal wage and earnings is most often rounded by 1000 FIM, with a 14% empirical probability of rounding to 5000 or 10000 FIM. Thus we would expect an average rounding error in the range of, say, 400-800 FIM.

5.2.5 Approach C): A reference value based on a regression equation

In order to overcome the problem and improve the model fit, a register-based value x_{reg} for monthly wage and earnings based on register data can be constructed (first published in Hanisch and Rendtel 2001, p.5):

$$(5.1) \qquad \hat{x}_{\text{reg}} = \frac{x_a - [\text{extra payments p.a.}]}{[\text{no. of working month}]} - [\text{extra payments p.m.}]$$

where x_a is the register-based annual income, "extra payments p.m." is an information from the interview, and "extra payments p.a." is calculated as: The sum of 13th + 14th salary + holiday pay + profit sharing bonus +

---

[3] Nordberg et al. (2001) have shown that non-proportional effects exist. They found relatively high discrepancies among persons with very low incomes according to the registers. Nordberg used a multiplicative error model with a different definition of ϵ_i, thus the results are not fully comparable to ours. For simplicity reasons, Nordberg's multiplicative error model was not used here.

income from company shares + income from other job + other lump-sum payments. All data on the right hand side of the equation are from the interview based survey. (p.a. = per annum, p.m. = per month.)

This value x_{reg} is already a useful predictor for monthly income based on register data, but we tried to improve the "fit" by including additional covariates. To exclude the effect of rounding on the estimation of coefficients (e.g. attenuation bias), only persons i with exact incomes in the questionnaire were included in the OLS estimation of the coefficients.

Implicitly it is assumed that the process of rounding is not informative for the relationship of annual and monthly data. For every combination of covariates the selection of rounded and exact cases is purely random and does not depend on reported income. In other words, the process of rounding has to be "Missing at Random" (MAR, see Rubin 1976) with respect to the above regression.

To reduce measurement error due to misreporting (other than rounding), several covariates are included in the regression models. Several variants of the model were calculated.

For Regression Model 2, we used z_1 as an indicator whether the person was working less than 12 month, z_2 as an indicator whether the person was doing other paid jobs other than main job, and z_3 is an indicator for "person is looking after children".

To reduce measurement errors not related to the problem, only persons who fulfilled the following restrictions were used to estimate the coefficients for the reference value equation: Register and survey wage and salary were valid information. The person has not experienced periods of unemployment in 1995. He had reported accurate (non-rounded) wages. The wage range was between 2000 and 30000 FIM per month, so very small and very large values with high leverage were excluded. Three outliers were excluded because the data seemed implausible.

For Model 2a, persons with income from self-employment work were excluded, too. The drawback is that only 230 persons have valid information for all variables and fit all inclusion criteria.[4]

$$(5.2) \qquad y \quad = \quad \hat{x}_{ref} + \epsilon$$
$$(5.3) \qquad \hat{x}_{ref} \quad = \quad \alpha \cdot x_{reg} + \beta_1 z_1 + ... + \beta_j z_j$$

---

[4] For details see Appendix A.3.

where x_{reg} is the monthly reference value from Equation 5.1, z_1 to z_j are covariates, and α, β_1 to β_j are coefficients that are estimated with an OLS model. ϵ is the residual difference between the final reference value $\hat{x}_{ref}$ and the survey interview value y.

The result for the estimated value of $\hat{x}_{ref}$ is (a positive coefficient could be caused by systematic over-reporting, negative values by under-reporting):

$$\hat{x}_{ref} = 0.985 \cdot x_a - 767.657 \cdot z_1 + 521.669 \cdot z_2 + 319.389 \cdot z_3$$

This yielded an acceptable result: The absolute difference between the reference value and the survey value had a mean of 647.11, with a minimum 0.88 and maximum 5596.32. For Finland, this is within a plausible range for what we would accept for the rounding error. The R^2 for this regression without intercept was 0.9931.[5]

On a substantive level, the main part of x_{ref} is determined almost precisely by the reference value (adjusted wage). The other characteristics do not play a major role to explain positive or negative differences: Though two characteristics have a significant effect in a statistical model, the regression fit does not decrease much when these are removed.

The standard deviation of the residuals $s_\epsilon = 932.64$ in Model 2 and 950.56 in Model 2a.) However, it somewhat increased the fit for those individuals where the respective covariates were not equal to zero.

5.2.6 Differences between reference values and survey values

Under the assumption $x_{reg} = x$, the difference between y_r (a rounded observation of y) and x_{ref} is the rounding error. A scatter plot of the absolute difference $|y - \hat{x}_{ref}|$ at different points of $\hat{x}_{ref}$ is shown in Figure 5.2.

It is the question whether the difference is really based on rounding. The rounding error is restricted by the location of the accurate value. An accurate value of 11073 could be rounded to 11000 (rounding error = 73) or to 11500 (error 437) or even greater values, but it could not be rounded with an error of, say, 200 (because 11273 is not a rounded value of 11073).

---

[5] For a no-intercept model, R^2 measures the proportion of the variability in the dependent variable about the origin explained by regression. This is different than R^2 for models with an intercept and cannot be compared. For the same model *with* intercept $R^2 = 0.9519$ (adjusted for the number of parameters).

To determine the amount by which a value has been rounded, or whether it has been rounded at all, several different rounding bases were used, the multiples of 500, 1000, 5000 and 10000. In the first step, it was determined whether y was a multiple of one of these rounding bases, and in the second step, if $|y_r - \hat{x}_{ref}|$ was less than the rounding base.

Figure 5.2 shows a scatter plot of the absolute difference between the monthly reference value and the survey interview value. Using the model coefficients estimated in the regression model, reference values were calculated for all persons, regardless whether they edited accurate or rounded income.

The absolute value of the error is shown on the ordinate, and the reference value is on the abscissa. If the reference value is truly x, then the difference is the rounding error. However, it is expected that an accurate value should be within a certain range around the rounded value.

For example, the accurate value of the rounded (rounded up, down, or mathematically) observation 4000 should be within the interval $[3000, 5000]$, while the true value for the rounded value 4100 is assumed to be within $[4000, 4200]$. Thus, only cases within such intervals were included in the figure.[6]

At medium income levels (7000-12000), rounding errors are most often in the range of less than 1000, but at higher levels of income, we see larger deviations from the true value.

To estimate the average absolute difference at different levels of income, the solid lines show LOESS scatter plot smoothers.[7] One line (upper, dashed) is for all individuals, the other (lower, solid) line only for values inside plausible rounding range.

Since more extreme values are excluded for the solid LOESS line, the estimate is systematically lower. However, the general shape is the same. From 5000 to 10000 the average difference is approx. 500 FIM (less than 100 EUR). Between 10000 and 13000 it rises to approx. 1000 FIM and stays at this level up to the maximum income scale (resp. slowly rises further when we look at the dashed LOESS line which includes values outside plausible rounding ranges).

---

[6] An alternative plot that shows which values are within the rounding interval, and which are not, is in the Appendix, Figure A.9.

[7] A short introduction to the LOESS (also called LOWESS) procedure can be found in Fan and Gijbels (1996).

Figure 5.2: Absolute differences between reference and survey value

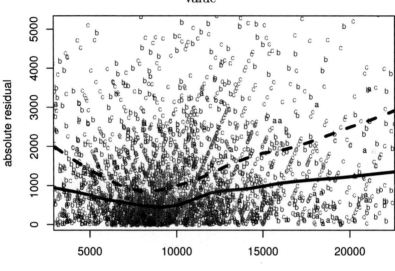

reference value

Scatter plot of absolute differences between reference and interview value superimposed with LOESS scatter plot smoothers. "a" marks values with no rounding, "b" marks values rounded to nearest 100 or 500, and "c" marks values rounded by 1000 or more. The solid line is a smoother for residuals within possible rounding range from the reference value, the intersected line is for all values.

This is further evidence for the hypothesis that rounding error is somehow tied to the level of income. However, the relation does not seem to be linear, because the difference between rounded value and reference value is great at low and high income ranges. Because rounding error and measurement error could not be separated very well, measurement error (e.g., misreporting) could play a role, too.

The "stepwise" rise around 10000 FIM in the LOESS function might suggest that the correlation is not simply proportional. Perhaps it rises when the accurate value is close to threshold values. Thus there is some empirical evidence for the hypothesis that respondents tend to use only a small number (1-2) of leading digits when reporting income and earnings.

5.3 Differences in the mobility of register and interview based incomes

5.3.1 Definition of income mobility

In a panel context, the change of income over time is of certain interest. In section 2.6.4, we have demonstrated in a simulated example that rounding can have a high impact on measurement of change . Since Finnish register and survey data for the panel years 1996 and 2000 is available, the empirical income mobility based on both data sources can be computed.

Given two incomes $x_{\tau,i}, x_{v,i}$ for the same individuals i for different periods τ and v where $\tau < v$, there are different measures for the change of incomes. For simplicity, we omit the index i. Also, the indices τ and v will be omitted when not necessary.

$$\delta_{\tau,v} = x_v - x_\tau$$

is the absolute change of the value x_τ from wave τ to v.

$$r_{\tau,v} = 1 - \frac{x_v}{x_\tau}$$

is the relative change of the value x_τ from wave τ to v. For $x_\tau = 0$, it is undefined.

Related to the measure of relative change is the following measure for individual *income mobility*.[8]

(5.4) $$m_{\tau,v} = \ln x_v - \ln x_\tau,$$

The measure m has several interesting properties. It is similar to the relative change rate: $m = \ln(1 + r) \approx r\%$ when it is close to zero (see Figure 5.3).

---

[8] This mobility measure is related to the concept used by Solon (1992) who uses the correlation coefficient ρ in $y_1 = \rho y_0 + \epsilon$ as a measure for income mobility.

Figure 5.3: Comparison of $ln(1 + r)$ and r.

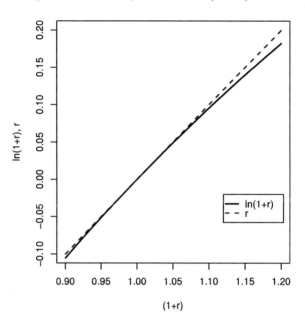

The solid line shows $\ln(1 + r)$ and the intersected line shows ∇ in the neighborhood to 1 (no change).

The second nice property is the fact that m is additive. Consecutive changes can be added to calculate the total change: $m_{1,2} + m_{2,3} = m_{1,3}$. And, if m is the dependent variable of a linear model equation, coefficients of the model can be easily interpreted with respect to their effect on the original value.

In section 2.6.2, we have demonstrated that rounding can have high impact on the measurement of change in a simulated example. In the following sections, we are analyzing the effect in a real data example.

5.3.2 Empirical distribution of income mobility in the Fin-ECHP

We want to compare the income mobility for individual persons based on values from two different sources. The first source is interview data from the Finnish sub-sample of the ECHP, wave 3 and 7. The second source is register data for 1995 and 1999 for the same persons.

In Table 5.3 is an excerpt from the two data sets. It is easy to see that register and survey values in corresponding rows (e.g. x_1 and y_1 are often very different from each other.

As mentioned in Section 5.2.5, the two sources are different with regard to the income period. In the Fin-ECHP data set, register values on wage and earnings are annual totals, while survey interview values are usually monthly averages. Only a very few number of persons reported their annual total, and these persons are different from the average population. One option was to use a reference value, but the simplest solution is to compare increases of annual register income with increases of monthly survey income.

Register values are annual totals, while the survey values are monthly averages, as has been mentioned before. If the monthly wage x is raised by a constant factor r, then it is plausible that the annual total x_a would increase by the same factor. As the annual income is the lump sum of the monthly incomes one might argue that the annual (register) incomes are somewhat more stable than the monthly incomes, thus the mobility would be more towards the mean increase. This would constitute a *regression-to-the-mean* in register data compared to survey interview data.

In statistics, regression-to-the-mean is a technical term which means that things tend to return to the mean. I.e., if the result from a random draw is very extreme and far away from the mean, then it would be likely that a repeated draw or second observation would be less extreme.

To see why regression to the mean can happen in an income study, let us consider an example. If you select the lowest 10% of the sample based on their income score, and then ask the people in the same sample about their income some time later, then you will find out that the lowest 10% are different. The reason is that many persons in the lowest 10% will now have higher incomes, and several persons in the other part of the sample will now have smaller incomes. In the ECHP, respondents are asked twice to report their income. First, they are asked to state their income to the

Table 5.3: List of individual values (examples)

Register		Survey		Mobility	
1995	1999	1995	1999		
x_1	x_2	y_1	y_2	m_R	m_Q
41000	72000	3333	6667	0.56	0.69
38987	117489	8050	9700	1.10	0.19
72498	113089	6350	8900	0.44	0.34
78141	99048	6537	7300	0.24	0.11
79767	95782	5132	7990	0.18	0.44
48545	108075	3763	7840	0.80	0.73
79864	100370	6972	8016	0.23	0.14
74741	86090	6150	7100	0.14	0.14
61275	126816	5730	10000	0.73	0.56
80913	89497	6633	7500	0.10	0.12
55353	159660	11350	14000	1.06	0.21
41400	116260	3400	4000	1.03	0.16
64872	60507	5045	5000	-0.07	-0.01
75491	82258	6250	8000	0.09	0.25
102569	93164	8120	6728	-0.10	-0.19
103911	82496	8960	9500	-0.23	0.06

List of empirical values of personal wage and income based on register (annual total) and survey (monthly average) from two different panel waves, and the respective mobility. Data: Sixteen randomly selected persons from Finnish sub-sample of the ECHP. m_Q: mobility according to survey values, m_Q: mobility according to interview values.

taxman, and then later, an interviewer asks them to report their income for the same year. However, since their true income is now different, it is very likely that they do not report the income for the report period, but an income more equal to the current income. In this situation regression-to-the-mean would have the effect that changes are reported less drastic than they really are, more towards zero change or average change. Extreme changes are less likely reported, regardless if it is an increase or a decrease. Thus, the average increase of incomes is approximately the same, at least if we exclude persons with periods of unemployment, with self-employed income, and others with very irregular income wages and earnings from analysis.

In what follows, we choose m_R, the mobility of log-earnings, for mobility based on register data, and m_Q for mobility based on survey interview data. For the analysis, persons with regular incomes from one main occupation in 1995 and 1999 were included, and the top and bottom 5% incomes according to register and survey were censored because they would cause a highly skewed empirical distribution.[9]

As we see from Table 5.4, the average increase amounts to 0.1604 ($\sim$16.0%) in the register and to 0.1549 in the survey.

If the average monthly income was about 10000 FIM,[10] then an increase of $m = 0.1604 \Rightarrow r = 1 - \exp(0.1604) = 17.4\%$ % amounts to 1740 FIM. This is an amount that is hardly rounded in zero, even with a scheme that rounds to multiples of 1000 FIM. As will be shown in the next section, the expected rounding scheme will be rounding to 1000 FIM. Therefore it is not surprising that the mean and the quartiles of the distribution of increase factors are quite similar for the register and the survey.[11]

However, the increase factors are far from being identical as indicated by the variances. Here we observe clearly a difference between the two measurements. Opposite to our a-priori notion that states a higher stability for the annual income, the register changes exhibit a higher variance than the survey changes.

The higher variability of the registers earnings carries over to the 5 percent

---

[9] The analysis includes only a balanced set of persons with valid income data in 1996 and 2000, and excluded persons with extreme personal wage and earnings. x_1 was between 36357 and 566715 FIM, $x_2 \in [36470, 614287]$ FIM, $y_1 \in [3000, 50000]$ FIM and $y_2 \in [3600, 55000]$ FIM.

[10] The unweighted mean in the sub-sample we used was about 11400 FIM, and the median was 10000.

[11] This may be different for lower increase rates across shorter time intervals. However, such information is not at hand.

Table 5.4: Marginal distributions m_R and m_Q

		m_R	m_Q
mean		0.1604	0.1549
std. error of mean		0.0082	0.0061
std. deviation		0.2964	0.2206
minimum	0%	-1.4549	-1.2993
percentile	5%	-0.2639	-0.1667
	25%	0.0690	0.0606
	50%	0.1427	0.1461
	75%	0.2413	0.2389
	95%	0.6310	0.5108
maximum	100%	2.1351	1.5041
N=			1322

Empirical statistics of marginal distribution of income (personal gross wage and earning) mobility for register (m_R) and survey (m_q) data. Data: Finnish sub-sample of ECHP, interview and register data, wave 3 and 7.

and the 95 percent quantiles which are more extreme than the corresponding survey quantiles. Figure 5.4 shows a Quantile-Quantile-Plot (Q-Q-Plot), which compares the quantiles of both distributions. It clearly reveals the longer tails of the register distribution. This means that according to register data, extreme income changes are more frequent than according to survey data.

5.3.3 Comparison of income mobility based on register and survey data

Even if the marginal distributions are very similar, large differences between m_{Ri} and m_{Qi} are shown in the plot of individual differences. The joint analysis of the observations by a scatter plot in Figure 5.5 reveals an enormous variation between the two measurements.

The (Spearman) correlation coefficient of mobility based on either register

Figure 5.4: Q-Q-Plot of m_R and m_Q

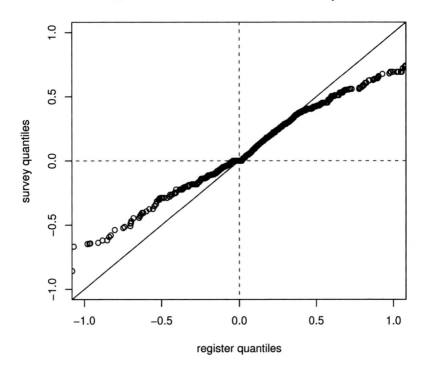

Q-Q-plot for marginal distribution of income (personal gross wage and earning) mobility for register (m_R) and survey (m_Q) data. Data: Finnish sub-sample of ECHP, interview and register data, waves 3 and 7.

or survey data is only $\rho_s = 0.504$. This is a relatively small correlation coefficient given the fact that empirical correlation coefficients for intergenerational income mobility are around 0.2 to 0.5 (Solon, 1992). We assume the register change is close to the true value and the difference is caused by misreporting (the respondent has made a false report about his wage and earning).

Figure 5.5: Scatterplot and LOESS regression line of $m_{Q,i}$ given $m_{R,i}$.

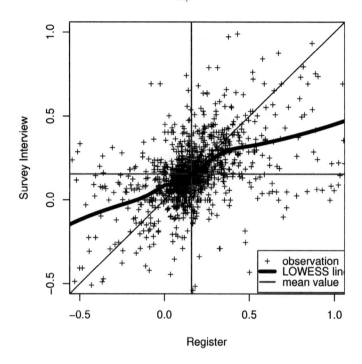

Data: Fin-ECHP 1995 and 1999, survey and register data.

Figures 5.5 display the means of both measurements together with a LOESS scatter plot smoother. In the ideal case of a perfect measurement by the survey all observations would be on the diagonal. However, the LOESS-line shows an small "regression-to-the-mean" effect: Above average increases (according to register information) shifted downwards to the mean and below average increases were upwards shifted.

A grouping with respect to observations from rounded and non-rounded income figures in Figure 5.6 reveals a special impact of rounding for income changes between 0 and below the mean. These changes are almost

Figure 5.6: LOWESS of m_{Qi} given m_{Ri} for rounded and
non-rounded responses

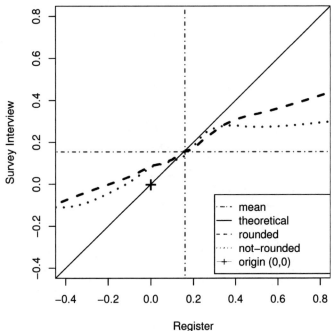

Data: Fin-ECHP 1995 and 1999, survey and register data. The
thick, intersected curve shows the LOESS line for rounded values,
the dotted curve is for non-rounded values. The straight lines
are at the cross-sectional mean values. The solid diagonal is the
equivalence line where $m_Q = m_R$. The small cross is at the origin,
the point of no change, where $m_Q = m_R = 0$.

rounded to an increase of ten percent. But the comparison reveals that
the regression-to-the-mean effect is not a mere rounding effect. For negative income changes and positive income changes larger than twice the

mean increase a similar pattern appears for both groups which cannot be attributed to rounding. However, the overall residual variance is enormous in these cases and the scatter plot does not show a systematic behavior.

The above findings are confirmed by regression models that includes different dummies for survey rounding and changes of the *register* income.

5.3.4 Regression of income mobility dependent on rounding

A subsequent linear regression analysis using several additional covariates in addition to m_R to explain m_Q shows that rounding has a small but significant effect.

The first Model (M0) is rather simple: $m_Q = \beta_0 + \beta_1 m_R + \beta_2 m_R^2 + \epsilon$.

Table 5.5: MODEL M0, $m_Q \sim m_R$

model terms	coeff.	std.err. coeff.	t-value	p-value
Intercept	0.088	0.006	15.428	< 0.001
m_R	0.414	0.017	24.344	< 0.001

Standard deviation of residual: $s_\epsilon = 0.034$. Adjusted multiple R^2: 0.309. *F*-statistic: 592.611.

Table 5.6: MODEL M1, $m_Q \sim m_R + m_R^2$

model terms	coeff.	std.err. coeff.	t-value	p-value
Intercept	0.090	0.006	15.671	< 0.001
m_R	0.436	0.019	23.025	< 0.001
m_R^2	-0.049	0.019	-2.598	0.009

Standard deviation of residual: $s_\epsilon = 0.033$. Adjusted multiple R^2: 0.312. *F*-statistic: 300.972.

In Regression Model M1, the estimated regression equation is:

$$\hat{m}_Q = 0.090 + 0.436 m_R - 0.049 m_R^2.$$

The income mobility observed in registers does not even account for 50% of the mobility according to the interview when using the adjusted multiple R^2 as a fitness criterion. The intercept is very high. In theory it should be equal to zero, but in this model it is significantly greater than zero (mean of $0.090\pm$ a standard error of 0.006). This implies a very high amount of noise or unexplained systematic differences. An analysis of income mobility could have very different numerical results depending whether it uses survey or register data.

Model M2 produces similar results for the basic variables: $\hat{m}_Q = 0.0965 + 0.4392 m_R - 0.0540 m_R^2 + \dots$. The coefficients for m_R and m_R^2 are not significantly different from each other in Models 0 to 2. The factors related to rounding and other effects contribute to the model in addition to the basic (quadratic) regression. However, the number of persons with different types of rounding is not balanced, and therefore the intercept coefficient in Model M1 and M2 are not fully comparable.

The coefficients for rounding effects are small compared to the total variance, but significantly different from zero. On the assumption that the response behavior might be different when the income situation has improved or not, we have calculated two sets of coefficients, depending on the information if mobility is greater or equal than zero (implying an income increase from 1996-2000), or less than zero (income decrease for the same period).

The dummy coefficients for rounding are cumulative, so if the coefficient for "y_1 is rounded by 10000" is equal to one, then the coefficient for "y_1 is rounded by 1000" is equal to one, too. The effects are additive.

The coefficients of rounding effects are rather different for positive and negative mobility: For negative income mobility (according to registers), three coefficients have a significant effect. If only the first value is rounded, and the second value is not rounded, then the mobility (according to survey) is lower. For negative values, lower means closer to the true value (on the average, absolute negative mobility is underestimated). If the first value is exact, and the second value is rounded, then negative mobility is closer to zero. If both values are rounded, then the effects cancel out each other.

Table 5.7: MODEL M2, Model M1 + rounding effects

model terms	rel. freq.	coeff.	std.err. coeff.	t-value	p-value
Intercept	*	0.0965	0.0110	8.7794	0.0001
m_R	*	0.4392	0.0225	19.5393	0.0001
m_R^2	*	-0.0540	0.0195	-2.7647	0.0058
coefficients based on rounding					
if $m_R \geq 0$					
y_1, by 1000	41.4%	0.0028	0.0114	0.2421	0.8088
y_1, by 10000	8.4%	-0.0266	0.0191	-1.3947	0.1633
y_2, by 1000	47.7%	0.0342	0.0113	3.0370	0.0024
y_2, by 10000	9.0%	-0.0538	0.0183	-2.9405	0.0033
if $m_R < 0$					
y_1, by 1000	7.6%	-0.1018	0.0258	-3.9473	0.0001
y_1, by 10000	1.6%	0.1778	0.0441	4.0282	0.0001
y_2, by 1000	7.7%	0.1047	0.0259	4.0463	0.0001
y_2, by 10000	1.6%	-0.0802	0.0442	-1.8134	0.0700
other coefficients					
CAPI interview	59.9%	-0.0305	0.0101	-3.0166	0.0026

Standard deviation of residual: $s_\epsilon = 0.032$. Adjusted multiple R^2: 0.338. F-statistic: 62.432. Rel. freq.: Relative frequency of observations fulfilling this category (if applicable).

For positive income mobility, only rounding of the second value has an effect that is significantly different from zero. Rounding by 1000 increases mobility, shifting it towards the accurate value (which is quite a surprise), while rounding by 10000 reduces it.

These linear effects of rounding behavior show only a simplification of the difference between the mobility of rounded and non-rounded response (compare Figure 5.6). A linear regression analysis only partially describes this effect.

Table 5.8: Example: Coefficients for $y_1 = 10000$ and $y_2 = 13000$
(Model M2)

value	by 1000	by 10000	coefficients
$y_1 = 10000$	yes	yes	+ 0.0028 - 0.0266
$y_2 = 13000$	yes	no	+ 0.0342
total =			+ 0.0104

In further regression analysis, a number of other panel-related factors have been examined with respect to their statistical effect on income increase measurement, but only one had a significant effect: The mode of interview in 2000. If interview mode in 2000 was "face to face CAPI interview", the observed mobility was 0.0311 greater on the average. The alternative interview mode used 2000 in Finland was "phone interview". This could be a psychological effect (e.g., persons who want to impress the interviewer). If other non-interview related factors where included in the model, then the result was a more substantial model. An example is shown in the Appendix, Table A.14. Several other characteristics like the level of education, whether the interviewee was looking after children[12], and the number of working hours, have an effect on income mobility. These characteristics correlate with rounding behavior in general, as will be analyzed in the Chapter 6 of this thesis.

5.3.5 Conclusions

We conclude that rounding has a small, but notable effect on income mobility. However, the overall discrepancies between mobility based on register values and based on interview values is much greater than the effect which could realistically be caused by rounding.

The effect of rounding can roughly be described as follows: A decrease in the accuracy of data (level of rounding increases) marks a decrease in the accuracy of mobility, while an increase in accuracy more often leads to values which are closer to the true value. While this is a trivial result, it should be noted that rounding is not necessarily the *cause* for low accuracy

---

[12] It is very likely that these are confounder effects because it is not very likely that looking after children is a real reason for income changes.

of income change, it might be an indicator of low data quality for other reasons, e.g., misreporting or uncertainty about the "true" value. Greater discrepancies between register and interview data are often accompanied by a greater level of rounding (as indicated by the number of digits or the greatest round denominator) in the reported in come data.

In an analysis of the measurement of change of a value, researchers should take the level of rounding into account. Empirical differences in income changes could possibly be explained by different rounding of the data. As a suggestion, a stratified analysis based on non-rounded data versus rounded data could be used as a sensitivity analysis.

In the Finnish ECHP data, the marginal distribution of mobility in the register and interview data was very similar in the range between the first and third quartile. Only the extreme values, especially the 5% lowest and the 5% highest values, were quite different. While it seems to be possible to calculate a cross-sectional reference value for monthly income based on register values, the measurement of mobility is more difficult. A (spearman) correlation coefficient of about 0.5 between register- and survey-based mobility is not very good. Regression models to predict survey-based mobility based on register values had R^2 coefficients of about 0.3. The greatest differences were observed for extremely low and extremely high income mobility. It seems possible that registers and interview-based surveys often measure significantly different dynamic income concepts.

CHAPTER6

Models for Response Behavior

In this chapter, the effect of panel conditioning and the correlation of individual characteristics with rounding behavior are examined. For this aim, various regression models with a qualitative dependent variable are used. As in previous chapters, data from the German and Finnish sub-samples of the ECHP (Germany: G-ECHP, Finland: F-ECHP), and the German Socio-Economic Panel (GSOEP) are used.

Several approaches are used, starting with a simple model (binary probit model) to more elaborate ones (ordered probit model). Additional analyses with other methods than regression are used when appropriate.

6.1 Methods

The analysis of rounding behavior does not have a continuous dependent variable, but an dichotomous (such as yes/no) or an ordinal dependent variable. The independent variable can be a single variable or several variables of any type. This type of model is also known as qualitative response (QR) model.

6.1.1 A dichotomous dependent variable

In an analysis with a dichotomous dependent variable, we limit the response to two categories only: rounded or not rounded. A dependent variable with two categories can be used as the left-hand-side of a logit or probit regression model.

Often, rounding is a matter of degree. For a dichotomous indicator, we define that values which are reported with one or two significant digits are "rounded", and values with three or more digits are "not rounded". Because of the "threshold" $B \leq 2$ digits, we call the indicator $B2$:

$$P(B \leq 2) \Leftrightarrow P(B2 = 1)$$

If the interviewee did not receive or report income in the current wave, then no valid information is available. For these people, no valid response category is available and they are ignored in the analysis.

Hence, the dichotomous indicator for rounding in wave t is defined as follows:

$$B2 = \begin{cases} 1 & \text{when } Y \text{ has no more than 2 significant digits,} \\ 0 & \text{when } Y \text{ is exact or rounded after 3 or more digits.} \end{cases}$$

6.1.2 A binary probit model

The binary probit model can be declared as:

$$(6.1) \qquad\qquad P(B2_i = 1 | \mathbf{z_i}) = F(\mathbf{z'_i}\beta)$$

where $\mathbf{z}$ is a vector of covariates usually consisting of a constant 1 and one or more additional covariates (e.g., the income value according to registers (if available) or survey interview, interview-dependent covariates, and covariates related to the individual i. The vector β are the regression coefficients. $F(\ )$ is a link function that maps the predictor $(\mathbf{z'_i}\beta) \in \mathbb{R}$ to probabilities $p \in [0,1]$. For the probit model, the normal distribution function $F(x) = \phi(x) = \int_{-\infty}^{x} \frac{1}{\sqrt{2\pi}} \exp(-\frac{x^2}{2})\, dx$ is used as the link function.

In other statistical areas, e.g., medicine or sociology, the *logit* model is used often instead of the probit model. The logit model uses the link function $F(x) = \frac{\exp(x)}{1+\exp(x)}$. Despite slight differences and a different parametrization,[1] they are very similar for the purpose of this paper.

6.1.3 An ordered probit model

The ordered probit model is an extension of the binary probit model. Instead of a dichotomous response variable (two categories), three or more ordered categories are possible. The ordered probit model has been described in numerous sources, for example, see Amemiya (1983).

---

[1] See Amemiya (1983) for a discussion of the probit and the logit model.

We use the following specification: Let $\gamma_j = Pr(b \leq j | \mathbf{x})$ be the cumulative response probability for the dependent variable b given one or more independent variables x.

The general model is given by $\eta_j = \theta_j - \beta' \mathbf{x}$ where η_j is related to the cumulative probability γ_j through the probit link function: $\eta_j = \Phi^{-1}(\gamma_j)$. The model location is defined by the threshold parameters θ_j and the location parameters β. Coefficients $\beta > 0$ imply that higher values of the independent variable are associated with larger outcomes of the dependent variable b, while $\beta < 0$ means a negative correlation.

6.1.4 A dependent variable with ordered categories

The construction of a dependent variable with more than two categories is more difficult than the construction of a dichotomous variable. For a dichotomous indicator for rounding, the ordering is unimportant. It does not matter whether one category or the other is the reference category. However, a dichotomous variable is not very informative and requires reducing the information available, by putting every possible response into one category or the other.

By using an ordered probit model, a dependent variable with more than two separate categories could be used. From a technical point of view, two options are available: either, the categories represent different levels of rounding, for example, by using the rounding indicator b. In this case, the analysis is restricted to persons who a priori are fully cooperating with the interviewer and are income-receivers. Or, the categories could include more different types of response, like income brackets and item and unit non-response. This requires some discussion.

Please recall from Section 2.2 that response (or non-response) in a survey is the result of a multi-stage process. As a result, different response options exist with respect to a question like "During 1995, what were your normal earnings *per month* worked?".

Following the questionnaire design, the interviewer first asks the person to give an exact value. Of course, the person has the choice to give an exact or an approximate (most likely a rounded) value. In the household questionnaire, someone refusing to answer this question is asked to choose one of several income brackets. If he refuses to answer this question, too, we speak of item non-response. In the personal questionnaire, there is no such follow-up question. Thus, an income bracket is only observed in the case of initial item non-response in the household questionnaire.

These options are not derived from a "natural" ranking order. While this is not a problem for a multinomial logit/probit model, we would have to make assumptions if we want to use them in an *ordered* probit model. To sort the options into a certain ranking order, three qualities are of importance: data quality with respect to precision and possible measurement error, questionnaire design, and the usefulness for further analysis.

An exact, non-rounded value Y is the response which combines the best of qualities. Exact values Y are continuous (at least $Y \in \mathbb{R}$), they are responses to the original question (and not a follow-up question), and they are useful for any type of further analysis. Rounded values are still a useful response, but with lower accuracy. The level of accuracy was implicitly chosen by the respondent, therefore rounded values are the second best response type. Income brackets are worse than rounded values. Instead of allowing the respondent to choose a level of inaccuracy (rounding off after 2 or more digits), he has to choose one of several predefined ranges of values.

Please note that *any* value, exact or not, could be false or just a rough guess. However, without further information, it is barely possible to indicate how much an answer is off the true value.

No answer is worse than any answer. However, unit non-response still has a higher amount of information because at least some information about the respondent is available.

Unit non-response is the worst response. We do not gain any information about the individual except for observing unit non-response. It is not only a refusal to answer the question, but refusal of being interviewed at all.

Thus, the following outcomes are possible, listed in suggested ranking order for an ordinal scale (not eligible is an exception and is put arbitrarily into the ranking):

1)   report an exact value
2)   report a rounded value
3)   choose an income bracket (only in the German ECHP)
4)   not eligible $\Rightarrow$ no value
5)   does not report a value
6)   refuse the interview
7)   non-contact

The options 1-3 imply values or value ranges (bracket). Option 2 could be specialized further by the level of rounding, for example rounding to multiples of 100 or 1000 (national currency units), or rounding after 1, 2 or 3 significant digits. Option 5 is called "item non-response", because the interviewee did not respond an item of the interview. Option 6 is called "unit non-response" because the person (or household unit) did not respond any item of the interview, and the case that an individual is not available for further interviews (usually, because he decides so) is called *attrition*. In addition to these options, technical difficulties could result in a non-contact unit non-response.

Regarding the achieved scale quality of income data, exact values are interval-scaled and therefore better than rounded values and income brackets, which have only ordinal scales. Therefore, exact values are better than the others. But are income brackets better or worse than rounded values?

A rounded value differs from the original value by an unknown amount less than or equal to the respective rounding interval. An income bracket contains the original value, but we do not know the exact location. Any point-estimator would miss the original value by no more than the range of the bracket. Thus, depending on rounding points and bracket range, either the rounded value or the income bracket has the higher quality of data (regarding scale and measurement error). If we would have to decide on one or the other in an ordinal scale, we would prefer to rate a rounded value higher than an income bracket, because the interviewed person – and not the questionnaire designer – chose the width of rounding interval. Therefore, we think it is justified to rank rounded values higher than income brackets with respect to accuracy.

6.1.5 Ordering of response categories

The categories discussed in the previous section represent ordered levels of quality or accuracy. An exact value is of the highest quality, unit non-response is of the lowest, and the others, like income brackets, are in between these extremes.

From a technical point of view, this could be modelled with a latent threshold model. We used the model as described in Fahrmeir et al. (1996, p.271–276). Here, quality is defined by a latent variable which cannot be observed directly, and the propensity to chose a certain category is determined by the value of the latent variable. If the value of the latent variable is increased by a certain factor, then the propensity of all categories is modified. If the value of the latent variable rises, then the propensity to chose higher categories rises and the propensity to chose lower categories drops. Technically, this is similar to the ordered probit model in Section 6.1.3.

However, the response categories are not necessarily chosen by the respondent. Rather, they are presented sequentially until the respondent chooses one (cf. Figure 2.1 on page 13). The sequence by which categories are presented to the respondent can play a role. Perhaps some respondents never chose the first category presented to them perhaps some never wait for the last. In these cases, the latent threshold model does not hold because a change in the latent variable would not have an effect on the propensity to chose these categories. Therefore, the results of empirical analysis should be interpreted with some caution.

6.1.6 Multidimensionality of response behavior

The social and psychological process during the interview which results in the observation of one response type or the other does not necessarily have to be one-dimensional. It is possible that the various response types are the outcomes of very different processes. And hence, it is possible that single factors do not increase or decrease the probability of the various response types in the same way for every person.

The interview situation is thought as a social process in which both, interviewer and respondent, want to achieve their goals. A theoretical framework to explain respondent behavior provides the Rational Choice theory (Esser, 1993) and the related utility theory. It is thought that some questions are more sensitive than others, and respondents are reluctant to report sensitive questions. They want to gain something in return. Rational Choice theory assumes respondents chose the type of response, and that their choice is based upon assessing all response options with respect to the consequences. Because in the ECHP interview, the respondents are not told all consequences, they learn from each interview. This is an explanation for possible panel conditioning effects.

Factors which correlate with the accuracy of the value provided are not necessarily the same factors that determine the type of response Imagine the interviewer calls a sample person and asks for an interview. A number of different factors could influence or correlate with the sample person's cooperativeness, his readiness to participate in the interview. If he participates, he will be asked a certain question during the interview, e.g., about his gross wage and earnings. Whether he provides a value or not, and how accurate this value is, does not (only) depend on his cooperativeness, but also on his knowledge of the value asked for, and his ability to edit a sufficient answer. Of course, this ability does not necessarily have to be highly correlated with his cooperativeness. And other factors, which correlate with his cooperativeness, do not necessarily correlate with his ability to provide a response. A factor perhaps correlates only with one or the other, or the correlation is of different strength.

Certain factors could correlate with one aspect, cooperativeness with the interviewer or ability to provide accurate answers, but not correlate in the same way with the other aspect. This would violate the assumptions of the ordered probit model, because these factors would have non-proportional effects on the propensities to observe certain categories in favor of other categories. An alternative would be to use a sequential model, but this will be left for future work. In a sequential model, each person's cooperativeness and ability to provide accurate answers could be described as a location in a one- or two-dimensional continuum. One dimension is for the willingness to participate and cooperate with the interviewer, and the other describes the ability to provide answers to the questions.

If these dimensions were not systematically dependent (i.e., a strong positive or negative correlation between co-operation with respect to participation and ability), then a variety of situations were possible. Figure 6.1 shows several possible combinations. Optimally, every person would have a high propensity for full cooperation and the ability to provide highly accurate answers. However, other combinations are possible. For example, a certain group of people could be very reluctant to participate in the interview, therefore we would observe a high level of unit non-response in this group, but if an individual participates, he fully cooperates with the interviewers and carefully answers all the questions with high accuracy. Another group could be highly willing to cooperate, but unable to provide answers with sufficient precision, resulting in a higher likeliness of of item non-responses and low precision in the values responded.

Of course, we could include additional steps in this model, for example, by including the contact step. Another factor is the eligibility of the question. Some persons do not receive income at all, and this correlates with various characteristics, too.

Figure 6.1: Cooperation in two dimensions

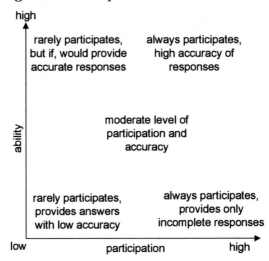

Figure 6.2 shall give some insight. To produce one response type or the other, a multi-stage process was necessary. At each step, different paths are possible.

Each response type requires a sequential path of events. For example, an "exact value" requires $A_1 = 1$, $A_2 = 1$, $A_3 = 1$, $A_4 = 1$ and $A_5 = 1$. The marginal probability of $A_5 = 1$ given $A_4 = 0$ would be zero (because this is an impossible combination). The possible path combinations are shown in the following list:

path	requires	description	values
A_1	—	contact	yes/no
A_2	A_1	participation	yes/no
A_3	A_2	question eligible	yes/no
A_4	A_3	question answered	yes/no
A_5	A_4	type of answer	precisely/rounded
A_6	$\neg A_4$	follow up 1	income bracket / non-response
A_7	$\neg A_4$	follow up 2	annual value / non-response

A model like this, with different functions for the various types of response

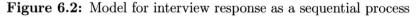

Figure 6.2: Model for interview response as a sequential process

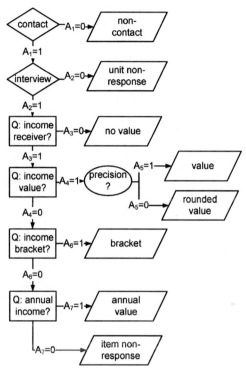

would be very interesting. However, a reliable estimate is possibly beyond the scope of the available data. Even models with only three different outcomes, like rounded value, accurate value and income bracket, implemented in SAS/STAT, PROC CATMOD yielded results which were difficult to use.[2] An example can be found in Nicoletti and Buck (2004), where the probabilities of establishing successful contact with the household and achieving a response from the household were separated.

---

[2] We decided not to include these models in the thesis because the results did not seem to contribute new information.

6.1.7 Some results from literature

Obviously, if the effects on the probabilities of the response types are different, then it would be more practical to treat the response types as categories of a nominally distributed variable. In this case, statistical models which could be deployed would be a contingency tables or log-linear models. However, these are more complex than latent threshold models and would require more model coefficients.

A more psychological view could be useful to understand why persons choose one response type or another.   Buck et al. (2004) deals with attrition and item non-response in the ECHP and analyzes national differences with respect to substantial differences and structural differences (explained by different coefficients).[3] For example, Nicoletti and Buck found that the contact and participation probabilities are different across the European member states, and that the biasing effect of initial non-response decreases in subsequent panel waves.

In a paper by Schräpler (2004), the author discusses item non-response with respect to two different causes: Either the interviewee does not know the answer to an income question and therefore is not able to report a value, or he knows it but refuses to tell it. With respect to a framework for interview response based on cognitive theory (Tourangeau et al., 2000), refusal can have one of three different reasons. The first reason is privacy. Personal income is a sensitive topic that is rarely openly disclosed in Germany. The second reason is concerns about confidentiality. E.g., if a respondent deliberately reported a taxable income different from the true income, then he might fear that the value he reports in a survey interview could be disclosed to third parties, especially the tax authorities.[4]

It is our working hypothesis that persons with high incomes are more likely to feel such concerns and would be more reluctant to state their income. The third and perhaps most important reason is social (un)desirability of the answers. Income is an important component of social rating. The

---

[3] Substantial differences can be related to differences in the distribution of the covariates in the population, structural differences are because of differen model coefficients.

[4] In spite of the fact that this would be an open violation of the data confidentiality required by authorities, the author of this paper himself has heard such concerns expressed to him even by an interviewee of the German Mikrozensus.

interviewee could be afraid of reporting a low income to the interviewer. A working hypothesis is that persons with low income have more reluctant to disclose their income.

6.1.8 Hypotheses

After discussing factors which possibly have an impact on the accuracy of responses, several working hypotheses can be formulated. The following factors could have an impact on rounding behavior and are therefore used as independent variables:

- Panel conditioning could have positive or negative effects on the quality of responses.

- An irregular job or periods of unemployment increases the difficulty of providing an accurate value.

- Very high incomes are not only more difficult to edit, they could also be associated with concerns on confidentiality.

- Very low incomes are possibly reported with low accuracy.

- Persons with technical or administrative professions or skills are more able to edit accurate values. Therefore, high education and certain occupation could be beneficial for the accuracy of responses.

- Higher age possibly means more stable job, and therefore a more stable income, causing a higher propensity for accurate values.

- The type of payment is a factor. Jobs with variable wages would require more guessing, the propensity to report rounded incomes would be higher.

- Gender is possibly a factor, at least as a result of differences in job types and education level.

To find evidence for or against these hypotheses, different models are used in the following sections. In Section 6.2, the effect of panel conditioning is examined in different panels. In several models, additional factors are used as independent variables, but the focus is on panel conditioning. In Section 6.4, a single model is build to examine various statistical effects on the rounding behavior. Some additional models which supplement the analysis are included in the Appendix A.3.

6.2   Empirical results: Panel effect and panel conditioning in the GSOEP

In Section 3.2, we have compared rounding in three waves of the GSOEP. To find more information on the effect of panel participation on accuracy, we focus our attention to the GSOEP, the German Socioeconomic Panel, starting 1984. A sample "A" of households and individuals was drawn in 1984. The units from the original sample were interviewed each year, and the panel has not ended yet. If panel participation had an effect on rounding behavior, then it should clearly show in this panel.

We are interested in the following questions: Is rounding stable, or does it change over time? Does it improve or worsen? Do common factors like sex, age and earnings have an influence on rounding behavior? What is the explanation for differences in the level of rounding in the German SOEP and the German ECHP survey?

6.2.1   Cross-sectional comparison of rounding

As a first step, we calculated the empirical frequency of rounded values for "personal gross earnings" for each wave:

$$h(b = j) := N_t^{-1} \sum_{i=1}^{N} \mathbf{1}\{b(y_{i,t}) = j\}$$

where N is the number of persons, $b(y)$ is the rounding indicator (see Section 2.5.1), $y_{i,t}$ is the reported income for person i in wave t and $\mathbf{1}\{A\}$ is the indicator function which is equal to one if the condition A is true, and 0 else, and N_t is the number of valid responses (excluding unit- and item non-response and persons without valid earnings) in wave t. j is an integer variable for the number of digits, values $j \in \{1, 2, 3, 4, 5\}$ are reasonable.

Graphical descriptions of the results are in Figures 6.3 and 6.4. The figures show stacked frequencies ($\sum_j h(b = j) = 100\%$). Tables with the frequencies can be found in the Appendix A.2.5.

In this cross-sectional comparison, we observed only a very slight trend towards less rounding in later waves. With the exception of the 7th and 8th wave, the relative frequency of rounded values was roughly equal from wave to wave. This result holds even whether all persons (including fresh sample members and persons with earnings in few waves only) were used,

Figure 6.3: Accuracy of values in earnings data (I)

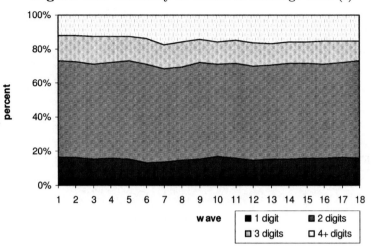

Plot: stacked frequencies, B=1 (dark shading) is at the bottom, B=4 (light shading) at the top. Data: G-SOEP, wave 1-18, personal gross wage and earnings. Sample size (valid N): 4361 (wave 1), ..., 2812 (wave 18).

or only selected persons with valid earning reports in every wave (balanced sample).

From this analysis, no evidence is gained that panel conditioning in the GSOEP improves the quality of data with respect to rounding. If rounding behavior is stable, then the differences between different surveys (e.g. GSOEP and German ECHP) would have to be explained by other factors like different fieldwork, questionnaire design and sample differences.

It could be argued that time and panel conditioning are not the only factors which have an impact on rounding. What if panel participation had an effect in one direction, and the change of time-dependent covariates had an effect in the other direction? For example, in the balanced sample all units are getting older, and age is perhaps correlated with rounding. Also, nominal prices have been steadily increasing since 1984, and an increase in incomes

Figure 6.4: Accuracy of values in earnings data (II)

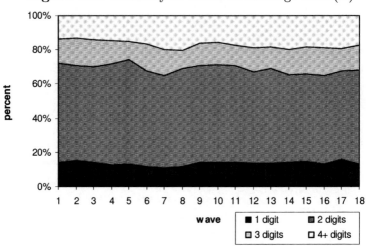

Plot of stacked frequencies: B=1 (dark shading) is at the bottom, B=4 (light shading) at the top. Data: German SOEP, wave 1-18, persons who participated and responded earnings in all waves 1 to 18 (balanced). Sample size (valid N): 497.

renders the report of income values more difficult. In fact, Figure 6.3 shows no clear improvement in accuracy. The only episode which seems to be remarkably different from the others is between wave 5 and wave 7. This can be seen better in Figure 6.5 which shows frequencies with 95% intervals of confidence around the observed frequency. The interval boundaries were calculated using the approximation $p_t \pm 1,96\sqrt{(p_t(1-p_t))/n_t}$ where p_t is the frequency of values in wave t reported with 3 or more digits, and n_t is the frequency of all values reported in wave t.

A possible explanation for this is a special set of questions used in SOEP wave 5, in which interviewees where asked to report figures about their wealth and assets. This caused unusual high non-response and attrition.[5]

---

[5] Source: Personal communications with Ulrich Rendtel who was responsible for

We think these questions caused an increased attrition of persons who also had a high propensity to report rounded values. It also seems that after a few waves, the rounding behavior in the sample population somehow returned to the previous levels.

Figure 6.5: Accuracy of values in earnings data (III)

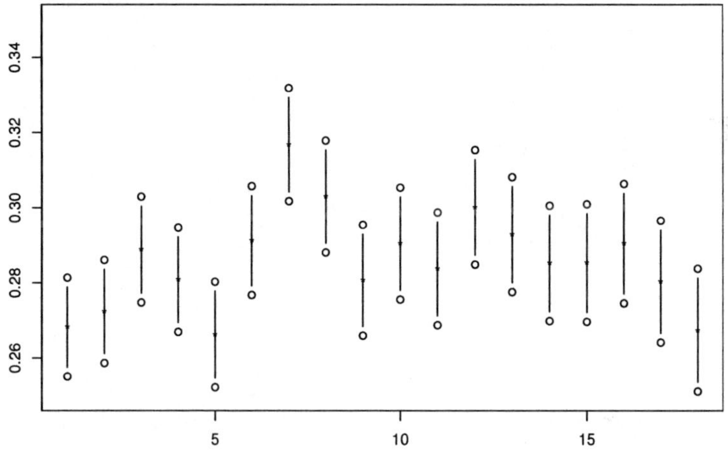

Relative frequencies of reporting 3 digits or more, with 95% confidence intervals. Data: German SOEP, wave 1-18, personal gross wage and earnings, all persons. Sample size: 4361 (wave 1), ..., 2812 (wave 18).

Evidence for the hypothesis whether the general increase of income has an impact on the overall trend should be detected when analyzing different income groups separately. Figure 6.6 shows the frequencies of values precise by $b = 1, \ldots, 4$ values in each wave by income range. In the lower two income ranges, the frequencies change a bit, but the changes are not much different from random variation.

SOEP methodology at the time.

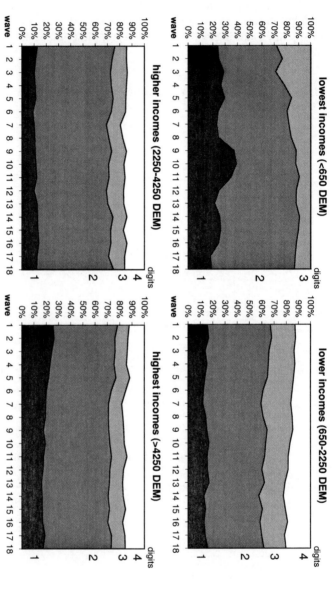

Figure 6.6: Precision of wage and earnings data (by income group)

Four plots of stacked frequencies: $B = 1$ (dark shading) at the bottom of each plot, $B = 4$ (lighter) at the top. Each plot is stratified by income range as given in the subtitles. Data: German SOEP, wave 1-18, all persons.

6.2.2 Probit analysis of rounding in early and late waves

After the cross-sectional comparison, we analyzed individual rounding behavior in consecutive waves of the German SOEP. The aim is to gather evidence about the stableness (or randomness) of individual rounding behavior. In this section, specific coefficient estimates are not of interest, just how good certain models fit at different points in time. An increase in stableness would imply a notable increase in model fit, if lagged values for rounding behavior in previous waves are included in the model.

Several different models with and without lagged rounding indicators from the previous wave(s) were calculated. Brief results are shown in Table 6.1. To evaluate the model fit, Akaike's Information Criterion (AIC) was used. It is defined as $-2LogL + 2(k + s)$, where $LogL$ is the Log Likelihood of the model fit, and $2(k + s)$ is a "penalty" term, k is the number of response levels (here: 2) minus one, and s is the number of explanatory effects (one for interval-scaled variables, one for each level of a category variable, excluding one).

The AIC is not explicitly calculated in the table, it is equal to the deviance plus the degrees of freedom "df" and can be interpreted as an adjusted measure of fit. The adjustment takes into account that introducing a new term in a model always decreases the degrees of freedom and also usually decreases the deviance. Therefore it is not advisable to include a model term which decreases the deviance only a little bit (less than the degrees of freedom).

The greatest improvement with respect to deviance as a measure of fit is the step from Model 1 (constant only) to Model 2 (a constant with 1 lagged variable), and a slighter improvement is observed from Model 2 to Model 3 (a constant with 2 lagged variables). Lag variables, of course, are correlated with individual covariates like sex, earning level and age. However, including other covariates like sex (SEX, male/female), year of birth (AGE) and earning level (Ygr, coded as factors for quartiles) improved the deviance only by quite small amounts. The fact that the lag variables improved the fit much more than the other covariates indicates that other effects which are not included in these models (or are perhaps not observed) play a bigger role than sex, earning level and age. Thus, we conclude that earning level is not the key factor for rounding behavior (because it contributes so little to model fit).

Table 6.1: Result for Probit Models for Rounding Behaviour in early and late waves. Dependent variable: $B2_t$

Model No. : Covariates	wave 3		wave 18	
	d.f.	dev.	d.f.	dev.
	residual			
1 : (constant)	3847	4386.1	4664	5336.3
	residual diff. to previous step			
1a : SEX + AGE + Ygr	-7	-37.6	-7	-29.8
2 : $B2_{t-1}$	+6	-323.2	+6	-711.7
2a : as 2 + SEX + AGE + Ygr	-7	-35.6	-7	-22.7
3 : $B2_{t-1} + B2_{t-2}$	+6	-31.3	+6	-199.1
3a : as 3 + SEX + AGE + Ygr	-7	-31.6	-7	-17.3

Data: G-SOEP wave 1-3 and 16-18 (dependent). df: degrees of freedom / change of d.f. compared to previous row, dev.: deviance / change of d.f. compared to previous row. SEX: dummy for male/female, AGE: age group (4 quartile groups), $B2_{t-1}, B2_{t-2}$: lagged response variables from previous two waves, Ygr: income group (4 quartile groups).

The values of the model fit and coefficients (see Table 6.2 for the model which had the best AIC) for the two waves shown in the model are different, but the model coefficients are basically the same: Response behavior in the past wave(s) is statistically the major determinant for response behavior in the current wave.

6.2.3 Contingency tables for rounding behavior in consecutive waves

During the explorative analysis of the data, a phenomenon related to panel conditioning was discovered: the statistical association of the precision for income reports in consecutive waves increased. In later waves, individuals were more likely to use the same response type respectively level of accuracy than in earlier waves.

Table 6.2: Coefficients for Rounding Behavior Model

coefficient	wave 3		wave 18	
	estimate	std. err.	estimate	std. err.
(Intercept)	0.2821	0.2678	-0.2519	0.1053
$B2_{t-1}$	**0.8264**	0.0507	**0.9193**	0.0481
$B2_{t-2}$	**0.4114**	0.0517	**0.7238**	0.0489
SEX(male)				
SEX(female)	**-0.2046**	0.0558	**-0.1388**	0.0481
AGE(Q1)				
AGE(Q2)	-0.2192	0.2605	-0.0088	0.0516
AGE(Q3)	-0.2860	0.2616	0.0417	0.0739
AGE(Q4)	-0.1464	0.2989	1.8723	1.8750
Ygr(Q1)				
Ygr(Q2)	**0.1736**	0.0685	0.0154	0.0640
Ygr(Q3)	-0.0472	0.0747	0.0571	0.0661
Ygr(Q4)	-0.0300	0.0770	-0.1140	0.0699

Data: G-SOEP, Sample A, Wave 1-3 and 16-18. Coefficients significantly different from 0 at $\alpha = .05$ are in **bold face**.

In each wave, a person has the option to report as many significant digits as he likes. There was no instruction during the interview how precisely he was expected to report earnings. However, many persons reported their earnings with exactly the same number of digits as in the previous wave. Figure 6.7 shows the relative empirical frequencies of persons with similar rounding in wave t and $t - 1$ $B_t = B_{t-1}$, together with the boundaries for the 95% confidence interval. Clearly, a trend towards higher frequencies is visible, and even the early and late confidence intervals do not overlap.[6]

Because of persons entering and leaving the panel, and other switching from employment to unemployment, the Figure 6.7 is based on a different sample each wave. Figure 6.8 shows the same statistic for a balanced sample. Here,

---

[6] Here, confidence intervals are used only in an explorative way and not as a test to test a hypothesis.

Figure 6.7: Relative frequency of persons who reported earnings with the same number of significant digits as in the previous wave

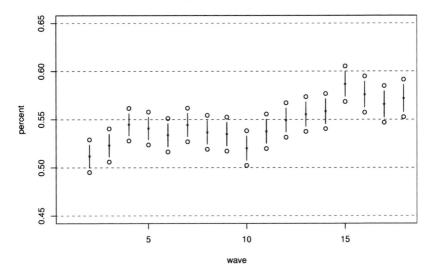

Data: G-SOEP, Sample A, waves 1 to 18. The asterisk gives the empirical frequency, and the circles denote upper and lower boundary for the 95% confidence interval for the proportion.

the confidence intervals are much wider and do overlap, but the general trend is the same.

To test the association between $B2_t$ and $B2_u$, we use two coefficients: The ϕ coefficient of association between two dichotomous nominal variables, and Pearson's χ^2 statistic for test of factor independence.[7] The empirical result is shown in Table 6.3, and Figure 6.9 shows the results for adjacent waves $\phi(t, t+1)$.

Right above the diagonal are the values for adjacent waves. At the start, the level of contingency in two consecutive waves is moderate, e.g., $\phi(t_1, t_2) =$

---

[7] For 2x2 tables, the phi coefficient ϕ is equal to the Pearson correlation coefficient.

Table 6.3: Summary of contingencies $B2_t$ given $B2_u$

$t \backslash u$	1	2	3	4	5	6	7	8	9	10	11	12	13	14	15	16	17	18
1	*	**.2783**	.2078	.2104	.1504	.1770	.1477	.1353	.1132	.1198	.1315	.1312	.0969	.0817	.0890	.0867	.0851	.1089
2	258.2	*	**.3232**	.3146	.2409	.2236	.2187	.2243	.2291	.1651	.1954	.2216	.2222	.1649	.2018	.2026	.1759	.1768
3	129.3	337.4	*	**.3706**	.2625	.2352	.2468	.2354	.2048	.2044	.2093	.1804	.2515	.1577	.2181	.1636	.2232	.2048
4	123.9	297.4	454.0	*	**.3609**	.2588	.2887	.2618	.2467	.2560	.2661	.2176	.2283	.1786	.2000	.2043	.2239	.2131
5	57.1	156.0	203.3	422.0	*	**.3310**	.3094	.2555	.2448	.2340	.2559	.2236	.2205	.2223	.2295	.1722	.2576	.2071
6	74.4	126.0	151.6	196.9	342.6	*	**.3594**	.3328	.2740	.2873	.2655	.2254	.2488	.2193	.2393	.2118	.2085	.2200
7	47.4	111.6	153.2	225.0	270.5	400.5	*	**.3806**	.3395	.3087	.2880	.2584	.3033	.2551	.2747	.2423	.2602	.2295
8	37.5	109.5	130.4	173.8	171.8	315.9	440.7	*	**.3477**	.3306	.2945	.3065	.3108	.2819	.2777	.2678	.2954	.2652
9	24.3	106.8	92.2	143.5	146.9	198.3	323.9	366.3	*	**.3712**	.3566	.3475	.3573	.2970	.2667	.2724	.2665	.2470
10	25.9	52.8	87.3	147.0	126.9	207.0	251.9	309.2	407.8	*	**.3998**	.3777	.3549	.3184	.3093	.2880	.3174	.2378
11	28.5	68.2	83.9	146.5	141.4	163.0	203.1	226.0	344.5	471.0	*	**.4121**	.3815	.3485	.3299	.2787	.3276	.2708
12	27.0	82.7	59.1	92.8	102.0	111.1	155.3	231.4	310.9	393.1	500.7	*	**.4332**	.3609	.3132	.3056	.3171	.2653
13	13.5	77.2	107.7	93.9	91.8	125.5	198.6	221.9	307.6	321.9	394.0	540.9	*	**.4274**	.4154	.3525	.3806	.3297
14	8.7	39.2	39.0	53.9	87.0	91.4	131.1	171.3	197.5	241.5	306.8	346.3	517.3	*	**.4566**	.3551	.3577	.3161
15	9.7	54.8	70.4	62.5	85.3	101.1	141.0	153.6	147.1	208.8	252.3	237.7	443.4	570.1	*	**.4526**	.4014	.3505
16	8.6	52.4	37.3	62.5	45.5	74.8	103.9	133.8	145.3	172.6	169.5	215.8	300.3	319.5	542.8	*	**.4259**	.3815
17	7.8	37.3	65.6	70.0	96.6	68.0	113.4	154.5	131.8	196.6	218.2	216.1	322.1	300.2	393.0	471.6	*	**.4277**
18	12.0	34.6	51.9	59.2	58.3	71.3	82.5	116.2	105.6	102.1	139.3	140.2	225.6	215.9	277.0	347.9	451.2	*

Upper right triangle: ϕ coefficient of association. Values for adjacent waves are in **bold face**. Lower left triangle: χ^2-statistic for test of independence between $B2_t$ and $B2_u$. Because the number of observations for each cell is very high (thousands), every coefficient is significantly different from zero (all p-values are less than 0.0001).

Figure 6.8: Result for the balanced sample

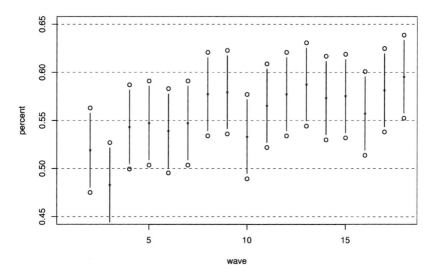

Data: G-SOEP, Sample A, waves 1 to 18. Sub-sample of persons who reported earnings in every wave. The asterisk gives the empirical frequency, and the circles denote upper and lower boundary for the 95% confidence intervals.

0.2783. It is not stable, but increases during panel duration, so $\phi(t_{17}, t_{18}) = 0.4277$, with a maximum $\phi(t_{14}, t_{15}) = 0.4566$. This is an indicator for less switches and more repetitions of reporting rounded/not rounded values in later waves compared to earlier waves.

Not surprisingly, the ϕ coefficient of association is lower for greater distances. However, for every combination of t and $t + j$ the coefficient shows a positive correlation which is significantly different from zero.

A preliminary conclusion is that rounding/not rounding is based on highly individual factors, but is subject to variation in time. Many persons tend to stick to a certain type of response for a while.

Figure 6.9: Phi-Coefficient for precision of income reports in adjacent waves

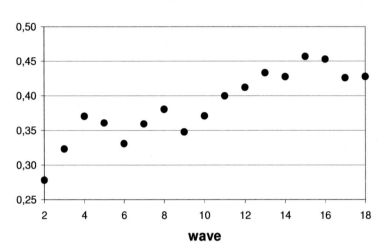

Data: G-SOEP, Sample A, waves 1 to 18.

6.2.4 Probit model for rounding behavior in consecutive waves

To gather more information on the individual component, we conducted an additional analysis. We calculated probit models with dichotomous response variable (rounding/not rounding) in wave t given response in previous waves $t - j$. Table 6.4 shows the results. The model is similar to the model in Section 6.2.2, but here the emphasis is on the consistency of the coefficients. The coefficients for income changes, but the coefficients for sex and for the lagged response (up to $t - 5$) are consistent with respect to sign approximative value. The fraction of deviance explained by the model increases, which confirms the result in Table 6.9, that the stability of response behavior increases (here, it peaks in wave 13).

We conclude that the process which leads to rounded responses to to the gross wage and earnings question in the G-SOEP is highly unpredictable.

Table 6.4: Summary of probit models

t	intercept	sex	$logY$	$B2_{t-1}$	$B2_{t-2}$	$B2_{t-3}$	$B2_{t-4}$	$B2_{t-5}$	dev. expl.
2	0.3318	-0.1145	-0.0319	0.7800					0.0628
	0.3260	0.0546	0.0406	0.0500					
3	0.2925	-0.2016	-0.0614	0.7762	0.4092				0.0960
	0.4061	0.0612	0.0500	0.0565	0.0578				
4	-0.5689	-0.1816	0.0025	0.8475	0.5650	0.3205			0.1610
	0.4991	0.0699	0.0607	0.0622	0.0639	0.0644			
5	-0.7495	-0.0611	0.0405	0.7820	0.3608	0.3299	0.0916		0.1361
	0.5455	0.0761	0.0658	0.0695	0.0705	0.0706	0.0704		
6	-0.824	-0.0123	0.0098	0.6594	0.3614	0.3396	0.2441	0.2371	0.1393
	0.6040	0.0812	0.0723	0.0734	0.0770	0.0751	0.0748	0.0729	
7	0.0095	-0.1741	-0.1259	0.7242	0.5202	0.3908	0.3246	0.2216	0.1929
	0.5996	0.0807	0.0715	0.0727	0.0771	0.0787	0.0770	0.0754	
8	-0.0444	-0.1575	-0.0991	0.7398	0.5814	0.2809	0.2150	0.2836	0.1970
	0.6285	0.0819	0.0744	0.0733	0.0749	0.0792	0.0798	0.0760	
9	0.9002	-0.0936	-0.2031	0.7059	0.5654	0.3074	0.2292	0.3021	0.2052
	0.6607	0.0842	0.0777	0.0758	0.0773	0.0782	0.0806	0.0783	
10	-0.1444	-0.1116	-0.0803	0.6904	0.4329	0.3865	0.3802	0.2130	0.2004
	0.6475	0.0831	0.0754	0.0776	0.0794	0.0787	0.0773	0.0791	
11	-0.9708	-0.0539	0.0086	0.7302	0.6342	0.2333	0.3487	0.2742	0.2239
	0.6492	0.0838	0.0752	0.0778	0.0805	0.0823	0.0797	0.0784	
12	1.2670	-0.2719	-0.2635	0.7429	0.4364	0.4862	0.4129	0.2322	0.2446
	0.6470	0.0831	0.0752	0.0784	0.0804	0.0817	0.0801	0.0801	
13	0.3836	-0.2559	-0.1676	0.6957	0.5038	0.3866	0.5545	0.3013	0.2724
	0.6432	0.0853	0.0739	0.0815	0.0829	0.0821	0.0820	0.0802	
14	0.9538	-0.2070	-0.2122	0.7656	0.4589	0.4218	0.3169	0.2271	0.2439
	0.6320	0.0848	0.0725	0.0811	0.0844	0.0833	0.0822	0.0830	
15	0.8922	-0.1312	-0.2186	0.7659	0.6688	0.1617	0.4087	0.3254	0.2639
	0.6462	0.0854	0.0740	0.0816	0.0847	0.0885	0.0854	0.0829	
16	0.3140	-0.0696	-0.1443	0.9427	0.3546	0.2918	0.3024	0.2717	0.2377
	0.6325	0.0847	0.0723	0.0828	0.0869	0.0885	0.0867	0.0858	
17	-1.2991	-0.0111	0.0323	0.7225	0.5552	0.3845	0.3958	0.3395	0.2649
	0.6510	0.0877	0.0738	0.0830	0.0889	0.0888	0.0905	0.0856	
18	0.6619	-0.1866	-0.1754	0.6303	0.5750	0.4656	0.3341	0.2663	0.2563
	0.6525	0.0878	0.0742	0.0868	0.0868	0.0919	0.0910	0.0900	

Coefficients for probit models of type $B2_t \sim \text{sex} + \log(Y) + B2_{t-1}..B2_1$ (rounding in wave t explained by sex, log earnings, and rounding in wave $t - u$). Column *dev. expl.* shows the fraction of deviance explained by model. Rows with smaller values below coefficients show estimated standard errors of coefficient.

However, it is not completely at random since it can be correlated with certain factors like job type. No strong trend towards better or worse accuracy with respect to rounding was found. However, the preference for one response behavior increases over time, interviewees tend to stick more to a rounding type in later waves.

6.3 Rounding in the German sub-sample of the ECHP

In the German ECHP, the amount of rounded responses to the gross wage and earnings question in the first three waves does not show a clear trend when compared wave by wave (see Table 3.5). With a binary probit model we analyze rounding on personal level.

In an explorative approach, we started with the simplest model and added several covariates and calculated the difference in deviance from step to step. As in the models for the G-SOEP data in Section 6.1 and Table 6.1, the covariates entered are age, sex and income. In addition, we used a coefficient called INTMODE for interview mode (CAPI/phone or proxy interview). The covariates used in the model where explained in Section 6.2.2. The results are shown in Table 6.5.

Table 6.5: Result of Probit Model for Rounding (G-ECHP).

Model No. : Coefficients		Residual		Diff.	
		df	Deviance	df	Dev.
0 :	(constant)	3660	2697.29		
1 :	Y_t	3659	2444.97	1	252.32
1a:	$\log Y_t + Y\mathrm{gr}$	3656	2323.52	3	121.45
2 :	AGE + SEX	3658	2628.21	-2	-304.69
2a:	(model 2) + $\log Y_t + Y\mathrm{gr}$	3654	2319.21	4	308.99
2b:	(model 2a) + INTMODE	3650	2309.85	4	9.36
3 :	$\log Y_t + Y\mathrm{gr}$ + SEX + INTMODE	3651	2309.98	-1	-0.12

Dependent variable: $B2_{t=3}$. Data: G-ECHP wave 3.

The fact that indicators for income groups are highly significant – even in addition to the effect of log wages – hints at an unusual correlation between the level of wages and earnings and rounding behavior.

6.4 Empirical Results: Ordered Probit Analysis

In a special analysis,[8] an ordered probit model (described in Section 6.1.3) was estimated using a sample of persons from the Fin-ECHP PDB, 1996. Instead of calculating a dependent variable with two categories, we use three: $B = 1$, $B = 2$ and $B \geq 3$.

Because of missing data and other problems, not all covariates could be included simultaneously in one model. Only persons with non-missing values for all model variables were included in the analysis.[9]

6.4.1 Marginal frequency of rounding

Figure 6.6 has already illustrated the differences in rounding behavior in four income groups. But income is not the only factor which statistically correlates with rounding.

Before calculating the more complicated ordered probit models, a few cross-tables (Tables 6.6 to 6.9) and means for subgroups with similar amount of rounding illustrate that there is in fact some correlation between rounding and basic characteristics.

Table 6.6: Crosstable sex by rounding

		No. of digits			Total
		1	2	3+	
male	Count	690	1025	497	2212
	Row %	31.2%	46.3%	22.5%	100.0%
female	Count	705	1081	435	2221
	Row %	31.7%	48.7%	19.6%	100.0%

Pearson Chi-Square-Test for factor independence: 5.757 on d.f. = 2. p-value (two-sided): 0.056

---

[8] The results of the analysis have been published in Hanisch (2005) and the following is quoted from Section 5.3 of that paper.

[9] During our research, we came to the conclusion that the correlation of personal characteristics with item non-response and rounding are different respectively non-proportional. We implicitly assumed that the propensity for editing rounded values and for item non-response are not systematically correlated.

Table 6.7: Crosstable interview mode by rounding

		No. of digits			Total
		1	2	3+	
CAPI	Count	1070	1757	806	3633
	Row %	29.4%	48.4%	22.2%	100.0%
telephone	Count	192	217	84	493
	Row %	38.9%	44.0%	17.0%	100.0%
proxy	Count	133	132	42	307
	Row %	43.3%	43.0%	13.7%	100.0%

Pearson Chi-Square-Test for factor independence: 44.228 on d.f. = 4. p-value (two-sided): < 0.001

Table 6.8: Crosstable interview duration (grouped) by rounding

int. duration (min)		No. of digits					Total
		1	2	3	4	5	
≤15	Count	261	266	51	11	2	591
	Row%	44.2%	45.0%	8.6%	1.9%	0.3%	100.0%
16-20	Count	416	597	197	28	10	1248
	Row%	33.3%	47.8%	15.8%	2.2%	0.8%	100.0%
21-25	Count	325	561	183	58	20	1147
	Row%	28.3%	48.9%	16.0%	5.1%	1.7%	100.0%
>25	Count	382	670	240	101	29	1422
	Row%	26.9%	47.1%	16.9%	7.1%	2.0%	100.0%

Pearson Chi-Square-Test for factor independence: 125.082 on d.f. = 12. p-value (two-sided): < 0.001

The differences between the rows are quite obvious for the three modes of interview (Table 6.7). On the average, respondents provide the most digits in CAPI interviews, and the least in proxy interviews.

Interview duration (in minutes) was put into four groups. The results in Table 6.8 seem to show that there clearly is a relation between longer interview duration and the number of significant digits reported. For higher

Table 6.9: Crosstable job type (grouped) by rounding

		No. of digits			Total
		1	2	3+	
1	Count	83	188	106	377
	Row %	22.0%	49.9%	28.1%	100.0%
2	Count	133	357	234	724
	Row %	18.4%	49.3%	32.3%	100.0%
3	Count	157	298	156	611
	Row %	25.7%	48.8%	25.5%	100.0%
4	Count	131	206	76	413
	Row %	31.7%	49.9%	18.4%	100.0%
5	Count	116	213	58	387
	Row %	30.0%	55.0%	15.0%	100.0%
6	Count	45	32	10	87
	Row %	51.7%	36.8%	11.5%	100.0%
7	Count	161	183	79	423
	Row %	38.1%	43.3%	18.7%	100.0%
8	Count	102	123	49	274
	Row %	37.2%	44.9%	17.9%	100.0%
9	Count	79	104	30	213
	Row %	37.1%	48.8%	14.1%	100.0%

Pearson χ^2-Test for factor independence: 154.326 on d.f. = 16. p-value (two-sided): < 0.001. "job" based on 1st digit of ISCO-88 code: 1=Legislators, seniors officials, 2=Professionals, 3=Technicians, associate professionals, 4=Clerks, 5=Service, shop and market sales workers, 6=Skilled agricultural and fishery workers, 7=Craft and related trades workers, 8=Plant and machine operators and assemblers, 9=Elementary occupations and armed forces.

interview duration, the fraction of persons who reported only one digit decreases, while the fractions of persons who reported three or more digits increases.

However, this relation is not stricly linear. What is not shown in the table is the observation that the average interview duration of all interviews in which five digits where reported was 26.8 minutes, while in very long interviews (one hour and more) more than 50% of the persons reported only one significant digit.[10]

The differences between the genders in Table 6.6 are more difficult to see. Because gender correlates with job type and interview mode, it is possible that other (unobserved) factors cause the difference between the two sexes. People with certain job types in Table 6.9 provide more digits, when their type of job is one of the first three categories, or less digits, especially when they are skilled agricultural and fishery workers.

Persons in the sixth category (skilled agricultural and fishery workers) reported the lowest number of digits on average. The table shows only empirical frequencies, but a 95% confidence interval for the percentage of persons who reported only one digit would still be 41.3%-62.0%, greater than the frequencies in any other category. In category two (professionals), the confidence interval for the probability to report three or more digits is 29.0%-35.8%, which is greater than any frequency in the other categories.

6.4.2 Model estimates

Before fixing the covariates for a final model, the following variables were inserted in the right-hand-side of the model: Start of current job, age of respondent, interview mode (Finland: CAPI, phone and proxy interview), interview duration, annual gross wage and salary from main job, type of main activity, recent change of main activity, number of working months, working hours per week, sex, citizen, change of interviewer (very rare in Finland) and job type. Only variables with a coefficient significantly different from zero for Finnish data were included in the final model.

The result of an estimation for the final model is shown in Table 6.10, calculated with Plum from SPSS Advanced Models. Nominal variables like interview mode and job type are simple contrasts with reference to the last categories. The sample distribution of the variables wage, age, and interview duration (int.durat.) is shown in Table 6.11.

The model confirms the results from the crosstables in the previous section. All parameters had coefficients significantly different from zero, even when used simultaneously.

---

[10] We could not reproduce this result for the German ECHP data, where differences in rounding across groups of equal interview duration were much smaller.

Table 6.10: Parameter estimates for the ordered probit model

Parameter	margin. %	Estimate	95% CI
θ_1	28.45	**2.7154**	(2.111, 3.320)
θ_2	48.61	**4.0954**	(3.485, 4.706)
(θ_3)	22.94		
wage	100.0	**0.4681**	(0.347, 0.590)
age	100.0	**0.0056**	(0.002, 0.010)
int.durat.	100.0	**0.0106**	(0.006, 0.015)
sex(male)	50.55	**0.1232**	(0.039, 0.208)
sex(female)	49.45		
mode(CAPI)	82.41	**0.2739**	(0.109, 0.439)
mode(phone)	11.46	0.0198	(-0.174, 0.213)
mode(PROXY)	6.13		
job(Techn./Manag.)	28.22	**0.2862**	(0.181, 0.392)
job(Professionals)	20.63	**0.4505**	(0.333, 0.568)
job(Clerk/Sales)	22.89	**0.1409**	(0.024, 0.258)
job(Agric./Fishery)	2.44	-0.1637	(-0.434, 0.106)
job(Worker/Operator)	25.82		

For ordinal parameters, margin. % is the marginal frequency of persons in this category. The first three rows are for the threshold parameters. The code of job is based on the ISCO-88 code: 1=legislators, seniors officials, technicians and associate professionals, 2=professionals, 3=clerks, service workers and shop and market sales workers, 4=skilled agricultural and fishery workers, 5=craft and related trades workers, plant and machine operators and assemblers, elementary occupations and armed forces. Coefficient estimates significantly different from zero (on 5% error level) are **bold face**. 95% CI=95% intervals of confidence for the estimates. Data: Fin-ECHP, $N = 3452$ complete cases.

Table 6.11: Descriptive statistics

variable	units	min	max	mean	std.dev.
wage	$\log_{10}$(FIM)	2.51	6.23	5.00	0.36
age	years	16	76	40.31	9.83
int.durat.	minutes	4	170	23.86	8.73

Data: Fin-ECHP 1996, only persons whose variables used in the ordered probit model have valid values.

Factors which did not add significant or relevant effects to the model were left out from this model, none played a relevant role in probit regression models with "number of significant digits edited" as the dependent variable.

The results for similar models for Finland, Luxembourg and Germany can be found in the Appendix, Section A.3.5.

6.5 Conclusions

After a number of different analyses dealing with rounding behavior, we try to summarize the results.

We started with several hypotheses in Section 6.1.8. The first hypotheses asked whether there is a panel conditioning effect. This hypothesis has been examined in Section 6.4 using the German Socio-Economic Panel (GSOEP). We could not find a panel conditioning effect with a marginal effect on the precision of the data. The relative precision of earnings data, defined as the number of significant digits, did not change significantly between the first and 18th wave. We drew the conclusion that panel conditioning has no noticeable effect on the marginal precision of earnings data in each wave. People who are longer in the panel do not seem to report earning figures with higher (or lower) precision just because they are longer in the panel than others. From the statistician's point of view, this is a good message because it implies that the persons in the panel would still be a "representative" population sample with respect to how they edit earning values.

However, besides marginal distribution of data, the panel units' response behavior does change in at least one respect. In the early years of the panel, the respondents seemed to be more variable from year to year with respect to precision. In later years, they more often sticked to a certain level of precision. Some people got used to report highly precise values, others reported highly rounded numbers. The contingency coefficients (see Table 6.3 and Figure 6.9) illustrated this phenomenon.

Among the many possible coefficients which could have had a effect on rounding behavior, marginal differences in rounding behavior could be found in the Finnish ECHP according to job type and interview mode. To a lesser degree, differences could be found according to the level of income, gender, age and interview duration.

A subsequent probit analysis had similar results. In an ordered probit model with multiple independent variables using the Fin-ECHP, all variables had statistically significant effects on rounding behavior.

Surprisingly, respondent's sex has an effect on rounding behavior. In Finland, males tend to be more precise in their reports. On the average, they use more digits than females. This could be national phenomenon specific to Finland and perhaps other northern European countries, because we could not confirm this result in an additional analysis for German and Luxembourgian data (c.f. Appendix A.3.5).

The mode of interview has an effect on rounding. As we would have expected, responses in (computer-aided) personal interviews have less rounding than proxy or phone interviews. Also, higher interview duration is correlated with higher precision. This seems a plausible result. If persons spend more time for the interview, more time relates to more information. However, the effect is rather small.

Older respondents tended to report more digits than younger ones, though the overall effect was quite small (0.0055 per year of age).

The fact that wage has a strong effect on the relative precision is not unexpected: Higher wages were reported with more digits than lower ones which is partly because the upper limit for the dependent variable b is determined by the level of wage.

An interesting result is the effect of job type. Professionals, managers, legislators and the like tend towards higher precision. Clerks and service workers are similar but with a smaller coefficients. Agricultural and fishery workers tend towards more rounding. Workers, operators, elementary occupations, and armed forces were combined into the reference category.

CHAPTER7

Conclusions

Rounded values and brackets – pre-defined ranges of values – are two types of incomplete income data. The extant statistical literature deals with the effects of rounding, e.g., on the variance and percentiles of a distribution.

The effect of rounding on statistical measures and social indicators can be demonstrated in simulations. Rounding can create substantial biases in the individual measurement of change: Small changes are often underestimated, and individual values are coarsely (or incompletely) measured. Aggregated measures are less affected, except for specific quartiles and the extreme values.

In the interview-based ECHP samples examined in this thesis, the German, Luxembourgian, and the Finnish national sub-samples, income values are frequently rounded. Gross wages and earnings are rounded by most respondents after the first two digits, and total household income is very often rounded after the first digit.

The most important determinant for rounding behavior is the value's original number of digits. A rounding indicator which is based on the absolute number of digits reported is suited as a descriptive measure for rounding.

A recommendation regarding the effect of rounding in income data: people should be cautious when they are analyzing rounded data. It is advisable to inspect the quality of data with respect to rounding first before drawing conclusions, especially when comparing results based on rounded data. Rounded data can be detected by tabulating the number of final digits equal to zero, or the number of significant digits (Section 2.5.1). Another option is to plot the average number of significant digits against the total number of digits (e.g., Figure 3.6).

These methods will possibly not work when the original raw data is not available, e.g. after transformation procedures. In these cases, a simple approach is plotting the kernel density with small bandwidth and a check of the result for patterns (e.g., Figure 2.4).

When data are rounded, caution is advised when comparing results from different sources such as different countries or different periods. On one hand, differences between samples could be caused by different rounding behavior. Therefore if one statistic is based on rounded data and the other is based on data without rounding, then the difference in an observed statistic such as the headcount ratio poverty measure could be caused solely by rounding. On the other hand, differences in two data sources could be blurred because rounded values are observed. Two median values could seem to be similar when rounded, even if the not rounded medians would have been different.

Conclusions regarding income brackets

In the national sub-samples of the ECHP, income brackets were used as follow-up questions when participants did not provide a value when asked about their income. The accuracy of income brackets is lower than the accuracy precise values and should be considered between the accuracy of rounded values and item non-response. The frequency of using income brackets instead of values was very different across the national sub-samples examined.

Not all panels offered income brackets as a response option, and it is the question whether choosing brackets instead of values could be correlated with determinants of the income value. In that case, a different distribution of values would be observed in panels where income brackets are offered compared to panels without brackets. When comparing the income values within the limits given by brackets observed in the German ECHP (offers values as well as brackets) and the German SOEP (offers values only), the result was that the distribution was similar. This is a good result with respect to the common practice to re-sample data for income brackets from valid responses, because the (unobserved) distribution of values reported as income brackets is similar to the (observed) distribution reported as income values. Also, it is a good result with respect to international comparisons, because the fact that the propensity to report income brackets instead of values can be different across countries does not affect the observed distribution of values. Income brackets are a good method to increase the amount of observed (albeit incomplete) data.

The middle of the bracket, i.e., (upper limit + lower limit)/2 is not a good estimate for the mean of income values reported as an income bracket. It is better to chose a parametric approach, e.g., by fitting a density function to the reported values, or by smoothing the values with kernel density estimation.

From the analysis of brackets a recommendation regarding the design of brackets can be derived (here: sets of values offered if the respondent refused to tell a value). It is common practice to use brackets with "round" limits, i.e. 1000−2000. It could have two benefits to use bracket limits which do not coincide with major rounding points: The quality of data would be increase by allowing a more precise imputation from the observed values without bracket use. Also, it would lessen the risk that the respondent chooses a wrong bracket. However, an experimental study would be advisable to analyze problems possibly introduced by these new limits.

In Germany and Luxembourg, income brackets were chosen more often among respondents with high incomes. A possible reason for this is that persons with high incomes are more likely to refuse to provide an answer to the initial income questions, and are then asked to provide an income bracket. However, in the Luxembourgian sub-sample of the ECHP, many respondents switched from providing brackets to values in subsequent waves, thereby the response gap between high income receivers and others was closing. As a result, the quality of income data increased.

Conclusions regarding register and survey data

In a register-supported survey (Finnish ECHP sample persons) virtually no values are rounded by noticeable amounts. Therefore, the accuracy of register and interview data is different with respect to rounding.

In our empirical analysis, we found considerable differences in the stability of incomes according to either survey or register data. But the cross-sectional distribution of changes was similar, with the exception of the tails which were different.

Individual register and interview data show considerable differences which cannot be caused solely by rounding. However, the presence of rounding (e.g., measured by the rounding indicator) seems to be correlated with other measurement errors which can cause greater differences between interview and register values.

Conclusions regarding rounding behavior

Besides the number of digits of the original value, several other factors correlate with rounding behavior: (a) Personal characteristics like sex, age and type of occupation. Professionals an clerks tend to be more accurate. (b) Survey characteristics like mode of interview and interview duration. Face-to-face interviews tend to produce higher accuracy than phone or proxy interviews. (c) Panel conditioning. plays a special role, in a way that persons tend to retain their response type from precedent waves.

We found only weak evidence for the hypothesis that panel conditioning would increase or decrease the propensity of respondents to provide rounded values. In the German SOEP, for example, which was started in 1984, the amount and the proportion of rounded values in gross earnings data first dropped (from about 71% in 1984 to 67% in 1990), and then climbed back (70% in 2001). The variations are probably because of opposing trends.

The statistical model presented in Section 6.4 accounts only for a fraction of the differences in rounding behavior between subjects. Though the above factors could be found in an ordered probit model, rounding behavior seems to be very individual. This is beneficial because the error caused by rounding would be worse when rounding was highly dependent on characteristics often used in socio-economic models like gender, age or employment status.

People who are doing empirical analysis using rounded data are advised to have a look at the amount of rounding in the sample and its correlation with factors used in statistical models. If the propensity of observing a rounded value is correlated with other factors, and therefore rounding is not completely at random, it might be fruitful to use an approach – such as multiple imputation of the "missing" digits of rounding – which takes explanatory determinants of rounding behavior into consideration in order to reduce the effect of rounding on the results.

Bibliography

Amemiya, T. (1983): Qualitative response models: A survey. *Journal of Economic Literature*, 19(4):1483–1536.

Atkinson, T., Cantillon, B., Marlier, E., and Nolan, B. (2002): *Social Indicators. The EU and Social Inclusion*. Oxford University Press. Oxford.

Basic, E. (2003): *Measurement Error and Attrition Bias in the Analysis of the Income Mobility*. Diplomarbeit, Johann Wolfgang von Goethe Universität Frankfurt am Main. Fachbereich Wirtschaftswissenschaften.

Behr, A., Bellgardt, E., and Rendtel, U. (2003a): Comparing poverty, income inequality and mobility under panel attrition. CHINTEX Working Paper 12, available via http://www.destatis.de/chintex/.

Behr, A., Bellgardt, E., and Rendtel, U. (2003b): The estimation of male earnings under panel attrition. CHINTEX Working Paper 11, available via http://www.destatis.de/chintex/.

Benford, F. (1938): The law of anomalous numbers. *Proceedings of the American Philosophy Society*, 78:551–572.

Biemer, P., Groves, R., Lyberg, L., Mathioweth, N., and Sudman, S. (1991): *Measurement Errors in Survey*. Wiley. New York.

Brachmann, K., Stich, A., and Trede, M. (1996): Evaluating parametric income distribution models. *Allgemeines Statistisches Archiv*, 80:285–298.

Brackstone, G. (1999): Managing data quality in a statistical agency. *Statistics Canada Survey Methodology, Catalogue No. 12-001-XPB*, 25(2).

Brugger, P. (1997): Variables that influence the generation of random sequences: An update. *Perceptual and Motor Skills*, 84:627–661.

Buck, N., Nicoletti, C., McCulloch, A., and Burton, J. (2004): Report on attrition analysis and item non-response. CHINTEX Working Paper 16, available via http://www.destatis.de/chintex/.

Carslaw, C. (1988): Anomalies in income numbers: evidence of goal oriented behavior. *Accounting Review*, 63(2):321–327.

Cowell, F. A. (1995): *Measuring Inequality*. LSE Handbook on Economics, Prentice Hall. Harvester Wheatsheaf.

Dempster, A. P. and Rubin, D. B. (1983): Rounding error in regression: The appropriateness of sheppard's corrections. *Journal of the Royal Statistical Society, Series B*, 45, Issue 1.

Dempster, N., Arthur P.and Laird and Rubin, D. B. (1977): Maximum likelihood from incomplete data via the (EM) algorithm. *Journal of the Royal Statistical Society, Series B*, 39:1–38.

Eisenhart, C. (1947): *Techniques of Statistical Analysis*, chapter 4.2, pages 185–224. McGraw-Hill. New York and London.

Esser, H. (1993): Response set: Habit, frame or rational choice? In D. Krebs and P. Schmidt, editors, *New Directions in Attitude Measurement*.

Eurostat (1999a): *ECHP User Guide*. Office for Official Publications of the European Communities. Luxembourg.

Eurostat (1999b): *ECHP variable list and code book*. European Commission, Eurostat, Directorate E: Social and regional statistics and geographical information system. Luxembourg.

Eurostat (1999c): *European Community Household Panel (ECHP): Selected indicators from the 1995 wave, 1999 Edition*. Office for Official Pulications of the European Communities. Luxembourg.

Eurostat (2003): NORIS - nomenclature on research in statistics. Source: http://europa.eu.int/en/comm/eurostat/research/viros/lknoris.html (accessed 2003). Luxembourg.

Fahrmeir, L., Hamerle, A., and Tutz, G. (1996): Kategoriale und generalisierte lineare Regression. In L. Fahrmeir, A. Hamerle, and G. Tutz, editors, *Multivariate statistische Verfahren*, chapter 6, pages 239–299. de Gruyter. Berlin, New York.

Fan, J. and Gijbels, I. (1996): *Local Polynomial Modelling and Its Applications - Theory and Methodologies*. Chapman and Hall.

Faris, P., Ghali, W., Brant, R., Norris, C., Galbraith, P., Knudtson, M., and the APPROACH Investigators (2002): Multiple imputation versus data enhancement for dealing with missing data in observational healthcare outcome analyses. *Journal of Clinical Epidemiology*, 55:184–191.

Fitzgerald, J., Gottschalk, P., and Moffitt, R. (1998): An analysis of sample attrition in panel data - the Michigan panel study of income dynamics. *Journal of Human Resources*, 33:251–299.

Frick, J. R. and Haisken-DeNew, J. P. (2002): *Desktop-Companion to the German Socio-Economic Panel Study, Version 6*. Deutsches Institut für Wirtschaftsforschung (DIW). Berlin.

Frick, J. R. and Haisken-DeNew, J. P. (2003): *Introduction to the German Socio-Economic Panel.* Deutsches Institut für Wirtschaftsforschung (DIW). Berlin.

Fuller, W. A. (1987): *Measurement Error Models.* Wiley. New York.

Hanisch, J. (2005): Rounded responses to income questions. *Allgemeines Statistisches Archiv*, 89:39–49.

Hanisch, J. and Rendtel, U. (2001): Preliminary results from the chintex project. CHINTEX working paper 6, available via http://www.destatis.de/chintex/.

Harms, T. (2003a): Calibration estimators for prediction of dynamics in panels. using longitudinal patterns to improve calibration estimates about development in panels. CHINTEX Working Paper 14, available via http://www.destatis.de/chintex/.

Harms, T. (2003b): Extensions of the calibration approach. calibration of distribution functions and its link to small area estimators. CHINTEX Working Paper 13, available via http://www.destatis.de/chintex/.

Heitjan, D. F. (1989): Inference from grouped continuous data: A review. *Statistical Science*, 4(2):164–179.

Heitjan, D. F. and Rubin, D. B. (1991): Ignorability and coarse data. *The Annals of Statistics*, 19(4):2244–2253.

Holt, T. and Jones, T. (1998): Quality work and conflicting quality objectives. Paper presented at the 84th DGINS conference in Stockholm.

Hovi, M., Nordberg, L., and Penttilä, I. (2001): Interview and register data in income distribution analysis. experiences from the Finnish European Community Household Panel Survey in 1996. *Reviews*, (9). Statistics Finland.

Hurd, M., McFadden, H., Chand, L., Gan, A. M., and Roberts, M. (1998): *Frontiers in the Economy of Aging*, chapter Consumption and savings balances of the elderly: Experimental evidence on survey response bias, pages 353–387. University of Chicago Press. Chicago.

IEEE Task P754 (1985): *ANSI/IEEE 754-1985, Standard for Binary Floating-Point Arithmetic.* IEEE, New York.

Jenkins, S. P. and Lambert, P. J. (1997): Three 'i's of poverty curves, with an analysis of UK poverty trends. *Oxford Economic Papers*, 49(3):317–327.

Jäntti, M. (2004): The effect of measurement errors, non-response and attrition on income inequality, poverty and mobility. In M. Ehling and U. Rendtel, editors, *Harmonisation of Panel Surveys and Data Quality*, pages 89–116. Statistisches Bundesamt.

Kakwani, N. C. (1976): Efficient estimation of the lorenz curve and associated inequality measures from grouped observations. *Econometrica*, 44:137–148.

Lee, C.-S. and Vardeman, S. B. (2001): Interval estimation of a normal process mean from rounded data. *Journal of Quality Technology*, 33(3).

Little, R. J. A. and Rubin, D. B. (2002): *Statistical Analysis with Missing Data.* Wiley, 2 edition. New York.

Manski, C. and Tamer (2002): Inference on regression with interval data on a regressor or outcome. *Econometrica*, 70:519–546.

Marek, I. (2002): *Die Anwendung von Sample Selection Modellen zur Behandlung des Problems der Panelmortalität.* Diplomarbeit, Johann Wolfgang von Goethe Universität Frankfurt am Main. Fachbereich Wirtschaftswissenschaften.

Moore, J. C. and Loomis, L. S. (2001): Using alternative question strategies to reduce income nonresponse. Source: U.S: Census Bureau, Statistical Research Division, Survey Methodology 2001-03.

Neukirch, T. (2002): Nonignorable attrition and selectivity biases in the Finnish ECHP II. CHINTEX Working Paper 8, available via http://www.destatis.de/chintex/.

Neukirch, T. (2003): *Attrition in panel surveys: Determinants, biases and weighting correction.* Doctoral thesis, Johann Wolfgang von Goethe Universität Frankfurt am Main. Fachbereich Wirtschaftswissenschaften.

Newcomb, S. (1889): Note on the frequency of use of the different digits in natural numbers. *American Journal of Mathematics*, 4:39–40.

Neyman, J. (1934): On the two different aspects of the representative method: The method of stratified sampling and the method of purposive selection. *Journal of the Royal Statistical Society*, 97(4):558–625.

Nicoletti, C. and Buck, N. H. (2004): Explaining interviewee contact and cooperation in the British and German household panels. In M. Ehling and U. Rendtel, editors, *Harmonisation of Panel Surveys and Data Quality*, pages 143–166. Statistisches Bundesamt. Wiesbaden.

Nigrini, M. J. and Metternaier, L. J. (1997): The use of benford's law as an aid in analytical procedures. *Auditing: a Journal of Practice and Theory*, 16(2):52–67.

Nordberg, L., Penttilä, I., and Sandström, S. (2001): A study on the effects of using interview versus register data in income distribution analysis with an application to the Finnish ECHP-survey in 1996. CHINTEX Working Paper 1, available via http://www.destatis.de/chintex/.

OECD (1982): *List of social indicators.* OECD. Paris.

Parzen, E. (1962): On estimation of a probability density function and mode. *Annals of Mathematical Statistics*, 33(3):1065–1076.

Pyy-Martikainen, M. and Rendtel, U. (2003): The effect of panel attrition on the analysis of unemployment spells. CHINTEX Working Paper 10, available via http://www.destatis.de/chintex/.

R Development Core Team (2004): *R: A language and environment for statistical computing*. R Foundation for Statistical Computing, Vienna, Austria.

Reilly, M. (1993): Data analysis using hot deck multiple imputation. *Statistician*, 42:307–313.

Rendtel, U. (1995): *Panelausfälle und Panelrepräsentativität*. Campus Verlag. Frankfurt/Main.

Rendtel, U., Nordberg, L., Jäntti, M., Hanisch, J. U., and Basic, E. (2004): Report on quality of income data. CHINTEX Working Paper 21, available via http://www.destatis.de/chintex/.

Rosch, E. (1975): Cognitive reference points. *Cognitive Psychology*, 7:532–547.

Rosenblatt, M. (1956): Remarks on some nonparametric estimates of a density function. *Annals of Mathematical Statistics*, 27(3):832–837.

Rubin, D. (1976): Inference and missing data. *Biometrika*, 63(3):581–592.

Sandström, S. (2002): The consequences of within household unit non-response in income distribution analysis. CHINTEX Working Paper 2, available via http://www.destatis.de/chintex/.

Schafer, J. L. (1997): *Analysis of Incomplete Multivariate Data*. John Wiley & Sons. New York.

Schräpler, J.-P. (2004): Respondent behavior in panel studies – a case study for income-nonresponse by means of the German Socio-Economic Panel (SOEP). *Sociological Method and Research*, 33(1):118–156.

Schweitzer, M. E. and Severance-Lossin, E. K. (1996): Rounding in earnings data. Federal Reserve Bank of Cleveland Working Paper, http://www.clev.frb.org.

Sen, A. (1976): Poverty: An ordinal approach to measurement. *Econometrica*, 44:219–231.

Sheppard, W. (1898): On the calculation of the most probable values of frequency constants for data arranged according to equidistant divisions of a scale. *Proc. London Math. Society*, 29:353–380.

Shorrocks, A. F. (1995): Revisiting the Sen poverty index. *Econometrica*, 63(5):1225–1230.

Silverman, B. (1986): *Density Estimation for Statistics and Data Analysis*. Chapman and Hall. London.

Singh, S. K. and Maddala, G. S. (1976): A function for size distribution of incomes. *Econometrica*, 44(5):963–970.

Sisto, J. (2003): Attrition effects on the design based estimates of disposable household income. CHINTEX Working Paper 9, available via http://www.destatis.de/chintex/.

SOEP-Group (2001): The German Socio-Economic Panel (gsoep) after more than 15 years - Overview. *Vierteljahreshefte zur Wirtschaftsforschung (Quarterly Journal of Economic Research)*, (1):7–14.

Solon, G. (1992): Intergenerational income mobility in the united states. *American Economic Review*, 82(3):393–408.

Spiess, M. and Goebel, J. (2004): A comparison of different imputation rules. In M. Ehling and U. Rendtel, editors, *Harmonisation of Panel Surveys and Data Quality*, pages 293–316. Statistisches Bundesamt.

Statistics Canada (2003): Statistics canada quality guidelines. available from Statistics Canada, Catalogue no. 12-539-XIE.

Statistisches Bundesamt (2004): *Harmonisation of Panel Surveys and Data Quality*. Statistisches Bundesamt. Wiesbaden.

Tourangeau, R. (1984): *Cognitive Science and Survey Methods:Building a Bridge Between Disciplines*, pages 73–100. Washington.

Tourangeau, R., Rips, L. J., and Rasinski, K. (2000): *The Psychology of Survey Response*. Cambridge University Press. Cambridge, New York.

Tricker, A. (1984): Effect of rounding on the moments of a probability distribution. *The Statistician*, 33:381–390.

Wand, M. P. and Jones, M. C. (1995): *Kernel Smoothing*. Chapman and Hall.

Weaver, W. (1963): *Lady Luck: The Theory of Probability*. Dover Publications. New York.

Winter, J. K. (2002): Bracketing effects in categorized survey questions and the measurement of economic quantities. Discussion Paper No. 02-35, Mannheim Research Institute for the Economics of Aging.

Yule, G. U. (1927): On reading a scale. *Journal of the Royal Statistical Society*, 90(3):570–587.

APPENDIXA

Appendix

A.1 Miscellanea

A.1.1 Software used for this work

GhostScript	production of PDF documents
LaTeX2e	typesetting, publishing
Microsoft Excel	figures
Microsoft Visio	flow charts
R	statistical analysis, figures and tables
SAS	data processing, statistical analysis
SPSS	statistical analysis, figures and tables
WinEdt	text editor

A.1.2 National Currency Exchange Rates

EUR fixed exchange rates:

Country	exchange rate		
Germany	1 EUR =	1.95583	DEM
Luxembourg	1 EUR =	40.33990	LUF
Finland	1 EUR =	5.94573	FIM

A.1.3 Eurostat definitions

Household "(DE: Haushalt, FR: Ménage). At community level, a household is defined in terms of shared residence and common arrangements, as comprising either one person living alone or a group of persons, not necessarily related, living at the same address with common house-keeping - i.e. sharing a meal on most days or sharing a living or sitting room. Not all countries adhere strictly to this EU definition. Persons currently residing in the household, persons temporarily institutionalized (health home, full-time education, military service) or absent for work or travel are included in all countries. However, in Denmark, persons in health homes are excluded." (Eurostat, 1999c)

Household's total net income. "Net income means amount [of income from all sources] as you receive it, which normally is after tax and contributions to social insurance and pension. If income varies between months, please give an average." (European Community Household Panel questionnaire, 1994, question H01076)

Income from work. "(DE: Einkommen aus Erwerbstätigkeit, FR: Revenu du travail). Consists of: (a) Wages and salaries ... include normal earnings from work as an employee or an apprentice and extra earnings for overtime work, commissions or tips. Additional payments such as 13th and 14th months salary, holiday pay or allowance, profit sharing bonus, other lump-sum payments and company shares are covered as well. (b) Self-employment income ... , such as own business, profession or farm is collected as the pre-tax profit, that is the profit after deducting all expenses and wages paid, but before deducting tax or money withdrawn for private use. This pre-tax profit is converted into net profit on the basis of a net/gross ratio (The net/gross ratio is estimated using a simple statistical procedure on the basis of reported ratios for income from employment, for which both the net and the gross amounts are solicited.)" (Eurostat, 1999c)

A.2 Additional tables and charts

A.2.1 Definition of nonresponse on wages

Figure A.1: Definition of nonresponse on wages

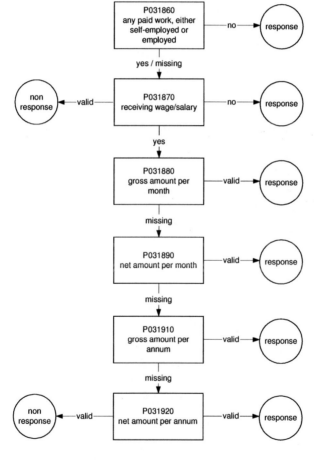

Source: (Neukirch, 2003, page 42)

Figure A.2: TIP curve for register data (unweighted)

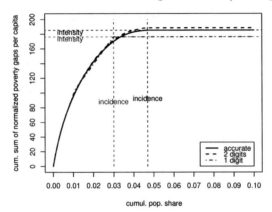

TIP curves based on register data. The solid line is for original data, dotted and intersected lines are for simulated rounded data (rounding after 1 respectively 2 significant digits).

Figure A.3: Density of gross wage and earning (empirical)

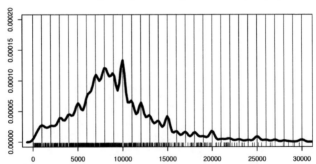

Density plot of household income (FIM). Data: Fin-ECHP 1996. (KDE using a gaussian kernel and a bandwidth of 1000).

A.2.2 Response on gross wage and earnings

As mentioned in Section 2.2, respondents could provide income values in many different ways: Gross or net, monthly or annual, values or brackets. In the various ECHP countries, wages and earnings are paid differently. In the UK, it is not uncommon to get paid weekly. In Luxembourg, many people do not know what they earn before taxes and only know the net value. This leads to different propensities in the response behavior.

Conditional on the (self-reported) information that a respondent did 1995 receive a wage, salary or other form of pay for work as an employee or an apprentice (Survey Question 132), he was asked to provide the normal amount of earnings. He was first asked for monthly gross or net value, then, if he did not know it or refused to answer, asked to provide an annual total, or (in Germany only) to choose one of the income brackets offered.

Table A.1 shows the frequencies of the different types of response in four national sub-samples of the ECHP wave 3.

Table A.1: Response type used in wage and earning question

		Finland		Lux.		Germany		UK	
		N	%	N	%	N	%	N	%
refused	(missing)	142	3.1	46	4.7	766	15.0	605	13.8
per month	gross only	23	0.5	49	5.0	69	1.3	9	0.2
(p.m.)	net only	49	1.1	538	55.0	610	11.9	12	0.3
	net + gross	4405	94.7	336	34.3	3663	71.5	3407	77.4
per annum	gross only	1	0.0	5	0.5	1	0.0	6	0.1
(p.a.)	net only	0	0.0	2	0.2	3	0.1	4	0.1
	net + gross	21	0.5	3	0.3	1	0.0	355	8.1
p.m.+p.a.	net or gross	10	0.2	0	0.0	1	0.1	1	0.0
Total		4651	100.0	979	100.0	5120	100.0	4399	100.0

Absolute and relative (adding up to 100%) frequency of responses. "refused": No value provided at all, item non-response. N: Number of respondents. %: relative to "Total N" per column, not to total number of respondents in the survey. Source: Own calculations. Data: ECHP wave 3 (1996).

The frequencies of the various response are very different among the four countries. For example, Finland is an example for very high quality of responses – 94.7% provided values for both gross and net incomes per month. 55.0% of the respondents in Luxembourg provided only a value for monthly net incomes. And both in Germany and the UK, the amount of item non-responses was relatively high: 15.0% and 13.8%. In some cases it seems that the interview process had deviated from the instructions given by the questionnaire, because respondents who already provided monthly values should not have been asked to provide annual values, too, but in fact this happened in ten interviews in Finland, in seven interviews in Germany and in one in the UK.

In Germany, the number of interviewees who did not provide a valid response is very large – 766 persons or 15%. However, the national questionnaire offered an income bracket in addition to the options given in the blueprint questionnaire. Not less than 568 out of 766 persons, or 11.1% of 5120, chose an income bracket. While this seems like a great success to reduce the level of item non-response, it is the question whether the inclusion of income brackets in the questionnaire perhaps had an impact on fieldwork and interviewer. Perhaps, the interviewer – knowing that he had the option to use income brackets – was less motivated to reduce the item nonresponse on the wage and earnings question.

It should be an interesting topic to analyze the differences with respect to causal factors, perhaps with a model similar to the one used in Schräpler (2004). However, it is outside the scope of this thesis.

A.2.3 Rounding of net disposable household income values

Table A.2: Rounding: Fin-ECHP net disposable household income

b	1996 N	(%)	2000 N	(%)
1	2353	60.27	1940	65.04
2	1330	34.07	963	32.28
3	150	3.84	69	2.31
4	66	1.69	10	0.34
5	5	0.13	1	0.03
total	3904	100	2983	100

Table A.3: Rounding: G-ECHP net disposable household income

b	1994 N	(%)	1995 N	(%)	1996 N	(%)
1	1105	27.37	1013	25.96	976	25.08
2	2452	60.72	2338	59.92	2341	60.16
3	329	8.15	370	9.48	380	9.77
4	152	3.76	181	4.64	194	4.99
total	4038	100	3902	100	3891	100

Table A.4: Rounding in German SOEP net disposable household income

b	1994 N	1994 (%)	1995 N	1995 (%)	1996 N	1996 (%)
1	1693	25.93	1684	25.45	1735	26.47
2	3764	57.64	3768	56.94	3788	57.80
3	723	11.07	790	11.94	662	10.10
4	350	5.36	375	5.67	369	5.63
total	6530	100	6617	100	6554	100

Table A.5: Rounding in Lux ECHP net disposable household income

b	1994 N	1994 (%)	1995 N	1995 (%)	1996 N	1996 (%)
1	105	20.08	82	15.59	91	15.24
2	240	45.89	262	49.81	236	39.53
3	138	26.39	136	25.86	179	29.98
4	16	3.06	6	1.14	41	6.87
5	18	3.44	23	4.37	27	4.52
6	6	1.15	17	3.23	23	3.85
total	523	100	526	100	597	100

A.2.4 Rounding of personal gross wage and earning values

Table A.6: Rounding in Finland, personal data

	1996		2000	
b	N	(%)	N	(%)
1	1396	31.47	970	30.78
2	2107	47.5	1533	48.65
3	673	15.17	511	16.22
4	199	4.49	85	2.7
5	61	1.38	52	1.65
total	4436	100	3151	100

Table A.7: Rounding in German ECHP, personal data

	1994		1995		1996	
b	N	(%)	N	(%)	N	(%)
1	729	19.73	702	18.27	700	18.73
2	2488	67.33	2578	67.08	2552	68.27
3	305	8.25	382	9.94	335	8.96
4	173	4.68	181	4.71	151	4.04
total	3695	100	3843	100	3738	100

A.2.5 Rounding in all waves, GSOEP wave 1 - 18

In Tables A.10 to A.12, only empirical frequencies are shown, not confidence intervals. Confidence intervals would have ranges between approximately $\pm 0.82\%$ for the empirical frequency of $h(b = 4)$ in wave 1 for the full sample, and $\pm 3.72\%$ for $h(b = 2)$ in wave 15 for the balanced sample. Tables A.10 and A.11 show the values required to construct Figures 6.3 and 6.4, and Table A.12 is for Figure 6.6, respectively.

Table A.8: Rounding in German SOEP, personal data

	1994		1995		1996	
b	N	(%)	N	(%)	N	(%)
1	822	14.57	802	14.2	795	14.38
2	3093	54.83	3135	55.53	3042	55.04
3	793	14.06	764	13.53	724	13.1
4	933	16.54	945	16.74	966	17.48
total	5641	100	5646	100	5527	100

Table A.9: Frequency of Rounding in Lux ECHP, personal data

	1994		1995		1996	
b	N	(%)	N	(%)	N	(%)
1	109	20.11	78	16.74	55	14.29
2	288	53.14	234	50.21	197	51.17
3	99	18.27	89	19.1	82	21.3
4	9	1.66	15	3.22	9	2.34
5	22	4.06	33	7.08	26	6.75
6	15	2.77	17	3.65	16	4.16
total	542	100	466	100	385	100

A.2.6 Rounding in all variables - Fin-ECHP

Table A.2.6 shows the numbers used to construct Figure 3.6 in Section 3.5. var is the variable name in the data base (variables with 10 valid observations or less were left out because of anonymity reasons.) B=1, B=2 to B=6 is the relative frequency (in percent) of values rounded after 1, 2... 6 significant digits. min is the observed minimum for this variable, mean is the mean of values, max is the maximum value, N is the number of valid values. maxh is the maximum relative frequency of a single value (the frequency of the mode). meanb is the mean number of reported significant digits.

Table A.10: Precision of values in GSOEP earnings data (all persons)

t	$h(b=1)$	$h(b=2)$	$h(b=3)$	$h(b=4)$	N_t
1	16.2%	57.0%	14.7%	12.2%	4361
2	16.2%	56.6%	15.0%	12.3%	4071
3	15.2%	55.9%	16.5%	12.4%	3984
4	15.6%	56.4%	15.5%	12.6%	4023
5	15.4%	57.9%	13.8%	12.8%	3812
6	13.2%	57.7%	15.2%	13.9%	3773
7	13.5%	54.9%	14.5%	17.2%	3671
8	14.6%	55.1%	14.6%	15.7%	3660
9	15.2%	56.7%	13.8%	14.3%	3573
10	16.6%	54.4%	13.5%	15.5%	3573
11	15.9%	55.7%	13.6%	14.7%	3478
12	14.6%	55.3%	13.9%	16.1%	3455
13	15.3%	55.4%	12.5%	16.8%	3400
14	15.3%	56.1%	12.8%	15.7%	3330
15	15.8%	55.6%	12.8%	15.7%	3196
16	16.0%	54.9%	13.8%	15.3%	3129
17	16.2%	55.8%	12.6%	15.4%	2960
18	15.8%	57.5%	11.7%	15.0%	2812
average	15.4%	56.1%	14.0%	14.5%	3570

Data: German SOEP, wave 1-18, personal gross wage and earnings, all persons.

The variable list and the corresponding interview questions can be looked up in the official documentation by Eurostat (1999b).

Table A.11: Precision of values in GSOEP earnings data (balanced)

t	$h(b=1)$	$h(b=2)$	$h(b=3)$	$h(b=4)$	N_t
1	14.3%	57.7%	14.5%	13.5%	497
2	15.3%	55.3%	16.5%	12.9%	497
3	13.9%	56.1%	15.9%	14.1%	497
4	12.5%	59.2%	13.7%	14.7%	497
5	12.9%	61.4%	10.5%	15.3%	497
6	11.3%	56.3%	15.5%	16.9%	497
7	11.1%	53.7%	15.3%	19.9%	497
8	11.3%	57.7%	10.5%	20.5%	497
9	14.1%	56.5%	13.1%	16.3%	497
10	14.1%	56.9%	13.1%	15.9%	497
11	14.1%	56.5%	12.1%	17.3%	497
12	13.5%	53.5%	14.3%	18.7%	497
13	13.7%	55.3%	12.9%	18.1%	497
14	14.1%	51.5%	14.5%	19.9%	497
15	14.9%	51.1%	15.5%	18.5%	497
16	12.9%	51.9%	16.5%	18.7%	497
17	15.7%	51.7%	13.5%	19.1%	497
18	13.3%	54.9%	14.3%	17.5%	497
average	13.5%	55.4%	14.0%	17.1%	497

Data: G-SOEP, wave 1-18, personal gross wage and earnings, balanced sample.

Table A.12: Precision of values in GSOEP earnings data, stratified

income range	B	\multicolumn{18}{c}{wave}
		1	2	3	4	5	6	7	8	9	10	11	12	13	14	15	16	17	18
<650	1	24	25	29	27	29	24	23	25	37	39	35	25	21	26	26	25	18	19
DEM	2	48	52	42	52	55	56	59	59	51	49	56	63	67	65	64	64	69	68
	3	28	23	29	22	16	20	18	16	12	12	9	12	12	9	10	12	13	13
650	1	16	17	14	15	14	12	12	14	15	17	15	16	17	13	14	13	14	16
-2250	2	51	51	52	50	51	49	47	47	49	46	47	44	45	45	46	46	46	46
DEM	3	20	20	21	22	21	24	24	24	21	20	19	22	17	20	19	23	19	18
	4	13	12	13	13	14	15	16	15	14	17	18	18	21	22	21	19	21	20
2250	1	13	11	10	11	11	9	10	11	11	11	12	10	13	13	13	14	12	12
-4250	2	64	63	62	62	63	64	59	60	63	60	59	59	58	62	60	59	59	63
DEM	3	9	12	14	12	10	12	11	11	12	13	13	14	13	11	10	13	13	9
	4	14	15	14	14	15	15	20	17	15	16	16	17	17	14	17	14	16	16
>4250	1	25	26	24	23	22	20	20	19	18	19	18	17	16	17	17	17	19	17
DEM	2	53	50	52	52	55	53	51	52	54	53	55	55	56	54	55	53	55	56
	3	9	11	10	10	11	12	11	12	12	12	12	11	11	12	13	12	11	11
	4	12	13	14	15	12	15	18	17	17	16	14	17	18	17	15	18	16	16

$h(B)$, by wave and earnings range. Data: G-SOEP, wave 1-18, personal gross wage and earnings.

Table A.13: Rounding of personal income variables in Fin-ECHP interview data

var	B=1	B=2	B=3	B=4	B=5	B=6	min	mean	max	N	maxh	meanb
P030340	31.5	35.3	27.0	6.1	0.1	0.0	41	1035	10833	907	0.01	2.08
P030380	16.7	33.3	50.0	0.0	0.0	0.0	140	236	452	12	0.00	2.33
P030460	42.2	38.2	17.6	2.0	0.0	0.0	20	629	6000	102	0.00	1.79
P030520	42.5	30.8	21.9	4.8	0.0	0.0	20	1052	10000	146	0.00	1.89
P030600	28.3	48.3	16.7	5.3	1.5	0.0	300	10629	100000	3453	0.03	2.03
P030610	35.8	54.3	5.7	4.1	0.1	0.0	300	6638	38000	3472	0.04	1.79
P031000	69.8	29.6	0.6	0.0	0.0	0.0	300	5320	20000	817	0.02	1.31
P031310	42.9	42.0	14.3	0.8	0.0	0.0	5	348	2666	119	0.01	1.73
P031880	31.5	47.5	15.2	4.5	1.4	0.0	80	9912	220000	4436	0.04	1.97

(cont.)

var	B=1	B=2	B=3	B=4	B=5	B=6	min	mean	max	N	maxh	meanb
P031890	36.3	54.0	5.5	3.9	0.3	0.0	80	6330	138000	4463	0.04	1.78
P031910	35.5	38.7	9.7	6.5	9.7	0.0	700	20130	84773	31	0.00	2.16
P031920	43.3	40.0	3.3	3.3	10.0	0.0	700	12893	65775	30	0.00	1.97
P031950	69.5	25.8	4.1	0.5	0.0	0.0	27	1772	25000	387	0.01	1.36
P031980	30.6	54.2	13.9	1.4	0.0	0.0	300	8516	48000	72	0.00	1.86
P032020	49.7	41.3	6.6	2.4	0.0	0.0	50	3794	30000	2696	0.04	1.62
P032040	62.4	33.3	3.3	1.0	0.0	0.0	30	10302	200000	306	0.00	1.43
P032060	56.2	38.0	3.3	2.5	0.0	0.0	100	10323	337000	121	0.00	1.52
P032080	71.4	21.4	7.1	0.0	0.0	0.0	350	26307	120000	14	0.00	1.36
P032220	33.5	42.0	12.5	2.7	4.7	4.5	173	99743	800000	528	0.00	2.17
P032270	44.0	33.0	16.7	5.7	0.5	0.0	10	1821	18965	209	0.03	1.86
P032290	49.0	39.0	8.8	1.5	1.7	0.0	40	13432	300000	467	0.00	1.68
P032320	26.0	53.0	11.5	9.2	0.3	0.0	118	3802	51481	773	0.01	2.05
P032350	14.3	41.9	20.2	23.6	0.0	0.0	160	1898	18300	475	0.01	2.53
P032380	31.7	46.2	15.4	5.8	1.0	0.0	60	2797	23487	104	0.00	1.98
P032410	57.1	21.4	21.4	0.0	0.0	0.0	3000	12922	50000	14	0.00	1.64
P032440	35.7	42.9	14.3	7.1	0.0	0.0	300	3258	17500	14	0.00	1.93
P032480	23.2	49.8	10.7	16.3	0.0	0.0	35	3953	18000	1097	0.01	2.20
P032510	20.0	50.0	15.0	15.0	0.0	0.0	18	1612	4000	20	0.00	2.25
P032600	20.7	48.8	17.9	12.3	0.0	0.4	20	5815	999998	285	0.00	2.23
P032630	39.6	33.3	25.0	2.1	0.0	0.0	160	1130	10500	48	0.00	1.90
P032670	19.2	46.1	17.4	17.4	0.0	0.0	50	1927	8200	167	0.00	2.33
P032820	21.1	42.1	31.6	5.3	0.0	0.0	200	1345	4280	19	0.00	2.21
P032860	8.0	42.3	35.3	14.1	0.3	0.0	200	1376	39600	1531	0.02	2.56
P032890	29.6	24.7	38.3	7.4	0.0	0.0	250	985	5200	81	0.00	2.23
P032920	22.2	54.1	7.4	14.4	1.9	0.0	200	3946	42000	257	0.00	2.20
P032950	24.6	73.7	1.8	0.0	0.0	0.0	500	741	860	114	0.01	1.77
P032980	20.5	26.8	37.5	14.3	0.9	0.0	200	1204	10800	112	0.00	2.48
P033040	19.6	58.8	8.1	12.5	1.0	0.0	1	2304	20000	296	0.00	2.17
P033080	31.2	39.5	16.6	9.6	3.2	0.0	300	4895	67585	157	0.00	2.14
P033110	32.1	57.1	3.6	7.1	0.0	0.0	200	2292	5000	28	0.00	1.86
P033140	34.2	36.8	13.2	10.5	5.3	0.0	80	6065	21714	38	0.00	2.16
P033170	25.9	53.4	7.1	13.6	0.0	0.0	432	3888	10000	294	0.00	2.09
P033200	50.0	35.7	14.3	0.0	0.0	0.0	100	4496	24000	14	0.00	1.64
P033240	14.2	33.8	35.3	15.2	1.5	0.0	80	7230	68040	521	0.00	2.56
P033270	43.2	47.3	8.1	1.4	0.0	0.0	150	1244	5000	74	0.00	1.68
P033300	73.9	21.8	2.9	0.9	0.5	0.0	100	5619	108000	551	0.01	1.32
P033340	61.5	30.8	4.3	3.4	0.0	0.0	20	7651	220000	1017	0.01	1.50
P033380	53.9	39.5	4.4	1.9	0.2	0.0	14	2716	64900	3993	0.03	1.55
P033520	44.2	44.0	11.7	0.2	0.0	0.0	1	129	2500	600	0.01	1.68

A.2.7 Rounding and bracket usage - Lux-ECHP

Figure A.4: Lux-ECHP final digits (modulo 1000)

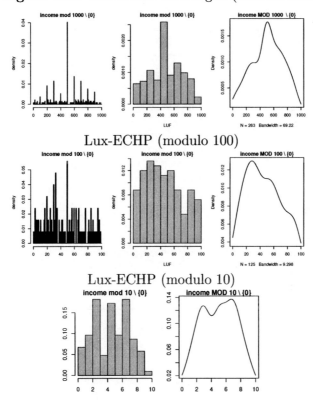

Histograms and a kernel density estimator of the final digit (modulo 10, excluding 0) Of net disposable household income value. Data: Lux-ECHP wave 1 to 3 pooled.

A.2.8 Rounding and bracket usage – German ECHP

Figure A.5: G-ECHP final digits (modulo 1000)

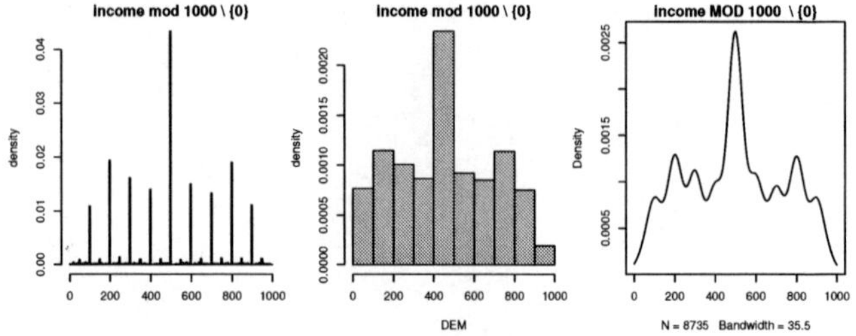

G-ECHP (modulo 100)

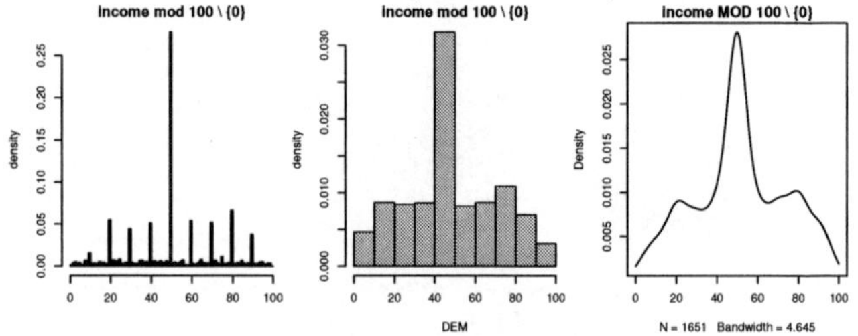

G-ECHP (modulo 10)

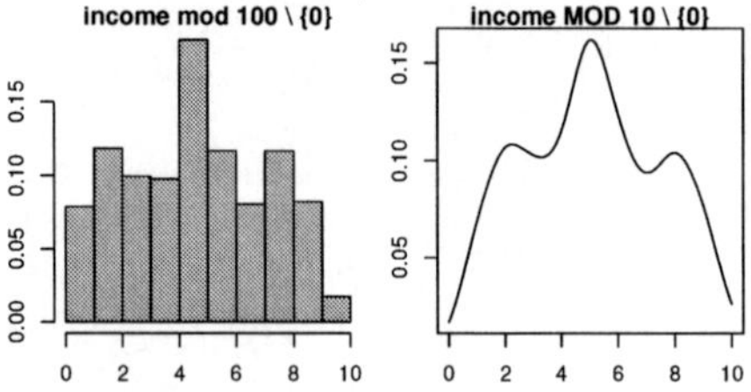

Histograms and a kernel density estimator of the final digit (excluding 0) of net disposable household income value. Data: G-ECHP wave 1 to 3 pooled.

A.2.9 Rounding and bracket usage - Finnish ECHP

Figure A.6: Fin-ECHP final digits (modulo 1000)

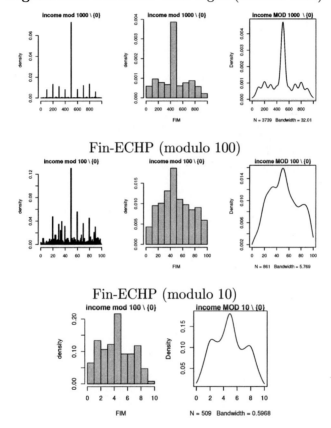

Histograms and a kernel density estimator of the final digit (excluding 0) of net disposable household income value. Data: F-ECHP wave 3 and 7 pooled.

Figure A.7: Fin-ECHP histogram of values in income brackets

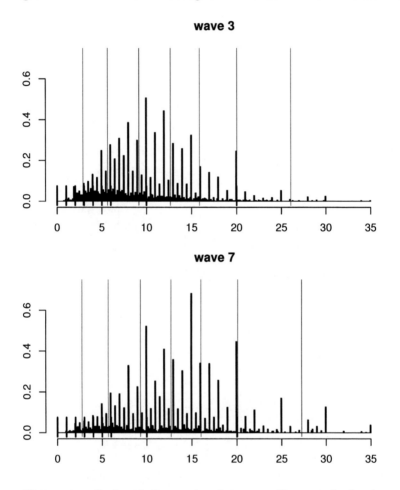

Histograms of values in income bracket range. Bars are the density
of bins, the short lines are at the borders of income brackets, and
the long thin lines indicate group means. Data: F-ECHP wave
3+7 pooled.

Figure A.8: Fin-ECHP histogram of values in income brackets

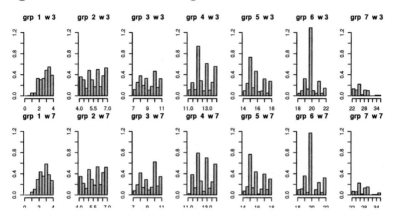

Histograms of values in income bracket range, by wave and income bracket. Data: Fin-ECHP wave 3 (1996) and 7 (2000).

A.2.10 Comparing reference value to survey interview value

A.3 Additional regression models used in the thesis

Regression Models 2, 2a and 2b predict personal gross wage and earnings value provided by respondents, given a reference based on the registers. In addition, several basic characteristics were used as predictors in Models 2 and 2b. Next, a model for the income mobility using the values provided by the respondents during interviews is calculated. Various characteristics are used as additional explanatory variables. Then a non-parametric model for rounding in the German ECHP given income, interview mode and sex is shown. In the last part of this section, the marginal correlation of rounding behavior with several co-variables is tabulated.

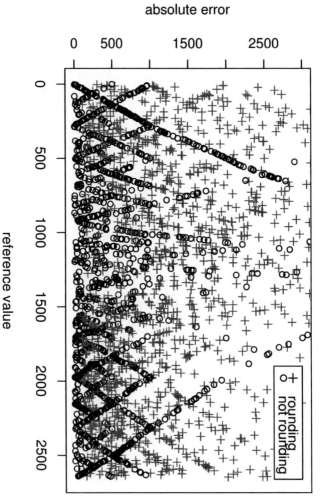

Figure A.9: Absolute difference between reference and interview value

Data: Fin-ECHP, wave 3, Finnish register data, 1995. Values where the difference is within one rounding interval are marked with circles, other values are marked with small crosses.

A.3.1 Regression 2: Survey income given reference income and two covariates

Model:

dependent:	$y :=$ gross wage and earnings (P031880)
predictor:	$x :=$ reference income (see Section 5.2.1)
	$z_1 :=$ dummy for "working less than 12 month"
	$z_2 :=$ amount of self-empl. income
model:	$y = \beta_1 x + \beta_2 z_1 + \beta_3 z_2 + \epsilon$ (regression through origin)
sample:	sample persons, wage earners (AMAS296 $= 1$),
	no unemployment in 1995, no secondary job,
	$2000 < x < 30000$ (exclusion of extreme incomes),
	rounding no more than nearest 50, 3 outliers removed.

Some additional predictors were discarded during the model-building process: Sex, education level, additional job, change of main activity, working hours per week and a dummy for looking after children. Depending on the model-building technique chosen, "looking after children" was sometimes in the final model, but this did not have a high impact on the other coefficients or the overall model fit, therefore it was disregarded.

Coefficients:

predictor	coefficient	Std. Err.	t-value	sign. (t-value)
x	0.9943	0.0058	170.876	< 0.001
z_1	-588.1995	227.3027	-2.588	0.010
z_2	-0.0049	0.0023	-2.140	0.033

ANOVA:

Model	Sum of Sq.	df	Mean Square	F	Sig.
Regression	2.7513e10	3	9.1711e09	10543.652	< 0.001
Residual	1.9658e08	226	8.6981e05		
Total	2.7710e10	229			

The result of the regression estimation is very good, measured by adjusted $R^2 = 0.993$. One comment: When the same model was calculated with intercept β_0, the estimation for the intercept was $\hat{\beta}_0 = 153.1264$ with a standard error of 163.5037, the adjusted $R^2 = 0.952$ and $\hat{\sigma}_\epsilon = 932.895$.

Figure A.10: Residual Scatter Plot for Regression 2a

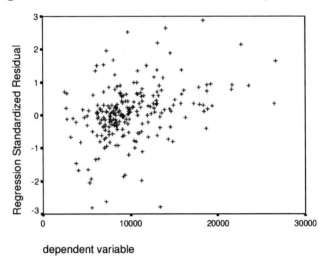

Both from a theoretical point of view and the fact that the intercept is not significantly different from zero, it is justifiable to use no intercept in the model.

A.3.2 Regression 2a: Survey income given the reference income value

Model 2a is the same as Model 2, but the only covariate is adjusted income.

Model:

dependent:	$y :=$ gross wage and earnings (P031880)
predictor:	$x :=$ adjusted income (see Section 5.2.1)
model:	$y = \beta_1 x + \epsilon$ (regression through origin)
sample:	sample persons, wage earners (AMAS296 $= 1$),
	no unemployment in 1995, no secondary job,
	$2000 < x < 30000$ (excluding roughly 3% extreme incomes),
	rounding no more than nearest 50, 3 outliers removed.

Coefficients:

predictor	coefficient	Std. Err.	t-value	sign. (t-value)
x	0.9887	0.0057	174.468	< 0.001

ANOVA:

Model	Sum of Sq.	df	Mean Square	F	Sig.
Regression	2.7510e10	1	2.7504e09	30439.274	< 0.001
Residual	2.0601e08	228	9.0356e05		
Total	2.7710e10	229			

Model Summary	R	R^2	Adj. R^2	$\hat{\sigma}_\epsilon$
2a	0.996	0.993	0.993	950.56

The results for Regression Model 2a are only a little bit different to Model 2. The two additional explanatory variables in Model 2 – working less than 12 months and amount of self-employed income – did not contribute much to the overall model fit. Together with the fact that the parameters were only slightly different from zero gives the impression that they are not important.

A.3.3 Regression 2b: Survey income given the reference income and several basic characteristics

For control reasons, we calculated Regression 2 for all persons, regardless of the level of rounding. Please note that we included a constant (intercept) in the equation. The number of persons is much higher than in Regression 2a, because the majority of values was rounded.

Model:

dependent: $y :=$ gross wage and earnings (P031880)
predictor: $x :=$ adjusted income (see Section 5.2.1)
             $z_1 :=$ dummy for "female"
             $z_2 :=$ dummy for "working less than 12 month"
             $z_3 :=$ dummy for working more than 38h/week
             $z_4 :=$ dummy for low education
             $z_5 :=$ dummy for very high education
             $z_6 :=$ dummy for change of main activity
excluded: additional job
           positive amount of self-employed income reported
           dummy for "looking after children"
model: $y = \beta_0 + \beta_1 x + \beta_2 z_1 + \beta_3 z_2 + ... + \epsilon$
sample: sample persons, wage earners (AMAS296 $= 1$),
           no unemployment in 1995, no secondary job,
           $2000 < x < 30000$ (not very small or very high incomes),
           3 outliers removed.

The difference between Regression 2a and 2b is striking: The coefficients
and the model terms are very different. The intuitively appealing model 2a,
where the slope coefficient for adjusted register income was 0.994, very close
to 1.000, cannot be found in Model 2b. Instead, a lot of coefficients have a
significant effect on the dependent variable. The distribution of residuals is
highly correlated with the dependent variable, as can be seen in Plot Figure
A.11. Finally, the standard error of the estimate $\hat{\sigma}_\epsilon$ in Model 2b is almost
three times as high as in Model 2a.

Coefficients:

predictor		coefficient	Std. Err.	t-value	sign. (t-value)
constant	1	5992.207	152.619	39.262	< 0.001
ajd.inc.	x	0.519	0.010	53.607	< 0.001
female	z_1	-1306.364	107.072	-12.201	< 0.001
work12m	z_2	-2920.978	383.045	-7.626	< 0.001
work38h+	z_3	49.571	6.624	7.484	< 0.001
lowedu	z_4	-986.606	114.674	-8.604	< 0.001
highedu	z_5	2006.322	418.939	4.789	< 0.001
mainchange	z_6	1104.072	380.363	2.903	0.004

ANOVA:

Model	Sum of Sq.	df	Mean Square	F	Sig.
Regression	3.3394e10	7	4.7705e9	667.893	< 0.001
Residual	1.9564e10	2739	7.1427e06		
Total	5.2958e10	2746			

Model Summary	R	R^2	Adj. R^2	$\hat{\sigma}_\epsilon$
2b	0.794	0.631	0 .630	2672.57

A.3.4 Regression M3: Income mobility depending on rounding and individual attributes

Figure A.11: Residual Plot for Regression 2b

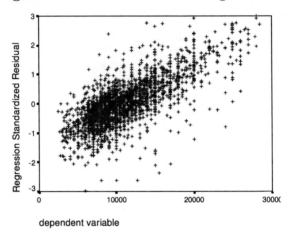

Table A.14: MODEL M3, Model M2 + individual attributes

model terms	coeff.	std.err. coeff.	t-value	p-value
coefficients based on registers				
Intercept	100%	0.107	11.463	< 0.001
m_R	100%	0.439	22.069	< 0.001
other coefficients				
interview mode	59.9%	-0.030	-2.758	0.006
children	7.0%	-0.152	-6.732	< 0.001
working 38h	100.0%	-0.002	-3.263	0.001
education level	15.6%	-0.054	3.647	< 0.001

Standard deviation of residual: $s_\epsilon = 0.032$, 1056 d.f. Adjusted multiple R^2: 0.332. F-statistic: 105.886. Working 38h is the number of working hours, positive values of this variable are hours above 38h/week, negative values are hours less than 38h/week. Education level is a dummy whether the person has an university degree (more than bachelor). Children is a dummy whether the person is looking after children.

A.3.5 Additional regression with an ordered categories dependent variable

In Section 6.4, an ordered probit model with a dependent variable for the degree of rounding (personal gross wage and earnings) has been estimated. We have calculated similar models for the Finnish, German and Luxembourgian sub-sample of the ECHP, wave 3. Table A.16 shows the result for the estimated model coefficients. It seems as if sex is the only "significant" factor in all three countries, but the results are not consistent across different countries. Table A.15 shows the degree of rounding among men and women in the three countries.

Table A.15: Crosstabulation of gender vs. number of significant digits (b) of reported gross wage and earnings

Stratum country	sex	b=1	b=2	b=3	b≥4	%	N
		\multicolumn{4}{c}{row percent (%)}	\multicolumn{2}{c}{total}	
Finland	male	31.2	46.3	17.6	4.9	100	2212
	female	31.7	48.7	12.8	6.8	100	2221
Germany	male	21.0	67.8	8.0	3.2	100	2052
	female	16.0	68.6	10.4	5.0	100	1578
Luxembourg	male	14.5	52.5	24.0	9.0	100	221
	female	14.0	49.4	17.7	18.9	100	164

Data: Fin-, Lux- and G-ECHP, panel wave of 1996.

Table A.16: Parameter estimates for the ordered probit models

co-variable	label	Finland	Germany	Luxembourg
α_1		**2.4441	-0.5672	1.8046
α_2		**1.3761	**2.0391	**1.5139
α_3		**2.2170	**2.6638	**2.2600
α_4		**2.7748		
sex	male	*0.1059	**-0.2180	*-0.3072
citizen	yes	0.2245	0.0066	-0.0756
int.mode	PAPI	–	0.0439	–
	CAPI	*0.2584	-0.0473	–
	self-adm.	–	0.3272	–
	phone	0.0049	-0.4546	–
age	(years)	*0.0059	-0.0020	0.0037
int.duration	(minutes)	**0.0117	0.0017	-0.0237
earnings	(log value)	**0.1849	0.0552	*0.6815
working $\geq$15h	yes		*-0.1756	0.0648
job	missing		0.2856	-0.2788
	1	*0.1969	-0.0225	
	2	**0.3338	0.1343	0.5272
	3	*0.2021	0.0708	-0.4335
	4	0.0875	0.3692	-0.7136
	5	0.0814	0.3114	0.1988
	6	-0.2460	0.9000	
	7	-0.0653	0.3335	-0.4240
	8	-0.0757	0.1750	-0.6305

Ordinal factors are contrasted to female, non-citizen, working less than 15h/week, job type 9, with proxy interview. Code of "job" is based on ISCO-88 code (1st digit): 1=Legislators, seniors officials, 2=Professionals, 3=Technicians and associate professionals, 4=Clerks, 5=Service workers and shop and market sales workers, 6=Skilled agricultural and fishery workers, 7=Craft and related trades workers, 8=Plant and machine operators and as-semblers, 9=Elementary occupations and armed forces. *reference* indicates the respective baseline category. The interview modes used were different in the three countries. Coefficient estimates significantly different from zero are marked with "*" ($\alpha = 5\%$ error level) or "**" ($\alpha = 0.1\%$).

A.4 Additional sections

A.4.1 Cards in the hat example

To demonstrate why probabilities decline from digit to digit, we use an example provided by (Weaver, 1963, p. 270–277): Write numbers on cards, start with 1 and end with 9,999. Each number is getting a separate card. Let $P :=$ the probability of getting 1, 2, 3, or 4 as the leading digit. Intuition suggests $P = 4/9$.

As we start numbering the individual cards and put them into the hat one at a time, the set of cards in the hat is changing from card to card. After each card, we may ask the question "What is the probability P that a card picked at random from the hat now will have a leading digit of 1, 2, 3, or 4?" [1] After the first four cards, the answer would be $P = 4/4 = 1$. This is trivial because every card in the hat now is a 1, 2, 3 or 4. After the fifth card, P has dropped to 4/5. By adding more cards, P falls further, until it reaches 4/9 or 44.4 percent after the ninth card, which was our overall intuitive level based on the entire batch from 1 to 9,999.

After the tenth card, however, P would rise to 0.5 since five of the ten cards have a leading digit of 1 through 4. Through 19, P rises to $14/19 = 0.7368$ since each card from 10 to 19 has the leading digit 1, and the original four cards are still in the hat. As cards 20 through 49 are added, P increases steadily to a maximum of $44/49 = 0.8979$. Starting with the 50th card, P declines until it reaches 44/99 with the 99th card. With the addition of the 100th card, P rises again. This rise and fall of P continues endlessly, and only rarely P is not greater than the intuitive value of 4/9. In fact, the lower digits 1 to 4 nearly always have a higher probability of occurring than 5 to 9.

Figure A.12 illustrates the rise and fall of probabilities P for single digits. The black, solid line at the bottom shows the probability to draw a card with the leading digit 1. Stacked on top of this line is an intersected line with the probability of drawing a card with the leading digit 2. Thus, the intersected line shows the probability for leading digits 1 or 2. The third line is for the digit 3. And so on. Probabilities for all digits stack to 1.0, of course.

---

[1] The example would be even more simple, if we would ask what the probability is that the final digit is zero.

Figure A.12: Cards in the hat example: Leading digit

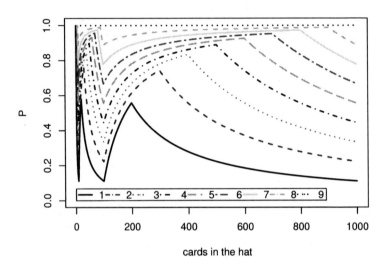

Stacked probabilities P for drawing a value with a certain leading digit.
Data: Batch of cards starting with 1 to number of "cards in the hat".

The distribution of the second digit can be illustrated in a similar way, however, the difference in the probabilities is much smaller. As an example, Figure A.13 shows the probability for drawing a value with a specific second digit from a batch of cards (starting with 10 cards).

The cards in the hat example is rather simple, but bears some resemblance with real world examples. Wages and salaries are not made up at random. They start at some entry level, and then (hopefully) rise in small steps during lifetime. Therefore, the distribution of starting digits follows similar rules like the cards in the hat example.

A.4.2 Rounding digit dy digit, household income

In Section 3.3, we presented a method to use the number of reported digits as a rounding indicator and presented empirical results for Lux-ECHP data. In this section, we present results from other panel data.

In the four different panels analyzed, we find roughly similar frequencies for rounding, but at different digits. In most cases, the first digit(s) are filled in, and then, at a certain digit, the number of rounded digits rises sharply.

To analyze this behavior in light of our sequential model, we compute ratio-like relative frequencies:

$$h(Di|Di+1) = \frac{N_{Di}}{N_{Di+1}}$$

where N_{Di} is the number of persons who filled in the i-th digit (starting to count with the lowest digit) instead of rounding off the value starting with

Figure A.13: Cards in the hat example: Second digit

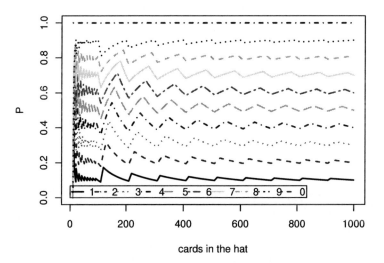

cards in the hat

Stacked probabilities P for drawing a value with a certain second digit. Data: Batch of cards starting with 10 to number of "cards in the hat".

Table A.17: Sequential rounding of net disposable household income

G-ECHP

ratio	1994	1995	1996
$h(D1 \mid D2)$	0.3393	0.3463	0.3509
$h(D2 \mid D3)$	0.1726	0.1959	0.2010
$h(D3 \mid D4)$	0.7310	0.7450	0.7573
$h(D4 \mid D5)$	0.9950	0.9938	0.9913

G-SOEP

ratio	1994	1995	1996
$h(D1 \mid D2)$	0.3444	0.3336	0.3745
$h(D2 \mid D3)$	0.2277	0.2414	0.2156
$h(D3 \mid D4)$	0.7534	0.7525	0.7432
$h(D4 \mid D5)$	0.9954	0.9952	0.9942

Lux-ECHP

ratio	1994	1995	1996
$h(D1 \mid D2)$	0.8846	0.8372	0.7818
$h(D2 \mid D3)$	0.3768	0.6056	0.4435
$h(D3 \mid D4)$	0.2054	0.2029	0.2995
$h(D4 \mid D5)$	0.6761	0.7014	0.7276
$h(D5 \mid D6)$	0.9503	0.9487	0.9531

Fin-ECHP

ratio	1996	2000
$h(D1 \mid D2)$	0.4912	0.3793
$h(D2 \mid D3)$	0.1287	0.0487
$h(D3 \mid D4)$	0.2609	0.2288
$h(D4 \mid D5)$	0.8699	0.8733
$h(D5 \mid D6)$	1.0000	1.0000

Frequencies of respondents who filled in a certain digits of the "net disposable household income" question, conditional on the fact that he has already filled in the next higher digit. Data: see title of respective table, household data.

digit j, $j > i$ and reporting only "zeros" for all following digits.

According to this table, we see remarkable similarities between the two German panel surveys, the G-SOEP and the G-ECHP. The other two surveys have different ratios: Luxembourg has more rounding at $D3|D4$, and Finland has very low ratios at both $D3|D4$ and $D2|D3$. Figure A.14 shows a graphical representation of the ratios.

The differences could probably originate from different numeraires: Today, each of the countries uses the same currency unit, the Euro, but until 2001, different currencies where in use. Thus, rounding off the last four digits in Luxembourgian Francs (LUF) is less "relative" rounding than rounding off the last two digits in German Mark (DEM).

We draw a second figure (see Figure A.15), this time by plotting ratios

Figure A.14: Plot of ratios $h(Di \mid Di + 1)$

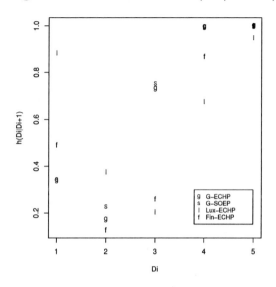

Data: German, Luxembourgian and Finnish (interview data) sub-sample of the ECHP and GSOEP. The panel year is 1994, except Fin-ECHP with 1996.

against the logarithm of the monetary value of each digit, divided by the exchange rate to the Euro.

Abscissa: $\log(10^i / NC)$

Ordinate: $h(Di \mid Dj) = \frac{N_{Di}}{N_{Dj}}$

NC is the fixed exchange rate of the respective national currency to the EURO, Di is the number of values where the i-th digit and all digits right of this are "zero".

Remarkably, the ratios from four different surveys seem to follow some U-shaped curve. If rounding is a sequential process, the probabilities for each digit are not proportional. The exact shape of the curve cannot be explained yet. We think It seems to be obvious that rounding of (income) values at a

Figure A.15: Plot of ratios corrected by log value of national
currency unit in EUR

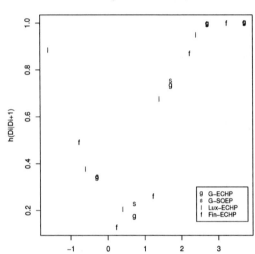

Data: Household income data from various panel surveys, see
legend.

certain digit is dependent on the real value of the numeraire. In addition, a
distinct point exists which is the most common rounding "unit" by which
most values are rounded. For monthly disposable household income, this
point is around 50-100 EUR (100 DEM, 500 FIM, 1000 LUF).

This result is based on tables from three different European countries. It
shows that there is a common rounding process which is at least dependent
on the level of income and the numeraire. If rounding is proportional to
numeraire, then the relative measurement error due to rounding is similar
across different countries. This is a positive result with respect to international comparability and harmonization of household surveys by questionnaire. If data is coarsened due to rounding, at least it is approximately
coarsened to a similar degree.

A.4.3 Rounding digit by digit, personal wage and earnings

We calculate a similar table to Table A.17 for normal personal earnings (wage and salary) per month. The result is in Table A.18, and visualized in Figure A.16.

Table A.18: Sequential rounding of personal gross wage and earnings

G-ECHP

ratio	1994	1995	1996
h($D1|D2$)	0.3228	0.2878	0.2921
h($D2|D3$)	0.1974	0.2320	0.2072
h($D3|D4$)	0.8338	0.8479	0.8377
h($D4|D5$)	0.9946	0.9984	0.9971

G-SOEP

ratio	1994	1995	1996
h($D1|D2$)	0.5355	0.5330	0.5531
h($D2|D3$)	0.3916	0.3939	0.3945
h($D3|D4$)	0.8770	0.8754	0.8738
h($D4|D5$)	0.9947	0.9957	0.9938
h($D5|D6$)	1.0000	1.0000	1.0000

Lux-ECHP

ratio	1994	1995	1996
h($D1|D2$)	0.8333	0.8333	0.8913
h($D2|D3$)	0.6364	0.7229	0.7077
h($D3|D4$)	0.1765	0.2578	0.2257
h($D4|D5$)	0.7262	0.7285	0.7869
h($D5|D6$)	0.9502	0.9485	0.9506

Fin-ECHP

ratio	1996	2000
h($D1|D2$)	0.5319	0.5526
h($D2|D3$)	0.1839	0.1357
h($D3|D4$)	0.5672	0.4897
h($D4|D5$)	0.9147	0.9085
h($D5|D6$)	0.9993	1.0000

Frequencies of respondents who filled in a certain digits of the normal personal earnings from wage and salary question, conditional on the fact that he has already filled in the next higher digit. Data: see title of respective table, personal data.

Figure A.16: X-Y-plot of ratios corrected by log value of national currency in EUR

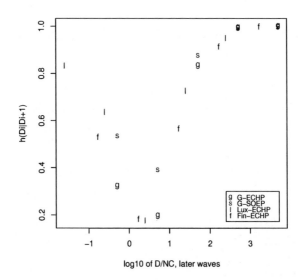

Ratios $h(Di|Di+1) = \frac{N_{Di}}{N_{Di+1}}$. N_{Di} Data: Personal gross wage and earnings data from various panel surveys, see legend.

A.5 Sample scripts and programs

A.5.1 Script used for Simulation 1 and 1a

Sample script written for R (http://www.r-project.org).

```
# user-defined function to compute descriptive

# function to produce statistics
statistics mystat <- function(x,na.rm=FALSE) {
  if (na.rm) { x <- x[!is.na(x)] }     # remove NA Values
  x.stat <- as.array(
          c(quantile(x)[1:3],mean(x),quantile(x)[4:5],sd(x),mad(x)))
  dimnames(x.stat) <- list(c("min(x)","x_{0.25}","x_{0.5}","mean(x)",
                    "x_{0.75}","max(x)","s_x","MAD"))
  x.stat                      # return vector of results
}


# generate random numbers for Simulations 1 and 1a
x <- rlnorm(n=10000, meanlog=8.0863, sdlog= 0.5268)

# Rounding with fixed number of final zeros in Simulation 1
xr.1    <- round(x)                 # rounding to integer
xr.100  <- round(x,-2)              # rounding by 100
xr.1000 <- round(x,-3)             # rounding by 1000

print(xr.stat <- rbind(mystat(xr.1),mystat(xr.100),mystat(xr.1000)))

# Probabilities for rounding to 1 to 4 sign. digits in Simulation 1a
bprob <- cumsum(c(0.25, 0.60, 0.10, 0.05))

result <- NULL                # initialize result vector
for (i in 1:500) {            # 500 simulation iterations
  dings <- runif(length(x))        # uniform random numbers
  bdigit <- rep(1,length(x))
  for (b in c(1:4))
    bdigit[dings > bprob[b]] <- b+1 # determine b= number of digits
  xb <- signif(x,bdigit)           # round after b digits
  result <- rbind(result,mystat(xb)) # add to list of results
}
```

```
# plot histogram of results

ptitle <- c("Min(x)","Q1(x)","Median(x)","Mean(x)","Q3(x)","Max(x)")
op <- par(mfrow=c(2,3))              # 2x3 plots on one page
hist(result[,i], breaks=13, col=i+2, freq=F,
  main=ptitle[i], xlab="x")
```

A.5.2 Program to construct and plot the TIP curve

This program is used in Section 2.7.3. It includes two useful functions to
generate and plot TIP curves from a vector of observations. Optionally, a
vector of weights w can be used.

```
# Functions to calculate and plot the TIP curve (Jenkins and
# Lambert 1997)
# written by Jens U. Hanisch, jhanisch@wiwi.uni-frankfurt.de
# last change 06.02.2004

TIP <- function(x, w=NULL, povertyline=NULL, normalized=FALSE,
  pname="cumul. pop. share", gname=NULL, xname="income" ) {
  # x    : vector of income values
  # w    : vector of weights (optional)
  # povertyline : poverty line threshold value (optional)
  # normalized  : normalized poverty line

  x.order <- order(x)      # order elements by income value
  x <- x[x.order]          # sort by income value

  if (! is.null(w)) {      # use weights ?
    w <- w[x.order]        # sort by income value
    n <- sum(w)
    popshare <- cumsum(w)/n
    if (is.null(povertyline))
      povertyline <- g.quantile(x=x,wt=w,prob=0.5)/2
    x.total <- sum(x*w)
  } else {                 # do not use weights
    n <- length(x)
    popshare <- 1:n/n
    if (is.null(povertyline)) povertyline <- 1/2*(median(x))
    x.total <- sum(x)
  }
```

```
    # optional normalization of the TIP curve
    if (normalized) {
        pg <- (povertyline - x)/povertyline
        pg[pg<0] <- 0
        if (is.null(gname))
            gname <- "cum. sum of normalized poverty gaps per capita"
    } else {
        pg <- 1-x/povertyline
        pg[pg<0] <- 0
        if (is.null(gname))
            gname <- "cum. sum of relative poverty gaps per capita"
    }

    if (! is.null(w))  g <- cumsum(pg * w)
                else g <- cumsum(pg)

    incidence <- popshare[povertygap==0][1]      # point of incidence
    intensity <- max(g)                          # height of intensity

    TIP <- list(g=g, p=popshare, povertyline=povertyline,
      incidence=incidence, intensity=intensity,pname=pname,
      gname=gname, xname=xname )
    attr(TIP,"class")<-"TIP-Curve"

  TIP # return the TIP curve
} # end of function TIP

# Procedure plot.tip plots the TIP curve with annotations
# It was written to be used in combination with the TIP function
#
plot.tip <- function (tip, angle = 45, on.x=NULL, col = "black",
    main = paste("TIP-Curve for", tip$xname),
    xlim = range(tip$p), ylim = NULL,
    xlab = tip$pname, ylab = tip$gname,
    plot.intensity=TRUE, plot.incidence=TRUE,
    axes = TRUE, labels = FALSE, add = FALSE, ...)
{
    if (! is.null(on.x)) { # plot curve over grid points
      x<-on.x
      y<-approx(c(0,tip$p),c(0,tip$g),x)$y
```

```
  } else {                     # plot curve over data points
    x <- tip$p
    y <- tip$g
  }
  if (is.null(ylim))   # make figure area higher than TIP curve
      ylim <- 1.1 * range(y, 0)
  if (!add) {               # make a new empty plot
      plot.new()
      plot.window(xlim, ylim, "")
      title(main = main, xlab = xlab, ylab = ylab)

      if (axes) {       # draw nice axes
         axis(1, seq(xlim[1],xlim[2],by=xlim[2]/10),
         col.axis = "blue")
         axis(2, seq(from=0,to=signif(ylim[2],1),
             by=signif(max(ylim),1)/10),
         col.axis = "blue")
      }
  }
  lines(x=c(0,x), y=c(0,y), col=col, ...) #  plot the TIP curve
  box()                                   #   draw box

  if (plot.intensity) {  # plot line for intensity
    lines(y=rep(tip$intensity,2),x=c(min(xlim,-.05),
          max(xlim,1.05)), lty=2, col=col)
    text(y=tip$intensity*.98,x=0,
          labels="intensity",cex=.8,pos=4,col=col)
  }
  if (plot.incidence) { # plot line for incidence
    lines(x=rep(tip$incidence,2),y=c(min(ylim,-.05),
          max(ylim,1.05)), lty=2, col=col)
    text(x=tip$incidence, y=tip$intensity/2,
          labels="incidence", cex=.8, col=col)
  }
  invisible()                       # return an invisible object
} # end of procedure plot.tip

# the following function by D. Brahm is used in the TIP function
# to calculate the weighted median if necessary.
# It was published on Feb. 8th 2002 in the R-help mailing list.
```

```
g.quantile <- function(x, wt, probs=seq(0,1,.25), na.rm=TRUE) {
  # by David Brahm,  brahm@alum.mit.edu

  if (missing(wt)) return(quantile(x,probs,na.rm))
  q <- !is.na(x) & !is.na(wt)
  if (!all(q)) {
      if(na.rm) { x <- x[q]; wt <- wt[q]} else stop("NA's!")
      }
  ord <- order(x)
  z <- list(y=x[ord], wt=wt[ord])
  z$x <- (cumsum(z$wt) - z$wt[1]) / (sum(z$wt) - z$wt[1])
      # 0 to 1 inclusive
  a <- approx(z$x, z$y, probs)$y
  dec <- if (length(probs)>1) 2-log10(diff(range(probs))) else 2
  names(a) <- paste(format(round(100*probs, dec)),"%",sep="")
  a # returns weighted quantiles
} # end of function g.quantile

# a simple example
x <- rlnorm(n=100, meanlog=8, sdlog=.7)
plot.tip( TIP(x), xlim=c(0,0.25))
```

Figure A.17: Sample plot from procedure plot.tip

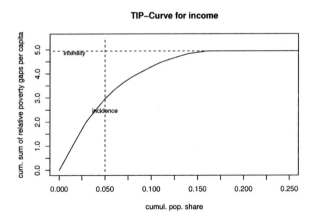

Schriften zur empirischen Wirtschaftsforschung

Herausgegeben von Peter M. Schulze

www.peterlang.de

Peter Lang · Europäischer Verlag der Wissenschaften

Uwe Sunde

Aggregate Returns to Individual Decisions

Development, Income Inequality and Competition for Jobs and Workers

Frankfurt am Main, Berlin, Bern, Bruxelles, New York, Oxford, Wien, 2003.
XVI, 236 S., 3 fig., num. tab.
European University Studies: Series 5, Economics and Management. Vol. 3005
ISBN 3-631-51726-2 / US-ISBN 0-8204-6516-X · pb. € 45.50*

In general, economic decisions are made in order to maximize individual well-being or, equivalently, to maximize the returns of these decisions to the individual. However, while taking their environment as given, the decision-makers often do not explicitly take into account what consequences their decisions have on the aggregate level. Many macroeconomic phenomena can be seen as unintended or unforeseen consequences, 'returns', to the decisions of rational individuals. This book presents several models in this spirit. The first part investigates the role of individual education decisions for long-term development and international differences in earnings inequality. The second part focuses on the consequences of individual search decisions on the labor market for the observed patterns of job creation.

Contents: Individual Education Decisions · Life Expectancy Decisions · Education and Earnings Inequality · Individual Search Decisions · Disaggregate Matching · Strategic Hiring and Search · Unobserved Bilateral Search · Regional Mobility and Job Competition

Frankfurt am Main · Berlin · Bern · Bruxelles · New York · Oxford · Wien
Distribution: Verlag Peter Lang AG
Moosstr. 1, CH-2542 Pieterlen
Telefax 00 41 (0) 32 / 376 17 27

*The e-price includes German tax rate
Prices are subject to change without notice
Homepage http://www.peterlang.de